Beyond The Hollywood Sign

Exposing The Counterfeit Kingdom

Alex Smith

Copyright © 2025 by Alex Smith

All rights reserved.

No portion of this book may be reproduced in any form without written permission from the publisher or author, except as permitted by U.S. copyright law.

"Special thanks to Pastor Chris Alford of Epiclesis Church—your wisdom, faith, and encouragement lit the spark that became this book."

Contents

1. Toddler's Toast — 1
2. Twisted Vines And Tangled Roots — 4
3. Sleepy Hollow — 8
4. Smoke On The Water — 12
5. Market Mischief — 18
6. Lifted By Darkness — 23
7. Ninth Grade: The Lakehouse Confessional — 27
8. The Devil's Chord — 31
9. Tenth Grade: The Road To Reckoning — 35
10. Eleventh Grade: Supernatural Electric Kool-Aid — 39
11. Fiberglass Deception — 44
12. Belly Of The Beast — 48
13. The Hollywood Hustle — 56
14. The Inglewood Giant — 62
15. Pow Wow Under The Indian Moon — 68
16. Cold Steel Raw Deal — 75
17. Santa Barbara Side Show — 78

18.	Tin Badge And American Idols	87
19.	Skid Row	103
20.	15 Seconds Of Fame	111
21.	A Foot Soldier's Journey	115
22.	Double Vision	123
23.	Neverland	131
24.	Lost Luggage	138
25.	Broken Cars And Big Stars	143
26.	Bus stops And Bullets	149
27.	Violation In The Valley	154
28.	The Road To Highland Grounds	160
29.	Bigger Dreams	170
30.	A Small Town Soul In A Big-City Show	176
31.	You Can't Handle The Truth, Or Can You?	180
32.	Five Lines For A Faustian Bargain	187
33.	Vanity And Vultures	191
34.	Roads Less Traveled	195
35.	New Jersey Blues	209
36.	Fiero And The Green Bible	215
37.	Haircuts And High Notes	219
38.	Filling The Void	224
39.	CIA And The Mark Of The Beast	228
40.	Whispers In The Dark	232
41.	Back To The Beast	236

42.	4.7 And The House Of Blues	240
43.	A House Without Light	247
44.	Bougie To Snooty	251
45.	Beneath The Hollywood Sign	254
46.	A Broken Band	258
47.	Strings Of Fate	264
48.	A Broken Wing	269
49.	A Black Crow And The Last Show	274
50.	Cold Steel Anger	280
51.	The Weight Of Darkness	284
52.	A Father's Final Chapter	288
53.	A Voice Of Evil	292
54.	The Dead Speaks?	297
55.	Window To The Soul	302
56.	The Invitation	305
57.	Haircuts To Honeymoon	308
58.	A Stroke Of Reality	315
59.	The Silent Battle Within	320
60.	From Fear To Family	324
61.	A Wake-Up Call From The Inferno	328
62.	Thundersnow And The Homecoming	334
63.	Embrace Christ's Freedom	338

Chapter One

Toddler's Toast

Martin Luther

"We are all conceived in sin and born in sin. Even children, from their mother's womb, are full of evil desire and inclinations."

I was born twenty days before man's first touchdown on the moon—June 30, 1969, in La Mesa, San Diego, California. That year, they dubbed it "the Summer of Love." Years later, I would joke with friends that I was born in the year of peace, love, and bell-bottoms. But as a member of the family of Christ now, I've since reconsidered that tagline. While it's a colorful narrative for my birthday, I sometimes wish I had emerged into the world a year earlier or later. But, as they say, God has a plan, and I'm thankful for the path I was given.

I was a lucky child, born into a family that loved me fiercely. My dad, Alex Sr., was a hardworking contractor with a flair for creativity—he could turn a pile of lumber into a work of art. My mom, Billie, was the heart of our home, dedicated to making sure we felt cared for, even if it was through a slightly burnt casserole or an endless supply of home run pies. My siblings, Kim, Shawn, and Scott, were fantastic in their own right, bringing laughter and chaos in equal measure. We were just below middle class, but we had clean water, food, and a roof over our heads.

But there was a glaring gap in our happy family portrait: the absence of a firm foundation in the Word of God. We owned a Bible, sure, but it mostly served as an impressive doorstop or an extra couple of inches for reaching the cereal on the top shelf. I know you're cringing at the thought, but that was the reality. My parents told me we were Christians, but what that truly meant was a mystery. I honestly didn't have a clue who Jesus was.

You see, when the scriptures say we are born sinners, I can confirm—it's true. I learned that lesson at a remarkably young age and played the role of a serial sinner throughout my childhood, preteen years, and even into adulthood. But before we dive into my transformative moment—when lust in the form of a pretty brunet invited me to her church—we must rewind to the earliest recollections of my childhood. It's essential to understand the backdrop against which my misadventures unfolded.

So, let's go back to around the age of three. I know, it's early, but it's the first memory that crystallized in my mind like a photograph. It was 1972, and I was at a wedding. Who was getting married? I couldn't tell you, but I remember the sights and sounds vividly: a large gathering of adults, laughter, and the unmistakable clink of glasses. Being only about three feet tall, everything was a world away. The drinks, in their colorful glasses, seemed to beckon from eye level on decorative white tables.

I knew I shouldn't, but temptation is like the shiny new object we all want and think we need. In my adorable blue suit, I reached out and began sampling the offerings. My tiny fingers wrapped around the glasses like a toddler with a prized toy. The tastes were revolting—I'm sure I was thinking why on earth are they drinking this stuff—but hey, they were all drinking, so why shouldn't I?

The effects didn't take long to kick in. My next memory? I was standing ankle-deep in a pond, surrounded by curious ducks, violently throwing up. I'm pretty sure that was one of my earliest encounters with clear disobedience. As I stood there, I had a nagging feeling that some unseen spirits were taking note of my reckless escapades, eager to make a home in this little sinner.

For years, I didn't touch alcohol again—not until I was about ten. Even at that young age, I had unwittingly opened a door to chaos, and those uninvited guests made themselves comfortable. My parents never heard about my wedding day debacle, and now that my mother has passed, I'm left wondering if I'll ever find the courage to share it with my father. Maybe it's the shame lingering in the shadows of my mind, or perhaps it's just a story that felt too embarrassing to reveal.

Little did I know, my journey had just begun, and those spirits weren't going anywhere anytime soon. This is about the time I think these unclean spirits realized I was clearly an easy target for harassment and even possession.

Chapter Two

Twisted Vines And Tangled Roots

Derek Prince

"A curse is like a spiritual legal claim, often rooted in generational sin, but Christ provides deliverance through His finished work."

I'm not saying I was born with a generational curse, but let's just say my family tree looks more like a cactus than a sturdy oak. I mean, I am the eighth Alex on my dad's side. Yes, the eighth. I like to think of us as the "Alex Clan," united by a name and a slightly questionable legacy. According to family lore—which I suspect was concocted over a few too many beers—my great-great-grandfather was a bank robber and a gangster riding with the notorious Quantrill Raiders back in the 1800s. Imagine that: a bunch of ruffians galloping through the Old West, and here I am, the latest in line, awkwardly trying to navigate life with a name that screams "criminal mastermind."

As a kid, I wore this familial badge of honor like a superhero cape, convinced it made me some sort of outlaw in training. Spoiler alert: it didn't. Most people with a shred of decency know that being a rebel is not exactly a commendable goal, and what does God say about rebellion?

Proverbs 17:11:

"An evil man seeks only rebellion, and a cruel messenger will be sent against him."

Great. Just great. So, if my great-great-grandfather was living it up in the land of lawlessness, I could only assume God was prepping a whole army of "cruel messengers" for my generation.

At the ripe age of four, my parents decided that Southern California was getting a bit too progressive for their taste, so they packed up the family and moved us nine hours north to Auburn, California—a quaint little historic town established in 1848. Talk about a change in scenery! From sandy beaches to Rivers and pine trees, I was about to trade in my flip-flops for snow boots.

Upon our arrival, I promptly began an impressive streak of illness. Fevers, sore throats, and an inability to swallow. Not what any kid or parent wants to deal with. It didn't take long for the 1970s medical wisdom to kick in: "Time to remove the tonsils!". In fact I think my brother was there with me having the same surgery. They put me in a crib-like contraption so I wouldn't try and make a run for it

I remember lying there, like a Virginia opossum, when in walked a nurse. I heard the eerie snap of latex gloves stretching on her hands—cue the horror movie soundtrack! She leaned over and, without warning, yanked my pants down. I was four! Naked from the waist down and unable to move, I had no idea what was happening until...surprise! Enema time! To this day, I believe that was the moment a spirit of fear entered my innocent little soul.

Cut to a couple of weeks later. My brother Scott was on the couch, flipping through channels until he landed on a movie. Not just any movie—The Trilogy of Terror. I was only four years old. Most kids my age would've been glued to something wholesome like Captain Kangaroo or Mister Rogers' Neighborhood. But not me. I was drawn to whatever Scott was watching, even if it was a horror film I had no business seeing.

The screen flickered, and there it was: a story about a demonically possessed African doll mailed to a woman in her apartment. The doll was no ordinary trinket. It was a vicious-looking, eight-inch figure, chained to a small wooden stand and clutching a sharp spear. Its jagged teeth and hollow, menacing eyes made my stomach churn, but I couldn't look away.

The woman on the screen pulled the doll out of its packaging, inspecting it with mild curiosity. She read the note enclosed—something about the chain keeping the evil spirit contained. But she shrugged it off like it was a gimmick. Setting the doll on the kitchen counter, she decided to hop in the shower.

The camera lingered on the doll, its beady eyes glinting in the dim light. Then the music started—low and eerie, with an unsettling rhythm that felt like it was crawling under my skin. The camera zoomed in, closer and closer. Suddenly, the chain fell away, clattering onto the counter.

The doll was free.

The next shot was a quiet apartment, the sound of water running in the bathroom. The woman stepped out of the shower, toweling off, oblivious to the nightmare she had unleashed. When she walked into the kitchen, the stand was empty. The doll was gone.

That was just the first ten minutes. The rest of the film was pure terror.

The doll wasn't just missing—it was hunting her. It scuttled across the floor, hiding in shadows, waiting for the perfect moment to strike. Its spear glinted as it darted out from under furniture, slashing at her legs. She screamed, running from room to room, barricading doors, only for the doll to find a way in. The tension was unbearable, and I could feel my tiny heart pounding as I watched her battle this relentless creature.

But it was the final scene that haunted me the most. The woman, somehow alive but clearly unhinged, called her boyfriend. Her voice was eerily calm, almost cheerful, as she invited him over to her apartment. But something was wrong—her smile was too wide, her eyes too vacant. The camera panned down with her crouched slowly stabbing the kitchen floor with a large butcher knife, waiting for the boyfriend. I had no idea that, for the next fifty years, that doll would hide in every dark corner of my life, planting seeds of fear. Seeds that would bloom into full-blown terror.

Meanwhile, my brother grew up with many of the same experiences I have had, and I'm sure shows like Trilogy Of Terror affected him because he was only 6 at the time, but our views on these events have shaped us on opposite sides of the spectrum. He ended up as an atheist, or at least agnostic, convinced that any fear he felt was just a learned behavior. I, on the other hand, have absolutely no doubt that it is spiritual.

Chapter Three

Sleepy Hollow

Charles Spurgeon

"The child left to himself will always choose folly over wisdom. Train him up in righteousness, or the world will train him in wickedness."

When I turned six, we moved again, this time to a charming little spot called Sleepy Hollow. No joke—the name was straight out of a horror story. It was about eighteen miles further north, to an even smaller town called Colfax. It had the best of both worlds. You had the ski resorts thirty minutes east and the ocean a couple of hours west. It was a big change because we were nestled in the middle of the forest, and we would be getting snow. As a child, that was a plus. The move was a good one. Our new home was surrounded by kids my age: Jennifer, Lisa, Dean, Billy, and Tony. A ragtag bunch, each with their own quirks, but together we were unstoppable—until, of course, we weren't.

One day, Dean had the brilliant idea to direct both Jennifer and myself to hop into an old sleeping bag. Naked. Yes, naked! Because what's childhood without a little questionable decision-making? Nothing at all happened between the two of us but I felt a spirit of sexual impurity settle over me that day, and I soon realized just how profoundly misguided our childhood adventures would become.

That year, I started the first grade, and from what I remember, I was already gaining a rebellious attitude towards life and authority. I would tell my mom I was heading to the bus stop, but instead, I'd hide in the bushes and watch the bus drive off. I would then play in the woods for the whole day. This became my new daily ritual until the gig was up and the school called, leading to a delightful confrontation where I had to confess my little charade. This pattern of rebellion seemed to be guided by forces I couldn't fully comprehend. It clearly showed I had an early dislike for school and authority.

I had my first cigarette at six; it was one out of Lisa's grandmother's purse. It was a Newport. I remember taking in the smoke with the menthol flavor. It was a rush. I just about choked to death. The nicotine high was overwhelming and powerful. We were under her porch when we lit it up and, with no experience in this sinful activity, tried following what we had witnessed the elders around us doing. It numbed and burned our throats. It was horrible. I wouldn't have another cigarette for thirteen years. It was like getting hit by a truck of bad decisions and adrenaline all at once.

But things really took a turn when I began my foray into crime. It was like I had found my calling! I started small, sneaking into neighbors' homes while they were out. I was a pint-sized burglar with no discernible plan. Lisa's house was my first target, and soon I was hitting every home in the neighborhood, including my friends.

The crown jewel of my juvenile delinquency was Tony's house. Knowing his dad kept Playboy magazines and, more importantly, guns; I was drawn in like a moth to a flame. A voice was whispering that I had to do it. When the opportunity arose, I crawled through and unlocked the kitchen window, muddy shoes and all. I found the magazines but not the guns. However, I did find some .44 Magnum ammo. With three bullets in hand, I felt like the king of the world. I made a clean break and headed to our makeshift clubhouse in the woods.

In a moment of pure genius—or sheer insanity—I decided to see if I could make a bullet explode by hammering it. Because, of course, that's what every six-year-old dreams of doing. I positioned the bullet on a rock and swung my dad's hammer down.

BANG! My ears rang like church bells. I felt a sharp pain in my knee as shards of metal lodged themselves in my flesh. Billie's mom rushed down, panic painted all over her face, while I scrambled to concoct a lie about boys playing with firecrackers. Somehow, I managed to limp back home, telling my parents I'd tripped over a log.

And while I sat nursing my wounds, I was blissfully unaware of the demonic seeds I had sown during that summer.

A few days later my dad was reading the Colfax Record about Tony's house getting burglarized while they were on vacation. Apparently, they found muddy footprints around the window. I can only imagine my face turning the color of a ripe tomato as I sat at the breakfast table, trying to appear nonchalant. That was the moment I learned that guilt could be a relentless companion. Through that summer, the three of us young boys would go into the fort and look through the Playboy magazines that I had stolen from Tony's house. Tony didn't even know that they had come from his house and that they were his dads. I never told the guys that I had broken into Tony's house. But I have to say, looking at the images in these magazines is not good for any man, let alone for a six-year-old child. I'm sure there was plenty of Demonic activity stirred as these young sons of Adam were starting their sinful journey. Not to mention, reading Playboy scars you in a way that makes you expect that all women should look like and act like the women on these pages. I truly believe doors were being unknowingly opened when we were engaging in these activities. Spirits of lust and just plain mischief were in full swing.

But looking back even as I tried to put on a brave face, deep down, I knew something dark was lurking beneath the surface. I wasn't just a little boy; I was a vessel for all the generational curses that had been passed down. And somehow, I knew this was only the beginning.

Chapter Four

Smoke On The Water

Charles Spurgeon

"If you leave a crack open for the devil, he will not hesitate to enter. Sin is always an invitation for the enemy to take up residence."

The '70s in the mountains were a magical time—if your idea of magic involved a lot of trees, the occasional mountain lion sighting, and snow and dirt being the pinnacle of play, then you were set. Our activities revolved around playing in the forest, and when the boredom threatened to swallow us whole, our parents would cart us off down the mountain side to the Auburn cinema. It seemed that parents in that time period had little fear of dropping their children off anywhere, but hey, it was the '70s—safety just wasn't a top priority, but most of us are still here.

Being in a remote town meant our cinematic adventures often involved watching blockbuster films a year or two after they hit the big cities. So, while everyone else was seeing Jaws or Rocky, we were settling into our sticky seats, popcorn in hand, for whatever old horror flick had finally made its way to our little town.

In 1974, The Texas Chainsaw Massacre was making waves in theaters, sending audiences into a frenzy. But we, the unlucky inhabitants of Auburn, had to wait until 1975. I was six years old when my siblings convinced my parents that we absolutely needed to see this film. "It's just a movie!" they insisted. I mean, what could go wrong? Let me tell you everything.

Sitting in that dimly lit theater, I was blissfully unaware that I was about to receive a masterclass in terror. The film unfolded, and before I knew it, I was peering through my fingers, desperately trying to shield myself from the horror on the screen. "This isn't what I signed up for!" I thought. But there was no escape. That night, I didn't just leave the theater; I left with a hefty dose of fear that settled into my bones like an unwelcome guest.

Later, I'd come to believe that maybe, just maybe, the Lord didn't intend for us to subject ourselves to this level of dread. But as things would turn out, this cinematic experience only paved the way for more horror films, and horror books. You could say there was a dark seed planted, and it was beginning to sprout. So, like clockwork, another Demon of fear entered me in that movie theater that night.

A couple of years later, we moved just a few miles west of Sleepy Hollow to a neighborhood and town called Applegate. I was around eight years of age. I thought we were remote on Sleepy Hollow, we were really remote now. There were around five homes and they were one hundred yards apart.

I found myself with no friends my age—just a few older kids who had no interest in hanging out with a loser little brother. My closest friends lived about three miles away from my house, so I didn't get to see them very often. However, I do remember spending time with one of my good friends, Bill. We went to the same school and were in the same grade.

One afternoon we decided to meet each other at the halfway mark from our houses. It was just a quick bike ride to a creek that had a beautiful waterfall and swimming hole. Little did I know, this day would set me on a path I never saw coming.

Bill arrived with a surprise: a joint he had pilfered from I don't Know where. I was thrilled—finally, I could live out the dream I had after watching "Up In Smoke" with my brothers. The film was a seventies comedy, filled with two stoner Mexicans on a ridiculous quest. The story line goes; An unemployed stoner loser named Chong who's an average drummer, leaves his strict parents and eventually meets his kindred spirit Cheech. While the weed smoking pair are soon arrested for marijuana, Cheech and Chong get released on a technicality, allowing them to resume their haphazard adventure and finally compete in a rock band contest, where they get to play the ear bleeding song "Earache My Eye." It was a total disaster, and I do not recommend watching it; yet it was still a perfect encapsulation of much of the seventies vibe.

So Bill lit up the joint, inhaled like a pro, and exhaled without a hitch. Meanwhile, I, on the other hand, gagged, choked, and coughed violently when inhaling just a small amount. Bill laughed so hard he nearly fell into the creek. But eventually, I managed to get the hang of it—sort of. As the smoke hit my system, everything slowed down, and the sound of the creek transformed into a full-blown symphony. I lay back in the sun, feeling utterly magical, as if I'd unlocked a new dimension of existence.

The sun was warm on my skin, and for a moment, it felt like the world had stopped spinning. We laid there, soaking in the light, and it was... magical. There's no other way to describe it. I had never felt anything so intense, so alive. But don't mistake this for some glorified ad for weed—because it's not. If anything, it's a warning.

Weed is a gateway drug, no doubt about it. It's not just a doorway to more substances; it's a doorway to something far more sinister. I didn't realize it then, but that afternoon, I stepped through a gate I could never close. A gate that I believe leads to dimensions we're not meant to meddle in. Dimensions where unclean spirits lurk in shadows, waiting for a chance to sink their claws into unsuspecting souls.

And that's exactly what happened.

I remember lying there, my mind drifting in a haze, and feeling... different. It wasn't just the high. It was deeper than that. I felt something shift inside me, like a tether snapping loose. Suddenly, the world wasn't just vibrant—it was unnervingly alive. Colors seemed sharper, sounds echoed longer, and the air itself buzzed with an energy I couldn't understand. But there was a dark edge to it, like the thrill of standing too close to the edge of a cliff.

I couldn't shake the feeling that something was watching me. No, not watching—waiting. Waiting for me to fall just a little further, to step a little closer to the abyss. And I did.

That afternoon marked the beginning of something I couldn't put into words at the time. A slow unraveling. A descent into addiction, but it wasn't just about substances. It was about the spirits I'd unknowingly invited into my life. I believe they were demons, plain and simple. They didn't just come knocking—they kicked the door wide open and walked right in, bold as anything.

The more I think about it, the more I'm convinced that weed wasn't just a drug that dulled my senses. It was a tool—a weapon—that opened me up to forces I couldn't control. Angels, demons, unclean spirits, heavenly beings... they're all out there, and weed can blur the line between their world and ours. The problem is, we don't get to choose which of them comes through that gate.

For me, it wasn't angels. It wasn't peace or enlightenment. It was something darker. The high wasn't just a high—it was the start of a long, treacherous road. And I wasn't the one driving.

After that day, my weekends morphed from innocent fun in the woods to desperate attempts to find that magical high again. Each little encounter with marijuana felt like dipping my toes in a pool that got deeper and darker with every visit. I started craving that sense of wonder, that connection to something beyond the mundane. But the more I chased it, the more I felt the pull of something insidious whispering in my ear, nudging me toward addiction.

The beautiful creek turned into a portal, and I was the unsuspecting traveler, blissfully unaware of the journey ahead. I'd always been the curious kid, prone to mischief and adventure, but this was a different kind of exploration—one that came with a price.

As the years rolled on, I continued to dance with the spirits that came knocking. Sometimes, they were playful and whimsical, showing me a world of imagination and creativity. But more often than not, they were dark and foreboding, taunting me with my own fears and insecurities. And through it all, I began to wonder: was I the one dancing with the demons, or were they leading the dance?

The line between joy and terror blurred, and I couldn't shake the feeling that this was just the beginning of a much larger struggle. And so, as I lay in the sun that day, I had no idea that I was not just a kid trying to have fun. I was a vessel for the unclean dimension, grappling with the weight of generational curses, fear, and a new addiction that had only just begun to bloom.

Chapter Five

Market Mischief

Augustine of Hippo

"Theft is not merely an offense against man, but against God, for it is He who has given to each his portion, and to steal is to challenge divine providence."

Later that year, when I turned nine, my dad picked a new house around the corner, perched atop the highest mountain in Applegate. This place was nothing short of magnificent—the kind of view that makes you feel like you're on top of the world, with a three hundred and sixty degree panorama of the Sierras. You could even see Sacramento, thirty miles away, which might as well have been another planet to me at that age. I remember sitting on the roof of our house, headphones clamped tight over my ears, dreaming of moving to the city and pursuing music. Little did I know, my dreams were about to collide with my spiraling reality in the most chaotic way.

All my siblings were still living at home, and while I battled my sin, I knew they had their own struggles too. But I had a feeling I was dealing with a bit more than they were—I could be wrong, but I think most humans feel this way. As summer rolled in, my mom had this delightful ritual of dropping my middle brother Scott and me off in town, where we'd walk to the public pool. After our swims, we'd meet her at the town market, which—let me tell you—was basically a gold mine for our mischief.

Each time we cruised through that market, I could practically hear the unclean spirits whispering sweet nothings in my ear, egging me on to elevate my game. The thrill of it all was intoxicating, and I fixated on the forbidden treasures: alcohol and tobacco. You know, the kind of stuff that screamed, "Don't you dare!" which only fueled my desire. That day, I decided to take my criminal antics to the next level.

With the finesse of a seasoned shoplifter—or so I imagined—I snatched a six-pack roll of Skoal chewing tobacco and rolled it into my beach towel. I quickly glanced around, tucked another can of Skoal into my shorts, and rolled up a bottle of Old Grandad whiskey in my towel. Scott was wide-eyed, watching me pull off this mini heist. I could see the fear etched on his face, but bless his heart, he didn't rat me out. Maybe he thought I was just "experimenting," or perhaps he knew I was already way too deep in the rabbit hole.

We bolted out of the store just in time to meet Mom, who had no idea that we were about to embark on a night of chaos. Back home, my brother elbowed me, probably trying to get me to reconsider my life choices. But it was a Friday night, and when the clock struck 9:30, my parents went to bed, leaving us to our own devices.

We cracked open the whiskey like it was a magical potion—because, in our minds, it was! We poured ourselves a small drink, and let's just say the first sip felt like drinking fire. But hey, humans don't drink whiskey for the taste, right? I didn't know how much to drink, so I figured more was better. I poured myself a full glass—like, a full cup—because what could possibly go wrong?

Spoiler alert: everything.

I woke up later to a cold wind brushing against my naked, curled-up body. The sun was just about to peek over the horizon, and I felt like I had time-traveled straight to the morning after a wild party. I was sprawled out in the bushes ten or so yards from my front door, surrounded by rocks, pine needles, and dirt. As I began comprehending my situation's absurdity, I realized I had somehow wandered outside after my reckless night and passed out.

My mouth felt like a desert, and all I could think about was water. What a glorious sight I must have been, a character out of one of Charles Darwin's twisted imaginations. Early man deep in the bush, dirt all over, pine needles in my hair, and in my whitey tighties! Or a cast member on Naked And Afraid. Stumbling inside, I found my brother Scott fast asleep on the couch, blissfully unaware of the chaos that had ensued.

A couple of weeks later, we hit the market again. This time, Scott wanted to join in the lawbreaking. You see, I think nicotine addiction was gripping him also. My heart sank a little. I just knew he wasn't cut out for this life of crime. But there we were, towels in hand, with about ten minutes to spare before Mom showed up. I stuffed my trunks with a can of Skoal and grabbed a roll of chewing tobacco in my towel, and Scott followed suit.

We headed for the door, but there was a plot twist—the store manager must have been watching us because, like a movie in slow motion, all three hundred pounds of him blocked our exit with a look that could curdle milk. "Alright, put the stuff on the counter," he said, and my heart sank. I'd never been caught before.

I can't say with certainty who got us caught, but if I was a betting man I'd have to say it was my brother, but I'm sure he'd day it was me. But I have to be honest it could have been me. We were herded to the front of the store, where the manager started interrogating us. And then, as if summoned by the universe itself, a police car rolled up. My stomach dropped.

"Are these the boys?" the officer asked, and I felt like we were cornered with no escape.

"Yes, you can take em," the manager replied, and that's when I realized we were in deep trouble. The cuffs clicked around our wrists, and I remember the cuff sound echoing in my mind—click, click, click, click. It was surreal. My older brother was visibly shaken, and I, in a moment of panic and disbelief, started laughing under my breath.

It wasn't out of cruelty; I think it was just the unclean spirits having a jolly good time at my expense. We were escorted to the Mayberry-style police station, where our mother pulled up to collect us.

Inside the station, we got a lecture that felt like it lasted an eternity. The officer sternly warned us he never wanted to see our faces in that station again. Afterward, we were handed over to our mom, who was not at all amused at our choices for the day.

At home, my mom sent us to our room. But the moment she shut the door, I motioned to Scott, pointing at my crotch. He shrugged, confused, until I pulled out the can of chewing tobacco and burst into laughter. His eyes widened in disbelief. "You're crazy!" he exclaimed, but he laughed along with me, our little conspiracy binding us even closer.

When my dad got home, we expected the worst—a severe reckoning for our escapades. But to our astonishment, he opted for a talk instead of a corporal punishment. He seemed to think the police intervention was punishment enough, and that was probably true for Scott. But for me, not so much.

The spirit of theft, nicotine, alcohol, and deception solidified its grip on my life that day. Thanks to our parents orders, the corner market by the pool became a no-go zone, like putting a giant "Danger: No Entry" sign on a playground. But as the nicotine cravings clawed at me, I had to find a new place to steal from, and I did. The game was afoot, and I was all in, spiraling deeper into a world of secrets and shadows, where the thrill of the chase mingled dangerously with the demons I could no longer ignore.

Chapter Six

Lifted By Darkness

St. Teresa of Ávila

"I have seen with my own eyes the work of the devil—he lifts the body as though mocking the miracles of our Lord."

A couple of years drifted by, and I found myself around eleven or twelve, sharing a cramped bedroom with my middle brother, Scott. Our room was simple with furniture constructed by my father and posters of that year's Raiders quarterback. One sweltering July night, as I lay there with nothing but a thin sheet to fend off the heat, I stumbled upon a revelation that would change my understanding of the universe forever.

It was a warm night, and by warm, I mean it felt like someone had thrown a blanket over a sauna. Scott was deep in the realm of snores, and there was no chance of my brother waking; he slept like a rock. I, on the other hand, was wide awake, staring up at our early seventies sparkly asbestos ceiling, which shimmered ominously under the glow of a full moon.

I closed my eyes, hoping sleep would find me when suddenly, I felt a grip on my wrists—firm, unyielding. At first, I thought it was just Scott playing a prank, his way of keeping me up for his amusement. But then I realized Scott was blissfully unaware, caught in his own world of heavy breathing and delightful dreams of whatever snoring brothers dream about.

Panic surged through me as I tried to pull my wrists free, but it was like being held down by a bully three times your size. I opened my eyes just enough to see the room, but everything was blurry like I was staring through a fogged-up windshield. I tried to call out to Scott and whisper for help, but my voice wouldn't cooperate—it was just a breathy undertone of sound coming out.

This was when I began to understand that I wasn't dealing with a typical sibling prank. The pressure on my chest was unlike anything I'd ever experienced—heavy, suffocating as that bully had just taken a seat on me.

And then, in a turn of events that would make any horror movie scriptwriter page, my legs were pressed together and slowly lifted into the air. My breath quickened, each inhalation a frantic gasp, and fear gripped my entire body. I felt helpless like being circled by great white sharks, completely at the mercy of something otherworldly.

The bizarre escalated even further when I realized my body—yes, my body—was slowly lifted and floating a few inches above the bed. It was surreal, like being in one of those cheesy sci-fi movies, except instead of aliens, I was pretty sure I was contending with demons. As I was gently carried or floated three or four feet away from my bed, my mind screamed for my brother. "Scott! Help!" But my voice remained a whisper, a mere puff of air lost in the chaos.

The moment I touched down softly on the ground, the grip on my body vanished. Just like that, the entities that had lifted me were gone. I slowly sat upright, sheet clinging to my skin, slightly wet from sweat. I glanced over at Scott, who was still blissfully snoring, completely oblivious to my supernatural ordeal.

I placed the damp sheet back on the bed, my heart racing. How could I explain this? How could I even begin to articulate what had just happened? I crawled back into bed, curling up in a ball, hoping the events of the night would somehow evaporate. But deep down, I knew I couldn't ignore it. I didn't tell my brother or my family; I was terrified of what these entities might do to me—or worse, to them.

Fast forward to today, and I'm in my 50s and filled with more life experiences than I can count, yet that night still haunts me. It defies reason and logic, a cosmic puzzle I still struggle to piece together. I used to wonder if it was aliens, like so many people claim. But after years of reflection and more than a handful of supernatural events, I realized it was most definitely demonic. Just as I believe the alien abduction reports are also unclean spirit encounters.

Some might dismiss my experience as childish imagination or the ramblings of a sleep-deprived mind. I get it; I wouldn't have believed it either if I hadn't lived through it. Even as I share this story today, a part of me still grapples with the reality of it all. But then I remind myself: thank the good Lord for the Holy Spirit, for without that divine guidance, I'd be lost in a sea of confusion, not being able to piece it all together. but now I can.

In that room, on that unforgettable night, I encountered something beyond comprehension, something that forever altered my understanding of the supernatural. It was the first time I realized that the universe is a far stranger place than I could have ever imagined. And while I still ponder the "what ifs" of that experience, I know one thing for sure: they weren't aliens. They were demons.

Chapter Seven

Ninth Grade: The Lakehouse Confessional

John Chrysostom

"Those who feast in excess, drink without restraint, and live for the flesh will find their souls weighed down, unable to rise toward heaven."

By the time I hit high school, my life had become a chaotic cocktail of chewing tobacco and weekend drinking. As I stepped into those hallowed halls of education, I was ready to trade in my innocence for a wild ride on the rollercoaster of adolescence. Over the next four years, I would find myself doing just about anything to score alcohol, marijuana, and, on one unforgettable occasion, a mind-bending trip with LSD.

To kick off our freshman year, Bill hosted a massive party the weekend before school started. And let me tell you, I was determined to make a grand entrance. But before diving into that chaotic night, I need to paint a picture of Bill's house and its surroundings, which were as beautiful as it gets.

Bill lived in a charming cabin right on a lake, nestled on a few hundred acres. The property was owned by the Catholic priesthood. That's right—his home was practically a holy enclave. The property was home to a retreat where young priests would come to spend their summers in serene contemplation (or, as we later discovered, not-so-serene mischief). The retreat featured a massive dining hall with a fully stocked kitchen with the finest cuts of meat, cheese, wine and beer. Also a two-story building where the priests could play games or pray—because nothing says "holy" like a game of bingo with a side of penance.

Bill's father was the caretaker of this retreat. He was a super kind hearted man who kept the whole place running smoothly. Bill's dad gave Bill the job of maintaining the small sewage system on the property. Bill told me that one of the problem with the sewage system was pulling condoms that were clogging the pipe out of the main line. So this means the young priests were definitely not following God's direction on living a holy, pure life.

1 Corinthians 6: 9-10

"Or do you not know that wrongdoers will not inherit the kingdom of God? Do not be deceived: Neither the sexually immoral nor idolaters nor adulterers nor men who have sex with men. nor thieves nor the greedy nor drunkards nor slanderers nor swindlers will inherit the kingdom of God."

Luckily there is God's forgiveness, forgiveness for anyone who repents and turns to him.

With the summer's end, the young priests had to go back to their churches and parishes, leaving Bill free to throw his bash in the grand prayer and game room of the retreat. The sun had set and I arrived armed and ready, with a Joint, booze, and—wait for it—a condom. Yes, a condom! I had no idea why I had it; I was a virgin, terrified of girls, and certainly not planning on using it anytime soon.

As I mingled with friends, I pulled out the condom and jokingly proclaimed that I was going to score tonight. Laughter erupted, and just as I was basking in the comedic glow of my bravado, a girl approached me. She whispered, "Do you have another one?" My heart raced, and I assumed she meant something else.

Before I knew it, she grabbed my hand and led me up the staircase to the second floor. I couldn't believe I was being whisked away like some romantic hero. The hallway looked like something out of an old hotel, lined with identical rooms that smelled Like mountain cabins. The Catholics established the retreat in the seventies, but I'm sure the place itself is over one hundred years old.

She opened one of the doors, and we stepped inside a tiny room that could only be described as 8x9—barely enough space for a bed, a nightstand, and, inexplicably, a large crucifix hanging over the bed, Christ watching our every move. It was all a bit too surreal, and I suddenly felt an overwhelming sense of dread—not from the alcohol or the weed, but from the sheer sacrilege of being in such a sacred place.

That's when she asked if I had another condom, and it hit me: this was not about weed. In a moment of sheer honesty, I admitted I didn't have one, having given the only one I had to a friend. But that didn't deter her; she moved closer, and we engaged in some incredibly inappropriate behavior right under the gaze of Christ himself.

When we finally stumbled out of that room, dress shirt un-tucked, tie untied, I felt a wave of humiliation wash over me. I was a mess—my clothes were disheveled, and I had the distinct feeling I was wearing the shame of a thousand lost souls. As I walked down the long staircase, it was like walking the gauntlet; upperclassmen and fellow freshmen eyed me like I was a prized catch, or maybe just a spectacle of teenage folly.

I burst out of the side door into the cool night air, desperate for a breather. My friends surged toward me, slapping me on the back and cheering as if I'd just achieved some monumental victory. "Congrats, man! You did it!" they exclaimed, assuming I'd just lost my virginity. But I wasn't about to correct them. Who would believe me if I told them the truth?

When I finally made my way home, the night replayed in my mind like a bizarre movie. My parents had a strict rule: no matter how late we got home on weekends, we had to check in with them. I was half expecting to be met with stern looks and lectures, but they were too preoccupied with their own lives to notice my internal turmoil.

Reflecting on that night, I think God must have a grand design for the memories we store in our brains. Maybe he allows us to keep them to humble us, teaching us lessons about right and wrong. And trust me, nothing about that night felt good. I stumbled through the chaos, guided by nothing but youthful bravado and a desperate need to fit in, but deep down, I knew I was playing with fire. The demons of my actions were waiting in the shadows, ready to remind me of my choices, and the party had only just begun.

Chapter Eight

The Devil's Chord

Billy Graham

"The devil will promise you the world, but he will leave you with nothing but chains."

As my freshman year progressed, my world began to revolve around music and the alluring shadows of the occult. While other kids were obsessing over their favorite sports teams or the latest fashion trends, I found myself enraptured by the darker side of existence, drawn in by Hollywood's glamorization of the Devil and his minions. It was as if the very fabric of my childhood was woven with tales of possession and haunting, while I had only a vague memory of Jesus—an elusive figure who felt more like a character from a storybook than a source of divine inspiration.

I remembered back to one fateful Sunday when my dad took us to a small church. I was around seven, and all I can recall is the plate being passed around, and wrestling with my brother over some inane disagreement. My focus was less on the sermon and more on the thought of snatching a bill or two from the collection plate, all while shooting furtive glances at my dad, who had perfected the art of The Look—the one that said, "You better behave, or you're in for it." Maybe that day planted a seed of rebellion, though I wasn't fully aware of it at the time.

Music, on the other hand, was the heart of my upbringing. R&B, pop, country, rap, rock—you name it, I loved it. But there was a catch: the singer had to have pipes! I fancied myself a decent singer, and while the world might debate my talent, I felt I had a grip on pitch, range, and rhythm. Yet, my musical diet was solely secular. The Beatles, Pink Floyd, Marvin Gaye, John Denver, Led Zeppelin, Sam Cooke—you get the idea. My cassette player was a shrine to musical gods, and it wasn't until the 2000's that I stumbled upon Christian music.

When I was six, I started playing the harmonica, and by the time high school rolled around, I thought I was a blues virtuoso. It was fascinating to learn about rock and roll history, especially when I later watched a documentary called "Rumble: The Indians Who Rocked The World." It exposed how much American Indians contributed to the blues genre, intertwining their rhythms and cultural heritage with music shaping generations. There is an agreement within the walls of music academia that early black slaves invented the Blues, and to some extent, they did. But after looking at the history of the Indigenous Indians' influence within the black communities of those early years, I would conclude American Indians might have had an even more significant hand in the formation of the Blues genre more so than their new neighbors.

It wasn't a leap for me to connect the dots and consider that perhaps there was a darker force behind the music I adored. The stories of musicians selling their souls for fame and fortune intrigued me—like the legendary Robert Johnson, who, according to folklore, made a deal with the Devil at the crossroads of Highways 49 and 61 in Clarksdale, Mississippi. To me, it was no mere myth; it felt tangible, real, like the vibrations of the guitar strings beneath my fingers. We even have movies like Crossroads with Ralph Machio. It highlights through film what might happen if you made a deal with the devil, then realized the impact of your deal and decided to try and reclaim your soul with a guitar contest with one of Satan's top guitarists, Steve Vai.

But I remember listening to Johnson's haunting melodies, feeling a chill run down my spine. It was as if each note carried a whisper of that fateful day when he bartered his soul for musical prowess. I believed, with every fiber of my being, that the Devil himself was involved in that transaction, the mastermind behind the curtain of rock 'n' roll. Guys like Carlos Santana or when Bob Dylan talks about his "deal with the chief commander." Many experts think he was referring to the Devil. It made me ponder—how many of my favorite artists were taking their cues from the darkness?

With my interest in music deepening, I became obsessed with JG Thirlwell, an Australian musician whose album "Scraping Foetus Off the Wheel" was a cacophony of chaos. Though his music might have been considered subpar by many, I couldn't shake the feeling that the Devil was all over it. I replayed that album endlessly, my mind swirling in a concoction of intrigue and unease.

At the same time, I was consuming horror films like they were candy, sneaking glances at our illegal satellite dish perched on the roof, my heart racing as I watched the screen flicker with images of demons, ghosts, and the grotesque. It was thrilling and terrifying, and I was addicted to the adrenaline rush.

As the months went by, I became increasingly aware of the crossroads I was standing at—the intersection of my musical passion and the lurking shadows of the occult. I could feel the tug of dark forces, whispering sweetly in my ear, enticing me to delve deeper into their world. Little did I know, this was just the beginning of a journey that would challenge my very soul, pushing me to confront not only the music that filled my life but also the darker aspects of my identity that seemed intertwined with every beat and every melody.

My fascination with the occult, fueled by my musical inclinations, was a cocktail of reckless abandon. I reveled in the thrill of it all, but somewhere deep down, a part of me felt the weight of those choices. The crossroads of California loomed larger than life, and I could sense that every decision I made would lead me further down a path of darkness or toward the faintest glimmer of light. I just had to figure out which direction I was headed.

Chapter Nine

Tenth Grade: The Road To Reckoning

John Wesley

"He that follows his own pleasure rather than God's will shall soon find himself a slave to his own desires."

With my freshman year in the rearview mirror, I was ready to tackle sophomore year head-on—specifically, by getting my driver's license. The prospect of freedom was exhilarating! My eldest brother Shawn, the life of every party, had just wrapped up his first year at the CIA—not that CIA, but the Culinary Institute of America in Hyde Park, New York. Before he packed his bags for chef school, he left me his 1974 Toyota Corona, which was undoubtedly the ugliest car ever made. I mean, it was a rolling testament to ugly, but hey, it had four wheels and a working engine. Looking back, I realize I didn't express enough gratitude to Shawn for his generous hand-me-down, but in the throes of teenage entitlement, I was more focused on the freedom that came with driving than the kindness behind the gift.

Getting my license felt like a rite of passage. For a brief moment, I was invincible—until I hit the road and realized that "reckless" was my middle name. The thrill of speeding down the highway with the wind in my hair and my friends crammed into the backseat was intoxicating. Despite numerous close calls (thank you, God, for my guardian angel), my erratic driving skills still left much to be desired, a trait I would carry well into adulthood.

The next three years zipped by like a roller coaster. My gang consisted of a motley crew: the twins Rob and Randy, Scott, Bill, Dana, Ernie and Jason. Ernie was a unique character—he was the only Black kid at our school, taken in by a couple of families in Colfax who fostered him. Growing up just 35 miles south in Sacramento, Ernie had weathered a rough childhood, and I felt a kinship with him that transcended our backgrounds. I could see his demons, and deep down, I knew there was that bond.

As the sophomore year came to a close, we entered a summer filled with reckless abandon. Ernie and I found ourselves chugging down Thunderbird wine and causing chaos—our playground was the local cemetery and neighboring schools. Waiting outside liquor stores for adults to buy us booze became old fast, so I did what any creative criminal would do: I altered the birthdate on my driver's license. Suddenly, I was the proud owner of a VIP pass to the world of underage drinking.

With the summer fading, we were gearing up for junior year, just a year away from graduation. School wasn't on my radar; all I cared about was partying and trying to fit in. Like many teens, I wanted to be part of the crowd, willing to dabble in whatever mischief came our way. One fateful weekend, I hatched a hair-brained scheme that would seal my status as a true rebel. I asked Ernie to join me in a nighttime adventure—breaking into a local dentist's office to steal a couple of nitrous oxide tanks.

Saturday night arrived, and with adrenaline coursing through our veins, we borrowed my dad's truck. We waited until darkness cloaked the world, backed up to the dental office in Auburn, and pulled out our trusty bolt cutters. Crack, crack, and we were in business! The nitrous tanks, stashed in little sheds outside, were practically begging for a home in our party circle. We loaded the tanks into the truck and sped off, visions of laughter and euphoric high filling our heads.

Nitrous parties became our thing—laughter, lightheadedness, and the joy of doing something absolutely illegal. But in retrospect, I shuddered at the thought of my actions. Deceitful? Check. Dishonest? Check. Criminal? And a substance that's out right terrible for a developing brain, Double check.

In our quest for thrills, we also began breaking into cars, making sure to venture outside of our own town to avoid any local heat. Auburn became our hunting ground, and we snatched up stereos and other small trinkets as if we were modern-day pirates plundering the high seas. There was a palpable dark force at work in us, a thrill that pulsed, but it was a dark thrill.

This might sound off-topic, but it isn't. I used to believe that babies were born innocent. This notion was shattered after watching toddlers interact. A child snatches a toy from another and shoves them down, without a second thought! It's like a tiny demonstration of human nature in its rawest form. When confronted, they would look up with wide eyes and a vehement "No!" while pointing blame at their innocent playmate. Those little angels knew exactly what they were doing.

It all points to the original sinners, Adam and Eve. We are hardwired to kill, steal, and destroy.

The truth is that we have to learn morals and standards from the start. This truth was meant to guide us—something I'd only realize years later. I think of Ephesians 6:4, which admonishes fathers not to exasperate their children but to raise them in the training of the Lord. Oh, how I wish I had soaked in that wisdom as a child! And we get these lessons for life from God's word, the Bible. That's where truth is learned. The Bible was given to us as a gift from our creator so we do not completely fall into sin and destroy our chances for salvation. Problem

Is I had never heard or read any of those passages from the Bible.

As summer wrapped up, I was left reflecting on the hot mess of my life. Here I was, a teenager teetering on the brink of adulthood, and instead of embracing responsibility, I was diving headfirst into a whirlwind of poor choices. It was exhilarating, terrifying, and incredibly reckless—a true cocktail of youth. But deep down, a part of me felt the tug of something greater, a call to step away from the chaos and find a different path.

Chapter Ten

Eleventh Grade: Supernatural Electric Kool-Aid

Paul Washer

"The moment you seek God through altered states, you have already chosen to worship a lie."

One of the spirits I know I had during my teenage years was a spirit of fearlessness. At first glance, this might sound admirable, but in reality, it was a very dangerous spirit. This spirit seemed bent on my destruction, pushing me to perform reckless and illegal stunts that not only endangered me but others as well. One example stands out vividly in my memory: the nights spent under the Forest Hill Bridge in Northern California. This towering structure, the tallest bridge in the state, spans 2,428 feet and stands an awe-inspiring 730 feet high. My friends and I, including my close buddy Ernie, would gather there on weekends. While they cringed and yelled at me to stop, I would free-hang from the center of the bridge—laughing, as though death was an abstract concept. Looking back now, I am certain angels worked overtime to keep me alive during those nights. Those poor angels were probably the highest-paid on God's payroll, and I'm sure I tested their patience.

Since becoming a believer, I've come to understand that my body is a temple of God, deserving of care and respect. Those days of reckless abandon now seem like a distant, foolish chapter—a time when I danced on the edge of destruction. But that spirit of fearlessness wasn't just reckless; it was a precursor to something far darker. It set the stage for encounters with forces I would come to recognize as spiritual warfare.

Fast forward to senior year, and the veil separating the physical and spiritual realms began to thin in terrifying ways. I'm fairly certain that's when I first saw the demons that had been stalking me. These encounters weren't limited to sleep paralysis, though that was a common feature. It felt as though these spirits were always watching, waiting for an opportunity to strike. I literally felt their gaze where ever I was.

It was around November of my senior year when a pivotal event unfolded. The air was crisp and foggy, and my parents had planned an overnight trip to Reno, an hour away from us. I decided this was the perfect opportunity to try LSD. Inspired by the works of Ken Kesey, Timothy Leary, and Tom Wolfe's Electric Kool-Aid Acid Test, and even Pink Floyd and Jim Morrison. I was eager to experience the psychedelic world they described. I called my more adventurous buddy Jason and invited him to join me on the psychedelic journey.

He eagerly agreed, and we quickly set our plan in motion. After a few phone calls and some backroom deals, we secured two hits of acid.

That evening, with my parents out of the house, Jason and I prepared for what we thought would be a night of mind-expanding adventure. We had music videos on VHS queued up, snacks on the table, and a sense of nervous excitement as we placed the tiny squares under our tongues. Then, as the hits of acid began to melt on our tongues the phone rang. It was my parents. We dropped the acid under our tongues and the phone ringes, what were the odds? They told us that they had decided to turn back due to heavy snow on the summit and would be home in thirty minutes.

Panic set in. I hastily told them I was going out with Jason and would stay the night at his house, so don't wait up for me, and hung up. Jason and I scrambled to leave the house, jumping into my hideous 1974 Toyota Corona. The effects of the LSD began to kick in just as we hit the road. At first, it was manic—a rapid-fire stream of nonsensical babbling. Then, everything slowed down, yet our minds raced at hyper-speed. It's hard to describe the sensation: a chaotic blend of mental overdrive and physical sluggishness.

We ended up at Bill's cabin, a decrepit 20x20 shack on the Catholic monastery property. Bill was heading out with Kenny and Jeff the guys that sold us the LSD, so we piled into Bill's 1975 yellow Ford Pinto. That's when reality began to unravel. Kenny, sitting in the front seat, turned to look at us—and horrifically transformed into a werewolf. This wasn't just a trick of the light or a subtle distortion. He physically morphed into the wolf man. I kept telling myself it was the drug, but he wasn't changing back to himself, so I leaned over to Jason, whispering, "Kenny just turned into a werewolf." Jason, now equally terrified, confirmed he saw the same thing. Kenny, overhearing us, began to growl and howl, and the car ride descended into pure chaos.

At a gas station, I looked out the window and a man at the pump next to us turned his head and face to us morphing into a clown. Not a friendly circus clown, but something straight out of a nightmare. I have later learned through podcasts and books that some historians have linked Clowns to the Nephilim. One person who has investigated this with thorough research is Paul Stobbs, and one of his many books on this, and one I recommend is The Nephilim Looked Like Clowns: Volume 1: The History. But seeing this abomination in combination of fear and hallucination made me feel like I was trapped in a carnival of horrors. By the time we returned to Bill's cabin, the trip had taken a darker turn. The walls seemed to breathe, shadows danced, and every sound had more importance. Then came the spiders.

At first, I noticed a single spider just hanging there in the entry way of the seventy five-year-old cabin. I studied it with rapt fascination. But soon, I saw spiders everywhere—crawling on the walls and on my skin. Desperate to escape the bad trip, I smoked as much weed as I could, hoping to dull the effects. It didn't work. LSD had taken full control, and there was no turning back. The spiders eventually disappeared, and things began to mellow out. The drug was so intense that it unlocked portions of the human mind that we have not yet fully explored. I was seeing equations and solutions to global issues that no human could understand. I'm sure this was intelligent designed giving me this information. Whether it was from God or an unclean spirit, I can not say. We spent the rest of the night sitting on sleeping bags. All we could do was ride it out until the sun rose.

After twelve hours, the effects finally subsided, and I drove home, utterly exhausted. I collapsed onto my bed, hoping for sleep. The effects of the LSD had subsided, and I was all but back to my normal cognitive self. This is when I was greeted by a vision that would haunt me forever. In the corner of my room, crouched atop my dresser, was a flame-colored creature with scaly, lizard-like skin. It had no hair, sharp teeth, and wore a medieval-looking outfit with a strap across its chest. This grotesque figure, about three feet tall, crouched grinning at me. Beside it stood a taller, less colorful creature, about four and a half feet tall. Though less detailed in my memory, its presence was equally unsettling. And even stranger I felt like I knew them.

They stared at me for what felt like an eternity before vanishing. Strangely, I wasn't afraid. I was perplexed. In hindsight, I believe these were the same demons that had plagued me during my earlier encounters. They weren't hallucinations; they were real.

This experience cemented my belief that psychedelics open doors to the spiritual realm. These substances are not mere chemical compounds; they are vehicles that grant access to dimensions we are not meant to traverse. When those doors open, you don't get to choose who or what comes through. For years, those demons remained a constant presence in my life, tethered to me by my choices and my sin. It wasn't until I surrendered my life to Christ that their hold was broken.

Looking back, I see God's hand in every terrifying, reckless, and chaotic moment. His angels shielded me when I was too foolish to protect myself. And though I wandered through darkness, He never abandoned me. These experiences, as harrowing as they were, became part of my testimony—a testament to God's unrelenting grace and the transformative power of His love and protecting nature.

Chapter Eleven

Fiberglass Deception

A.W. Tozer

"You may hide your theft from men, but never from God. He sees, and His justice will not sleep forever."

Hats and tassels filled the air as I stood among my classmates, a bittersweet mix of relief and uncertainty washing over me. I had officially made it through high school—not with flying colors, mind you, but I was standing there all the same. While my brothers and sister had their futures mapped out—college, careers, the whole nine yards—I was staring at a blank canvas. My grades weren't exactly scholarship material, and the only thing I was certain of was that I wasn't ready for the next chapter.

So, like many eighteen year olds grasping at a semblance of direction, I enrolled in the local JC. It wasn't glamorous, but it felt safe, a way to buy time while figuring things out. Little did I know, life had other plans—or, rather, my dad did.

That summer, my father extended an intriguing offer: move to Southern California to help him start a fiberglass pool company. He and his high school best friend had partnered with the friend's brother, and they needed an extra set of hands—cheap labor, to be exact. It wasn't a career path, but it was a fresh start and a chance to escape the rut I felt I was in.

Proverbs 10:9 says, "Whoever walks in integrity walks securely, but whoever takes crooked paths will be found out."

At the time, I didn't realize how prophetic those words would be.

Moving to Thousand Oaks felt like stepping into another world. The sunlit streets and cooler weather were a welcome change from the sweltering heat in the summertime and the chilly winters in my hometown. My job was simple: walk neighborhoods in Simi Valley and Valencia, handing out brochures for "America Fiberglass Pools." It wasn't glamorous, but I took pride in the work, knowing I was part of something bigger.

To my surprise, the calls started rolling in almost immediately. Within weeks, we had broken ground on a handful of pools. By the end of the first month, there were twelve projects underway, and business was booming. Watching my dad thrive was the best part. He was energized, driven, and for the first time in years, I saw a spark of pride in his eyes.

But life has a way of throwing curve balls when you least expect them.

Just as we were hitting our stride, and had almost twelve pools in the ground and awaiting to pour concrete for the foundations, the business crumbled beneath us. My dad's best friend's brother—the one managing the financial side—had been siphoning money from the company. Every deposit we'd received for labor, materials, and time was gone. He and his wife fled to Mexico, leaving a trail of chaos and betrayal.

The situation spiraled quickly. Not only had he stolen from us, but we learned he'd also borrowed heavily from the mafia to cover gambling debts. He'd used the stolen money to repay a fraction of what he owed, but it wasn't enough. Word got back to us that he hadn't made it far in Mexico before meeting a grim end with a bullet in the back of the head. Not sure if it was the mafia or federales.

As shocking as that revelation was, the aftermath was even more devastating. Dozens of pools were half-built, customers were furious, and lawsuits poured in like a relentless storm. My father's best friend—already grappling with the stress—was diagnosed with cancer. Whether the stress accelerated the disease or it was simply cruel timing, he passed away that summer, leaving a gaping hole in our hearts.

My parents were left with nothing. Every penny they had poured into the business was gone, and they couldn't even pay the rent. Watching them go through this was agonizing. My father, who had always been my rock, seemed utterly defeated.

One night, as we sat around the dinner table in our near-empty apartment, I felt a conviction in my heart. I had to do something, even if it wasn't much. I told my parents to take the $1,300 I had earned that summer. It wasn't a fortune, but it was all I had.

I can still see the look on my father's face as I handed over the cash—part pride, part heartbreak. He didn't want to take it, but he knew he had no choice. I kept $75 for myself, though I didn't tell them how little I was holding onto. If they had known, they never would have agreed to the plan.

There was one condition: the T-Bird. My parents had two vehicles—a truck and the old Thunderbird. I told them to take the truck and head back up north, where they had contacts and a chance to start over. I'd take the T-Bird and figure out my next steps on my own. The T-bird was actually worth more than $1,300, so I was thankful they had the extra car.

The day we parted ways is etched in my memory. My parents packed what little they had left into the truck and hugged me tightly. And we said our goodbys.

As I watched them drive away, a lump formed in my throat. I was scared—terrified, really—but there was also a flicker of hope. I climbed into the T-Bird, started the engine, and headed south.

The road to Hollywood stretched out before me like an open book, each mile a blank page waiting to be written. The future was uncertain, but one thing was clear: this was the beginning of a new chapter, one where faith, resilience, and a whole lot of grit would be my guiding lights.

I didn't realize it then, but God was already at work, shaping me through the trials. Like Job, I was about to face some unholy trials and tribulations.

And so, with $75 in my pocket, a T-Bird, and adventure in my heart, I drove toward an uncertain future, ready to face whatever came next.

Chapter Twelve

Belly Of The Beast

King Solomn

"Truthful lips endure forever, but a lying tongue is but for a moment."

I had $75 to my name and an incredible, pink-champagne, fully restored 1972 Thunderbird with a white leather interior. It was a head-turner—like a movie star in chrome form. All my worldly belongings were stuffed in the trunk and backseat as I rolled into Hollywood.

Getting off at Cahuenga Boulevard, I took a left on Franklin and then a right onto Vine Street. The city felt alive—its pulse humming through the pavement and into my chest. As I pulled into a gas station to top off the tank, a sharply dressed man approached me. His tailored suit screamed old-school Hollywood, and his cologne hit me before his voice did.

"Beautiful car," he said, gesturing toward the Thunderbird. His tone was as smooth as a jazz saxophone. "I work in the film industry, and I'd love to buy it off you. Eleven grand, cash, right now."

I froze. $11,000.00?! That was more money than I'd ever seen, let alone held in my hands. But something inside me, perhaps divine intuition or sheer stubbornness, said no. I thanked him but politely declined. His expression twisted into one of pure disbelief, as if I'd just turned down a winning a million dollar lottery ticket.

"You sure about that?" he pressed, his voice laced with incredulity.

"Ya I'm sure," I replied, trying to sound confident.

As he walked away, shaking his head, doubt gnawed at me. What am I doing? With $65 left after putting $10 in the tank, I could have used that money to get a place, eat something other than gas station snacks, and maybe even jump-start my Hollywood dreams. But hindsight's a funny thing—it always wears rose-colored glasses.

Back in the car, I drove down Vine, taking in the neon signs and the gritty allure of the city I'd dreamed about since I was a kid. Hollywood the birthplace of cinematic legends. As I rolled onto Hollywood Boulevard, I spotted the Walk of Fame. Those small stars were embedded in the concrete like headstones in a graveyard that seemed to whisper stories of glory, heartbreak, and a time that flickered in the past.

I stopped outside Hollywood High, my mom's alma mater. It looked different now—graffiti sprawled across the walls like scars. It broke my heart to see it. Mom used to tell me stories about her time here, hanging out with Natalie Wood and Stefanie Powers, and their infamous graduation prank of cutting down a historic tree that stood at the schools entrance. I could almost hear her laughter as she recounted it.

Shaking off the melancholy, I decided to drive up to Runyon Canyon. With the Sunday paper I'd grabbed at the gas station, I scoured the job listings. My eyes landed on a peculiar ad: limo driver for Universal Studios. "Flexible hours. High pay." It sounded perfect, except for one minor detail—The city was entirely unknown to me.

That night, I parked the Thunderbird at Runyon and tried to sleep. Hollywood's nightlife was a symphony of chaos—horns blaring, sirens wailing, and voices shouting into the void. Around 2 am, a homeless man tapped on my window with what I think was a ring or maybe a bottle. He offered me a trade: a bottle of whiskey in exchange for the backseat to sleep in.

"Sorry, man," I muttered, waving him off. My heart pounded as he lingered for a moment before shuffling away.

By morning, I was groggy but determined. After a quick breakfast at Denny's, I drove to Universal Studios and found the office listed in the ad. Inside, a stunning receptionist greeted me. Her accent was foreign and melodic, unlike anything I'd ever heard.

She smiled. "Are you here for the limo driver position?"

"Yes, ma'am," I said, trying not to sound too green.

Moments later, a short, animated man with slicked-back hair and a thick East Coast accent burst out of the office.

"You the kid here for the driver position?" he barked.

"Yes, sir," I said, standing straighter than a soldier at attention.

"You know the city?" His sharp eyes locked onto mine.

"Absolutely," I LIED, praying he wouldn't ask for specifics.

"Great. Tonight, you're taking me and some friends out for drinks. Be here at 6."

"Six. Got it," I replied, though internally I was screaming, Oh no. What have I done?

As I left the office, panic set in. I didn't know Hollywood. The streets might as well have been a labyrinth. I was about to lead a pack of wolves through it that evening, and as the sun dipped behind the hills, I could feel the pressure.

The day stretched out before me like a blank canvas, and I spent it aimlessly driving around the city. I needed to clear my mind, and I thought a little sightseeing might do the trick. Griffith Park was the first stop, and as I stood at the observatory looking down at the sprawling city below, I was amazed by how massive it all was. The city was an endless ocean of lights, concrete, and dreams, and it felt like it could swallow me whole if I didn't get a hold of myself. I stood there for a while, imagining what it would be like to own this town, to walk down these streets with my head held high, a local legend.

The thought flickered in and out of my mind as I drove through the winding roads of the Hollywood Hills. I thought to myself, I'm gonna conquer this town. I'm gonna own this place. I had an arrogant confidence that wasn't earned, but I wore it like armor.

I drove around aimlessly for a bit more, stopping by the YMCA to take a quick shower. It wasn't much, but it was something. I was starting to feel like I had a handle on things, even though I was far from it. The clothes I had weren't exactly "hip." The Nor Cal style was a bit behind, and my wardrobe was a mix of hand-me-downs from my brothers, but I figured it'd have to do. The money was running low, so I pinched pennies at Denny's, ordering the smallest meal I could get away with. My stomach growled, but I tried not to think about it.

When I finally showed up back at Universal Studios, the guy looked at me like he could see straight through me. He probably noticed my outdated clothes, my scuffed shoes, the weariness in my eyes that I couldn't quite mask. And then he laughed—just a quick chuckle, but it stung.

"All right, let's head out to the car," he said.

I followed him outside, trying to pretend that everything was fine. There, under the towering Universal Studios Hotels, was a sight that took my breath away—a charcoal gray Lincoln limousine. It was pristine, gleaming in the light, every inch of it flawless.

I think I started sweating.

Tony, the guy who had been giving me the tour, noticed my Thomas guide and raised an eyebrow.

"Why do you have that?" he asked.

"Just for reference," I said, feeling a pang of guilt.

It wasn't for reference, not really. It was for survival.

Tony and his friends—two incredibly attractive women and another guy—climbed into the back, and Tony gave me a quick crash course on how to drive this massive machine. He talked about the partition, the stereo, the windows, like he was explaining the controls of a jet. It was all over my head, but I nodded along. The confidence was fading, replaced by the realization that I had no idea what I was doing.

The plan was simple: take them to the Rainbow Room. The man and his entourage piled into the limo, laughing and chatting like old friends. I gripped the steering wheel, staring at the maze of streets ahead.

"Let's go to Spago," one of them said, throwing out the name of a restaurant I'd never heard of. They flipped the script, but I had to roll with it or be found out.

"Sure thing," I replied, trying to sound confident while discreetly flipping through the Thomas Guide map that my dad gave me before we parted. We didn't have GPS this was the late eighties.

The night unfolded in a blur of wrong turns, near-misses, and silent prayers. Each stop felt like a minor victory, though my passengers didn't seem to notice my inexperience. By some miracle—or divine intervention—I managed to get them to Spagos.

As the night wore on, I realized something: Hollywood wasn't just a city. It was a beast—a creature that could swallow you whole if you let it. But maybe, just maybe, I was strong enough to tame it. I had a feeling I was in trouble, but my pride was too strong, and my sin too great to admit it. The idea of telling the guy that I was lying—that I didn't know what I was doing—was simply unbearable. So, I swallowed my guilt and nodded along when he told me to go park and come back at 9, after they had finished eating. After an hour I pulled up to the front of Spagos and they were standing and waiting. They pilled back into the limo and Tony assured me he knew a shortcut to the Rainbow Room.

We were off and finally reached Sunset Boulevard, and Tony told me to turn left. Another mile down, the neon sign of the Rainbow Room blinked to life. My heart raced, not from excitement, but from sheer anxiety. The car felt like a rolling coffin as I pulled up in front, hoping nothing would go wrong.

The crowd outside was a wild sight—long, greasy hair, studded jackets, leather pants. The true essence of rock 'n' roll. I watched Tony and his friends disappear into the night club, and then I went to find parking. I must've done ten loops around the block. My anxiety was skyrocketing.

Eventually, I found a spot, parked, and waited. An hour passed, then another. When they finally came out, I had already received the page on the limos pager, so I rushed to the front. They looked buzzed, laughing, and I did my best to mask my frustration.

"Take us to Pink's," Tony said, rolling the partition closed before I could ask a single question.

My mind was racing. What on earth is Pink's? I'd never heard of it. Was it a nightclub? A record store? I rifled through my Thomas guide, flipping through pages desperately, but it was nowhere to be found.

I wasn't going to admit that I didn't know. I couldn't.

But after about eight minutes of dead silence, Tony's voice broke through the partition.

"You don't know where you're going, do you, kid?"

It felt like the ground dropped out from under me. I could feel my face turn beet red as he laughed. Not a little chuckle. Oh no. This was full-on, gut-busting laughter.

"You've got a lotta balls," he said in his thick New York accent. "Pink's is the most famous hot dog stand in the world!"

His friends didn't laugh. They just stared at me in awkward silence. I was mortified.

I couldn't help myself. I mumbled, "I'm sorry. I really don't know where it is."

"Take us back to the hotel," Tony said between laughs.

I didn't even try to argue. I turned around, retraced my steps, and made the drive back to the hotel. My mind was swirling, but I kept my focus. I wasn't going to screw this up any more than I already had.

When we finally arrived, I looked at Tony. My pride had been shattered, but I needed this job.

"Please forgive me," I said. "I really need a job."

Tony looked at me, still grinning.

"Don't worry, kid," he said, his voice softening. "After this, you'll do just fine."

I looked at him, almost in disbelief. "And please don't tell the owner about this."

He looked at me like I was insane. "I am the owner."

We shook hands, and that was it. I had no idea what to say. But one thing was for sure—I wasn't going to forget this night.

Chapter Thirteen

The Hollywood Hustle

Augustine of Hippo

"He who deceives others is first deceived himself."

I returned to my car, parking under the shadows of a tree at Griffith Park. The day had drained me, and exhaustion seeped into my bones as I reclined the seat as far as it would go, trying to make peace with my situation. Sleep came sporadically, interrupted by distant city noises and the unease of knowing my reality—no job, no home, and dwindling funds.

Morning arrived with sunlight piercing through the windshield, a reluctant wake-up call to face another day. My stomach growled, but I ignored it, pulling out the crumpled newspaper I'd snagged the day before. The classifieds section was a sea of words, most of them irrelevant or unattainable. But one ad caught my eye: **"Extras needed for film and TV. No experience required."**

It wasn't stable, nor was it a long-term solution, but it was a glimmer of possibility. The office wasn't far—just down Bronson and Sunset—so I pulled out my trusty Thomas Guide, charted the route, and started the car.

The address led me to a small plaza across from Fox KTTV. At its center stood a modest hotel with faded letters spelling "The Hollywood Hotel." I parked cautiously, taking a moment to grab my prized possession, a JVC camcorder. I couldn't afford to have it stolen—it was expensive and an item I cared a lot for. Clutching it tightly, I ascended a wrought iron stairway to the second floor.

The office was unassuming—a single room with two desks and walls plastered with 8x10 headshots. An attractive young woman greeted me with a smile and a faint accent. "Are you here for casting?" she asked.

"I am," I replied, placing my camcorder on the desk and trying to exude confidence.

Before I could say more, the door creaked open, and in walked an older man. He was short and fragile-looking, his presence commanding but peculiar. My eyes were drawn to his right eye, scarred and clouded—it was unmistakably glass. The sight triggered a memory of my mother, who had lost her eye to glaucoma at fifteen, the same year she lost her father. My mother had a glass eye and so did this gentleman.

The man extended his hand. "I'm Jack."

I shook it firmly. "Alex."

Jack moved to the other desk, sat down, and began a rapid-fire monologue. His voice was raspy but full of energy, like a salesman who had mastered his craft. He rattled off his resume, a cascade of titles from the '70s and '80s: *The Best Little Whorehouse in Texas, Cannonball Run, Godfather 2* and countless others.

I tried to keep up, nodding as he pitched me the dream of being in film and TV. He said all he needed was a Polaroid and a $25 registration fee to start submitting me to casting companies.

It was a compelling pitch, but reality hit hard. I had $65 to my name, no job, and no roof over my head. I couldn't afford to gamble. "I'm sorry, I can't sign up right now," I said, careful not to reveal how dire my situation was.

Jack's face twitched with frustration, but then his gaze shifted to my camcorder. "Is that yours?"

"It is," I said, a hint of pride in my voice.

His expression softened as an idea sparked. "Maybe we can make a deal," he said. "If you're looking for work, you could spend a few hours a day shooting videos of clients for their registration. In return, I'll help you get rolling with some TV and movie gigs. And maybe a couple extra bucks"

It wasn't the solution I'd expected, but it felt like a lifeline. "That could work," I said, trying to mask my relief.

Jack leaned back in his chair, satisfied. "Where do you live?"

"Close by," I lied, knowing the truth—that I was sleeping in my car—would probably scare him off.

"Great. Come back tomorrow," he said.

I spent the rest of the day wandering the streets near the Hollywood Hotel, conserving gas and weighing my options. I found a YMCA nearby and managed to grab a shower, scrubbing off the grime and anxiety of the past day. Dinner was another $5 meal at Denny's, and with my funds down to $55, I parked my car in the alley behind the hotel and prepared for another restless night.

The alley was eerily quiet, save for the occasional scurrying of rats or the muffled hum of passing cars. Sleep came fitfully, my mind racing with uncertainty.

Morning broke early, and I headed into Denny's again, but this time I didn't spend a dime. I grabbed a free newspaper someone had left behind and pocketed a few ketchup packets, squeezing them into, and stirring them in a warm cup of water for a makeshift meal. Desperation makes you resourceful, I thought bitterly.

When the time came, I climbed the stairs to Jack's office, camcorder in hand. This wasn't just another day; this was a gamble, a test of whether or not I could make something out of nothing. As I opened the door, the young woman smiled again, and Jack looked up from his desk, his scarred eye-catching the morning light.

"All right, kid," he said. "Let's see what you've got."

he grabbed the camcorder I had brought and waved it lazily in my direction. "Whenever you're ready."

He gestured me over and spread out a pile of papers across the desk. They were mock scripts for clients to read during their auditions. One of them, I remember, read something like, "When I choose a drink, I always choose Coke," or another equally uninspired line that made me wonder what these people were getting themselves into.

That day was a parade of faces—eight people in total. Most of them were young kids, their wide eyes sparkling with dreams of stardom. A couple of adults came through as well, all hoping that Jack's promises would open some golden door to fame. What struck me though was how many of them were Black. I learned later that Jack was advertising in areas like Compton, Englewood, and South Central because he could get cheaper ad rates there. It was a grim realization, but at the time, I was too focused on filming and surviving to dig deeper.

Jack worked the room like a seasoned showman, delivering the same high-energy spiel to everyone who walked in. His pitch was magnetic. They'd read the script, I'd record them, and Jack would pocket $25 from each hopeful. In return, they got a flimsy sheet of paper with a list of other casting agencies—essentially his "competitors." It baffled me at first, but I realized it was part of his strategy to maintain goodwill while ensuring they left with something tangible.

By the end of the day, Jack had made $200. He handed me $25, almost half of what I had to my name. It wasn't much, but to me, it was a lifeline. I thanked him, and he waved it off. "Don't worry about it," he said in his thick New York accent, one that I'd only ever heard on TV growing up. It was oddly comforting, almost cartoonish in its familiarity.

Gabriella was there, too, manning the phones with an air of elegance that seemed out of place in Jack's tiny operation. Her accent gave her an air of sophistication, and I couldn't help but chuckle inwardly. Jack clearly knew the power of perception.

As the days went on, I started piecing together the reality of what we were doing. It didn't take long to realize that this was all a scam. The cheesy scripts, the unfulfilled promises, the token sheet of paper handed to every client—it was all smoke and mirrors. And yet, I stayed. I was broke, far from God, and willing to compromise my morals for gas in my tank and food in my stomach.

I was still sleeping in my car, parked in the same alley behind the Hollywood Hotel. One day, Jack noticed the duffel bags in my back seat. He stopped, pointed, and let out a raspy laugh. "You sleeping in your car?"

I shrugged, trying to play it off. "Yeah."

He laughed harder. "The Hotel T-bird!"

I chuckled. "It's not that bad. Got AC, heat, and an entertainment center. The price is right!"

Jack wheezed out another laugh. "Kid, this isn't exactly the safest city. Why don't you crash in the office with me?"

I blinked in surprise. "With you?"

"Yeah," he said, his laugh tapering off. "I sleep in the office. He winked, the price is right!"

His words caught me off guard. I'd assumed Jack had a place of his own, somewhere far removed from this cramped little office. When we got up to his office I said "Where?" I asked, glancing around the single room. Its large glass window faced the walkway balcony, leaving little privacy.

Jack smirked. "Behind the desk. Got a mat and a sleeping bag. It's all I need."

It was strange hearing that from him. Jack had an air of authority, of someone who had the world figured out. But here he was, living as humbly as I was. Maybe even more so.

The offer was odd, but after a homeless man had banged on my car window late one night, scaring me half to death, I realized Jack might be right. This city wasn't safe, and the office, bizarre as it was, offered some protection.

I accepted his offer. That night, I moved in.

The arrangement was far from ordinary, but I was grateful. I rolled out a sleeping bag behind Jack's desk and lay down, staring at the ceiling as the hum of Hollywood buzzed faintly through the glass. For the first time in weeks, I felt a tiny flicker of stability, even if it came in the strangest of forms.

It wasn't home, but for now, it was enough.

Chapter Fourteen

The Inglewood Giant

Charles Spurgeon

"Better to be poor with integrity than to be rich by deceiving others."

The hustle was in full swing, and Jack seemed reinvigorated by my youthful energy. My camcorder, bulky but state-of-the-art for its time, added a thin veil of legitimacy to our operation, fooling the desperate hopefuls who came through the door. Jack always justified his scam by pointing to the sheet of paper he handed out—a list of legitimate casting agencies, as if that made everything else above board.

It didn't take long to discover Jack had another layer to his hustle. He had a photographer named Jeff working with him. Jack would up-sell the clients(victims) who came in, convincing them that their chances of landing a commercial or movie role would skyrocket with professional head shots or a Zed card. Today, you'd just upload everything online, but back in the '80s, it was all about tangible, glossy 8x10s and neatly printed cards. It wasn't cheap, but Jack's silver tongue ensured almost no one left the office without paying for at least one of the two: a registration fee, a photo shoot, or sometimes both.

Jack was slick, the kind of New Yorker who could sell ice to an Eskimo. And his ads targeted struggling neighborhoods—places where hope was a rare commodity. They weren't looking for stardom; they were looking for a lifeline.

One day, a guy named George walked into the office. George was massive, easily 6'6" and three hundred pounds. His size made me nervous. I couldn't shake the image of him realizing we were conning him and deciding to take his frustration out on us—physically. But George turned out to be a gentle giant. He smiled warmly, shook my hand like I was an old friend, and listened intently as Jack spun his web of promises. George didn't just fall for the pitch; he paid for the registration fee and a headshot session. My relief was almost palpable.

To Jack's credit, Jeff was a talented photographer. The headshots were high-quality, and even though the rest of the operation was shady, at least the clients got something worthwhile. When George's photos were ready, Jack handed them to me. "You've got a car," he said casually. "Drive these over to George's place."

I had no idea what I was in for.

I'd never been to Inglewood or Compton, and I didn't know what to expect. Growing up in my small-town bubble, these were just names I'd heard on the news, places whispered about with a mix of fear and misunderstanding. I pulled out my trusty Thomas Guide, mapped the quickest route to George's house, and set off.

The L.A. freeway system was a labyrinth of interchanges and concrete rivers, and I was still learning its quirks. The chaos of it all—cars darting in and out of lanes, horns blaring, endless signs—made me feel like a fish swimming upstream.

About ten minutes into the drive, I noticed my gas gauge dipping dangerously low. I had no choice but to pull off the freeway at Florence Boulevard and find a gas station.

The moment I pulled into the station, I felt a shift in the atmosphere. The air felt heavier, the stares sharper. I was out of place, a skinny white kid with a classic Thunderbird, sticking out like a sore thumb. A group of guys stood near the entrance, their voices loud and their body language confident, bordering on intimidating.

I got out of the car, trying to project an air of calm that I didn't feel. The gas pump was ancient, one of those with the spinning dials instead of a digital display. As I filled the tank, I kept my head down, avoiding eye contact. But I could feel their eyes on me. I didn't bother surveying my surroundings at the gas station—a rookie mistake, given how out of place I was. The reality hit when a black woman in heels and a glittering, tight-fitting outfit hurried toward me, her urgency slicing through the air.

"Hey, white boy," she said, her voice sharp but oddly protective. "What are you doing up here? You betta move on outa here, or you gonna be sorry."

Her words pulled me out of my bubble. I glanced around and saw it—young angry black men slowly moving in my direction. I was the only white guy there, and their glares made it clear that my presence wasn't welcome.

I froze for a moment before shoving the gas nozzle back into the pump, heart pounding like a drum in my chest. I looked back at the woman, who was still urging me to leave, then at the men closing the gap between us. My survival instincts kicked in. I jumped into my car, slammed the door, and stomped on the gas.

The tires squealed as I tore out of the station. My heart was still racing as the woman in heels grew smaller in my rear view mirror. It hit me then: she was a prostitute. The sequins, the demeanor—it all clicked. I'd only seen depictions of women like her in movies or TV shows, and seeing one in real life was a jarring experience.

But what haunted me more was her face. She looked like she was in her 30s, but her eyes told a different story. The lines around her mouth, the wear on her skin—it all screamed a life of hardship and despair. She radiated pain, anger, and fear, as if her very soul was carrying the weight of her struggles.

Back then, I didn't fully understand the spiritual battles people faced. I wasn't in a place to see how God's light could heal the darkness in her life—or mine, for that matter. But even in my ignorance, I felt a pang of sadness. I would've prayed for her if I'd known how, but truthfully, neither of us had God on our minds that day.

Still, I was grateful for her warning. Without it, I might have found myself in a situation far worse than a few angry stares.

Back on the 110 Freeway, the incident replayed in my mind, but I pushed it aside as I navigated toward George's house in Inglewood. The Thomas Guide was a lifesaver, its pages crinkled and smudged from constant use.

The sun was high, casting sharp shadows as I pulled onto George's street around 1 PM, just as I'd promised. George must've recognized my car because he came outside, waving and signaling for me to stay in my car.

Confused, I cracked the door open, but he jogged over before I could step out and leaned into my car window. "Thanks for bringing these by, but you're not safe here."

His words made me sit up straighter. I scanned the neighborhood and noticed groups of young men hanging out on porches, their eyes trained on my car. Some held bottles of beer, laughing loudly, but their glances in my direction weren't friendly.

The gas station incident came rushing back. I felt the same unease. George tried to smile, probably to put me at ease, but it was clear he was serious.

"Oh, right," I said, fumbling for words. "Well, here are the photos. I think they came out great—you're going to turn some heads with these."

George opened the box, and his face lit up as he sifted through the glossy prints. "Man, these are perfect," he said, his grin wide. For a moment, the tension in the air faded.

He looked over his shoulder at the young men on the porches, then back at me. "I'd ask you to come in," he said, laughing nervously, "but...you know."

I nodded, understanding more than I wanted to. Growing up in the mountains, I had never experienced racial tension. My small town didn't have the kind of divides I was witnessing now. The realization that I wasn't welcome here—not because of anything I'd done, but simply because of who I was—saddened me.

George must've seen the look on my face because he chuckled. "I think you're the first white guy to ever drive into this neighborhood."

I laughed, though it felt hollow. "Well, I'm honored," I said, trying to lighten the mood.

"Stay safe, man," George said, stepping back as I started the car.

The drive back to Hollywood was slow, the traffic as thick as ever. The nine miles felt like an eternity, giving me plenty of time to think. The day had been a roller coaster of emotions—fear, gratitude, sadness.

As I navigated the congested freeway, I decided I might try to get some headshots done for myself. Maybe I'd even submit them to one of the legitimate agencies on Jack's list. The idea was a small flicker of hope, a reminder that even in the chaos of my life, there were still paths worth exploring.

But one thing was clear: I'd never forget the faces I'd seen that day—the woman in heels and George's quiet determination. They were both reminders of a world I was only beginning to understand, a world that would shape me in ways I couldn't yet imagine.

Chapter Fifteen

Pow Wow Under The Indian Moon

A.W. Tozer

"Entertainment, when not tempered by holiness, becomes a distraction that blinds the heart to the voice of God."

When I got back to the office, Jack was sitting with Gabrielle, flipping through one of the casting lists. I decided to ask him what it would cost for some head shots.

"For you? Next to nothing," Jack said, grinning.

"Great. Let's do it," I replied. He called the photographer, Jeff, and scheduled it for the following evening after our usual "work" routine. As much as I hated to admit it, scamming people had become the job.

That night, Gabrielle left, and Jack announced he was going out. "You can stay here, but I only have one key, so..."

"I'll head out too," I said, pretending I had plans. Truth was, I had no idea what to do. As Jack locked up and disappeared down the stairs, I felt the city calling.

Hunger won out first. Just below Jack's office was a tiny Thai restaurant. I'd never had Thai food before, so I walked in, hoping for the best. The menu was in Thai, which might as well have been hieroglyphics to me.

I pointed at a random item. "Chicken?"

The man behind the counter nodded and soon brought out a steaming bowl of soup. I didn't want soup, but I figured, why not? One spoonful and I was hooked. The flavors were complex and unfamiliar, but they worked. That little bowl of soup became my gateway to Thai food for years to come.

After finishing, I cracked open the fortune cookie, paid the man, and stepped outside. As I looked up, I saw the towering Hollywood Hotel, its rooftop glowing under the marquee lights. I remembered reading there was a bar and restaurant up there.

"Why not?" I thought. I wasn't twenty one yet, and my brother gave me his driver's license and had another one issued to him so I could use it for clubs and booze.

The elevator doors opened on the 20th floor, and I felt like I'd stepped into a seventies time capsule. Purple booths, teardrop lights, and a faint whiff of stale carpet gave the place its retro charm. I found a seat at the bar, ordered a Miller, and handed over a few crumpled bills.

As I sipped my beer, a voice from behind startled me.

"What are you doing up here?"

I turned and saw Gabrielle flanked by an attractive woman and two men with striking features—long black hair, traditional leather outfits, turquoise embroidery, and feathers. They looked like they had stepped straight out of a historical epic.

Gabrielle smiled and introduced me to her friend, a fellow Swiss traveler, and the two men. They were Native American Indians, their presence commanding without a word.

"We're heading to Malibu for a small powwow by the ocean," Gabrielle said. "Want to come?"

I had no plans, so I shrugged. "Sure."

She laughed. "Great, because our car's too small. Can you drive?"

I laughed too. "Why not?"

We picked up two more people—another Indian man and woman—along with a couple of ice chests. Gabrielle, her friend, and one of the men rode with me while the others followed in a second car.

We took Santa Monica Boulevard to the beach and then cruised along the Pacific Coast Highway. The moon hung low and enormous over the ocean, casting a silver glow on the waves. By the time we pulled into a public lot in Malibu and backed my car onto the sand, it was nearly 9 PM.

One of the men handed me a cassette tape. "Play this."

I popped it in and cranked up the volume. The opening riffs of Deep Purple's *Smoke on the Water* blasted through my custom speakers from the opened trunk. The group erupted in cheers, the music fueling the fire they built just a few yards from the car.

For the first hour, it felt like a casual beach party—beers, music, laughter. Then things shifted. The music went silent, and one of the men lit a joint, passing it around. I sat between Gabrielle and her friend Gina, learning more about their travels. They'd planned a three-month stay in the US before heading back to Switzerland.

Then one of the Native men returned from his car carrying a drum adorned with feathers. The other two joined him, and together, they began a rhythmic beat around the fire. The talking ceased. The night grew still except for the drum's haunting cadence and their chanting voices.

I was transfixed. The rhythm pulled at me, its hypnotic power impossible to resist. It felt ancient, otherworldly—like a ceremony I had no right to witness.

That's when the atmosphere shifted again. The air grew heavier and colder. A shiver crawled up my spine as I stared into the flames. The chants and drumbeats seemed to reach into a part of me I didn't know existed, pulling me toward something dark.

Looking back now, I believe unclean spirits were present that night. At the time, I was too naive to understand, but I felt their weight, their pull. These spirits stayed with me for years, haunting my dreams and decisions.

Through the flames and the shadows, I glanced at the people around me. Their faces blurred in the firelight, and for a moment, they didn't look like people at all. The rhythmic chanting became more intense, almost maniacal. I couldn't move, couldn't speak—just sat there, a fragile mind in a fragile body, staring into a fire that felt alive.

If there had been a lens to reveal the spiritual realm, I have no doubt the beach would've been swarming with grotesque creatures that night.

Around midnight, the ceremony ended as abruptly as it began. The drumming stopped, and the spell broke. We packed up in silence and headed back to Hollywood.

That drive home felt like a blur, the events of the night playing on repeat in my mind. I had witnessed something ancient and powerful, something I didn't understand but knew would linger with me.

And linger it did. We drove back to the hotel and dropped off the Indians, but I couldn't help noticing the guy with the long black hair lingering behind, clearly reluctant to let Gabrielle go. She was soaking up his attention, smiling and playing coy. Gina, her friend, rolled her eyes and muttered something sharp in Swiss German. Gabrielle laughed, said her goodbyes, and got back in the car.

"I don't know where you live," I said awkwardly, turning to them.

"Just around the corner," Gabrielle replied. "Friend's condo. He's in Iran right now. The power's off, but the plumbing works."

We pulled up to the small complex, and Gabrielle said, "Stay the night. It's too late to go back." I hesitated but realized Jack probably wouldn't be thrilled about being woken up in the middle of the night. "Sure," I said, trying to sound casual.

The condo was simple—one bath, and a lone king-sized mattress on the floor. My first thought: *Where am I going to sleep?* I asked, and they both laughed.

"With us, of course," Gabrielle said, her tone matter-of-fact.

The fear that struck me was immediate. I was a virgin. Sure, there was that one awkward experience at Catholic retreat, but this? *This* was terrifying. I tried to mask my panic with a nonchalant, "Oh, yeah, of course," as if I was totally cool with it.

They lit candles for light, their soft flickering making the space feel surreal. Gabrielle and Gina went into the bathroom, chatting and laughing in Swiss German. When they came out, they slid under the covers.

My turn. I took my time in the bathroom, splashing cold water on my face, trying to get a grip. When I finally climbed into bed, I was so tense I thought my heart would burst out of my chest. I could sense their expectations, but I was paralyzed. I did nothing.

Relief washed over me as the night passed without incident.

In the morning, we all woke got ready and headed to the casting office, and soon the chaos of the day began.

Jack pulled me aside and said, "You can head over to the photographer if you want." Grateful for the break, I left.

The shoot was an experience—posing in awkward angles, swinging a golf club, even trying a fake laugh for some "candid" shots. When we finished, the photographer handed me the negatives and directed me to a nearby shop for prints. It cost me $45 to get one hundred 8x10s, which felt like a fortune.

Back at the office, Jack greeted me with a sly grin. "Good night last night, huh?" he teased, winking.

Embarrassed, I stammered, "Oh, it was really nothing."

He chuckled. "Relax, I'm not judging."

"Seriously, nothing happened," I insisted, but he just laughed and walked away.

Later, I called my brother; he was attending the University Of Santa Barbara (UCSB) from a pay phone. His roommate, Don, picked up, and we chatted a bit. This is when he invited me up to the legendary Isla Vista Halloween party on the Tuesday coming up. "Bring beer," he added. "It's impossible to get alcohol on holloween."

I headed back to the office and told Jack about my Santa Barbara plans. He laughed, saying, "That party's a global event. Come back in one piece."

After grabbing dinner at the Thai place downstairs, I went up to the bar again. Just as I sat down with a beer, someone tapped my shoulder. Gabrielle and Gina.

"What are you doing tonight?" Gabrielle asked.

"Nothing," I replied.

"Come with us," she said. "Let's check out Hollywood Boulevard."

We wandered through tourist traps, laughed at ridiculous trinkets, and ended the night playing pool at Hollywood Billiards. It was light, fun, and exactly what I needed.

But when I returned to Jack's office, the night took a darker turn. The door was unlocked, and the office was eerily silent. In the dim light, I noticed the bathroom door was ajar. I walked closer and froze.

Jack was slumped against the wall, legs outstretched, his glass eye open, staring blankly while the other was shut in sleep. A rubber bungee was tied around his arm and some tin foil, lighter, and a syringe was laying beside him.

My stomach churned. I'd seen drugs before, but this? This was different. This was heroin.

I backed away, the sight burning into my memory. I couldn't stay there anymore, so I just planned on sleeping in my car from here on out.

Chapter Sixteen

Cold Steel Raw Deal

David Wilkerson

"God does not promise to keep us from trials, but He promises to be with us in the midst of them."

The night was quiet, but my mind wasn't. I couldn't shake the feeling that I needed to pick up a little weed for the Santa Barbara trip. Showing up empty-handed felt like a rookie move, so I grabbed my keys and headed out into the city. The streets were dimly lit, shadows stretching long under the occasional flickering streetlamp. I cruised aimlessly, looking for a spot that felt discreet but not entirely deserted.

After a few minutes of driving, I spotted them—a couple of black guys standing on a corner, illuminated by the glow of a nearby convenience store sign. They looked rough around the edges, their postures casual but their eyes sharp. I hesitated for a moment but brushed it off. I was young, confident—invincible, or so I thought.

I pulled up to the curb and rolled down the window. "Hey," I said, trying to sound casual. "Know where I can score a little smoke?"

The guy in the light tan jacket stepped forward, his eyes narrowing. "You a cop?" His tone was sharp, almost accusing.

I let out a nervous laugh. "No, man, just looking to buy."

He stared at me for a beat, then nodded. "I don't got any on me, but I can get it. Wait down there." He pointed to the end of the block.

I agreed, telling him I needed an eighth or a quarter, and drove to where he indicated. My heart was pounding, though I wasn't sure if it was nerves or adrenaline. The area was too quiet now, the kind of quiet that makes you feel exposed.

Minutes dragged by, each one heavier than the last, until he finally reappeared. He walked up to my car, his movements quick, almost frantic. Something about his demeanor put me on edge.

"Thirty-five," he said curtly, holding a small bag.

"I've only got twenty," I replied, keeping my voice steady.

His jaw tightened, and for a moment, I thought he might walk away. But then he nodded reluctantly. "Fine. Let me see the money."

I held up the twenty, and he snatched it from my hand, shoving the bag at me before walking away. Something felt off. As soon as he was out of sight, I opened the bag and took a sniff. Oregano, or some other garbage meant to fool idiots like me.

Anger flared in my chest. Without thinking, I got out of the car and started after him. My strides were long and purposeful, my pulse thundering in my ears. His friend, the other guy on the corner, noticed me approaching and stepped into my path.

"Where you going?" he asked, his voice low and threatening.

"That wasn't weed," I snapped, my frustration boiling over. "Your buddy just scammed me."

He didn't respond. Instead, his hand went to his waist, and in one fluid motion, he pulled out a gun and pressed it hard against my side.

"You're gonna go, boy," he hissed, his eyes cold and unflinching.

The reality of the situation hit me like a freight train. I wasn't invincible. I wasn't in control. I was standing on a dark street corner with a gun in my ribs over twenty bucks.

I raised my hands slightly, palms out. "Okay," I said carefully, my voice trembling. "I'm going. No problem."

I backed away slowly, my legs barely holding me upright. He watched me until I reached my car, then turned and disappeared into the night like a shadow.

I climbed into the driver's seat, my hands shaking as I fumbled to start the engine. My breath came in shallow gasps, and my heart felt like it might burst out of my chest. Twenty dollars lighter and a whole lot wiser, I drove back to my spot, parked, and sat in silence.

Sleep didn't come easy that night. Every time I closed my eyes, I saw the glint of that gun and felt the cold metal pressing against my side.

The next morning, I left for Santa Barbara, determined to leave Jack's demons—and maybe a bit of my own—behind.

Chapter Seventeen

Santa Barbara Side Show

John Chrysostom

Drunkenness and revelry are the devil's nets, and those who are caught in them are dragged to destruction."

My trip to Santa Barbara to visit my brother was straightforward—two hours tops. I left at 9 am, aiming to arrive at 11.

The T-Bird, with its four twenty nine four-barrel engine, was a beast—a relic of raw American muscle. At nineteen, I pushed it to its limits, weaving through California highways as though I owned the road. It was 1989, and Halloween fell on a Tuesday so I'd Hang out with my Brother and his roommates a day early just to catch up with everyone. Santa Barbara was infamous for throwing what many considered the wildest Halloween party in the world. Tens of thousands of college kids flocked there, drunk, high, and surging with hormonal chaos. Nothing could possibly go wrong, right?

Except everything did. Overdoses, fights, sexual assaults—it was the kind of pandemonium that kept the police and faculty on high alert. By the nineties, they'd had enough and brought the hammer down, effectively choking the life out of those infamous celebrations. But this was 89, and I was a reckless, unclean-spirit-filled youth with "fun" on my mind. That fun, of course, was anything but virtuous.

By 10:45, I rolled into my brother's apartment complex, fifteen minutes early. It was Friday, so most of the students were in class or buried in books—choices far wiser than mine. My brother wasn't home, but his roommate Don was.

"Don, great to see you, man!" I said, shaking his hand with enthusiasm.

"Likewise!" he said, grinning. "Glad you decided to come. This is gonna be an unforgettable weekend."

"That's why I'm here," I replied, smiling big and stepping inside.

I had picked up a twelve pack of Miller on my way out of Hollywood, a meager contribution to the weekend's debauchery. Don warned me to keep it close. "Stuff like that has a way of growing wings and disappearing around here," he said with a smirk.

As we chatted, another roommate shuffled out of one of the bedrooms. He looked like a caricature of a big Victorian orphan—thick glasses that magnified his eyes to cartoonish proportions, mismatched clothes that seemed straight out of a Dickens novel. He flopped onto the couch like he'd been surviving on spite and coffee.

"Who's this guy?" he asked, his voice flat.

"I'm Scott's brother," I replied.

He squinted. "Oh, the Hollywood one. Meet any stars?"

I laughed. "Not yet."

"Figures," he said with a shrug. Then, without warning, he pulled out a baggie of mushrooms and dangled it like bait.

"Whoa," I said, raising an eyebrow. "Are those what I think they are?"

He grinned, sly and toothy. "Sure are. You sticking around? Ten bucks gets you a share tomorrow."

A strange voice inside me whispered, *Do it.* Looking back, I know exactly where that voice came from, and it wasn't divine. Against my better judgment, I fished out a crumpled five and five ones, handing them over.

"Fair portions," he promised, tucking the cash away. "You won't regret it."

Oh, but I would.

Don and I killed time chatting about life. He was a law student, articulate and focused. The Victorian roommate, surprisingly, was an English major with a history minor, though he looked more like a mad poet. Their worlds felt light-years ahead of mine.

By 1 pm, my brother finally arrived, his face lighting up when he saw me.

"Don said you might come, but I didn't believe it," he said, pulling me into a quick hug. "Great to see you! We're gonna have some fun this weekend."

He tossed his bag onto the couch. "I'm done with school for the day, so let's hang out. A buddy invited Don and me to go surfing in about an hour. You in? He's got an extra board and wet suit."

I hesitated. Surfing wasn't exactly in my wheelhouse, but the prospect of an adventure was too good to pass up. "Absolutely," I said, trying to sound more confident than I felt.

My brother disappeared into his room to grab his gear. Soon, we were en route to Rincon Beach. The salty breeze carried a promise of freedom, the kind that only the ocean could deliver.

At the beach, I slipped into the borrowed wetsuit, which smelled like a decade of bad decisions. The zipper was busted, and it fit me like a saggy garbage bag.

"You'll be fine," my brother said, laughing as I waddled awkwardly toward the water.

The first wave hit me like a freight train. I tumbled off the board, sputtering seawater. Over and over, I tried to catch a wave, each failure more spectacular than the last. But there was one thing I just couldn't shake I couldn't get the Shark images looming in my mind to leave. And I know now it was a spirit of fear. Most likely from either Jaws or any one of the aquatic horror movies that I had the unfortunate pleasure to watch as a child. But Jaws was the one that was buried in my mind. So I just laid on the board for a few minutes watching how the other surfers started off into paddling before a decent size wave came behind them. Then I watched them maneuver themselves onto their knees to a standing position then effortlessly carved the wave to the shore. I felt like I understood the process I gave it ago. Finally, I managed to stand—briefly. For a few glorious seconds, I rode the wave like I belonged there. Then I wiped out so hard I was sure my ancestors felt it. I crawled back onto the board, laid on it, then back out, I did this about three or four times. I finally caught a decent size wave and I was standing and riding it when I fell one final time. and when I fell this last time, I hadn't realized that each time I fell from the board into the ocean my suit was filling up with water.

That's when I heard a man yelling on the shore: "Shark. Everyone out of the water."

My heart stopped. The ocean suddenly felt enormous, dark, and alive. My brother and his friends were already up on the beach, but I was stuck, the waterlogged wet suit pulling me down like an anchor.

I paddled with everything I had, my arms screaming, my mind racing with images of fins slicing through the water. The shore felt a million miles away.

I don't remember how long it took for me to get to the shore, but it felt like an eternity and every foot or so I made I could sense a shark, just within shredding range. After what seemed like forever took place I finally made it to the shore, and to be totally honest I was holding back tears. I unstrapped the surfboard, threw it on the sand, and as the water drained from the wetsuit, I fell on my face in the sand I later learned that there was a school of great whites that were going across the beach and they wanted everybody out of the water. Or at least that is what a guy told me on the beach. That was the last time I ever went surfing. And more demonic fear had been injected into my body. My brother his roommate and his friend did not see my ordeal.

I rinsed the sand off me, grabbed the surfboard, and we headed into downtown Santa Barbara, had a beer, and then headed back to my brother's apartment. That night, we relaxed on the couch, nursing beers as I recounted stories from Hollywood, embellishing them for flair. My actual life in Hollywood was far from glamorous, but I wasn't about to admit that. The couch I crashed on that night was lumpy and smelled faintly of mildew, but it felt like a king-sized bed compared to the car I'd been sleeping in.

The next day, we grabbed a couple of bikes, and my brother gave me a tour of the UCSB campus. The sprawling university was alive with students, bikes weaving through paths, laughter echoing in the California sun. For a brief moment, I felt normal, like I belonged there.

By evening, we regrouped at his apartment. The Halloween party was about to explode. My brother's roommate handed me the mushrooms I'd purchased earlier. Don and my brother passed on taking any. It wasn't my first time dabbling in substances, but my first time taking mushrooms. I heard a voice in my head saying, *What are you doing?* But I ignored it, chasing the promise of a night I'd never forget—or regret, depending on how it ended.

At 8 p.m., the mushrooms went down, chased by the bitter foam of cheap beer. The air buzzed with Pink Floyds Money blaring through the stereo. The party was about to begin, and so was the next chapter of my reckless adventure. I had my video camera with me that night, hoping to capture the wild and festive Halloween atmosphere. The streets of Isla Vista were a chaotic swirl of costumes, loud music, and youthful energy. I don't think any of us dressed up, but that didn't matter. The city was alive with energy, and I could feel it buzzing in the air. As we stepped out of the apartment, the crowd on the street was impossible to ignore. The costumes ranged from creative to completely inappropriate, especially the young girls who seemed to have confused Halloween with a strip tease show.

One of the guys suggested we head down the street to a party with a live college band. The idea sounded good enough, so we set off. By the time we got there, I could feel the psychedelic mushrooms slowly starting to take effect. The world around me seemed to shift slightly, colors a little brighter, edges a little softer. We could hear the music from a block away, and while it wasn't the best quality, it was live, so that was something different. I was game for whatever.

We arrived at the party, and it was a scene straight out of every college movie I had ever seen. Young people drinking beer, smoking, laughing, and trying to have what they called a "good time." Looking back, it seemed so empty—like they were all just filling the space between them with noise and substances. But in that moment, it felt like the only thing that mattered.

I started filming everything. The more I captured, the more I felt part of it all. People started noticing, some irritated by the camera, others posing for it. As we moved through the party, I caught sight of an altercation. Without thinking, I zoomed in on it, eager to capture the drama. What I didn't realize, until it was too late, was that it wasn't just some college spat—it was a drug deal gone bad.

UCSB had its share of visitors during Halloween—gangs that would come into the city to sell drugs and other paraphernalia. The man involved in the altercation didn't look like a student; he looked like someone from the streets. I'm sure he wasn't a stranger to violence. He caught my eye through the lens of the camera and zeroed in on me with a look of pure anger.

He marched over, his eyes locked on mine. "Give me that tape," he growled.

I was high and buzzed from the beers and mushrooms, but I was still foolish enough to refuse. I probably added some sarcastic remark, not realizing the trouble I was inviting. In a split second, he snatched the camera from my hands, slammed it to the ground, and crushed it under his boot.

I stood there, frozen in disbelief. My mind screamed at me to fight back, but my body knew better. This guy was twice my size, and I wasn't exactly in fighting shape. I guessed from his demeanor that he was part of a Mexican gang. He pushed me, rattling off something in Spanish—words I couldn't understand. I felt small, insignificant, and helpless.

Just then, my brother and his friends appeared from the party and noticed me standing there, staring at the remains of my camera. They asked what had happened, and I told them. My brother and his friends were sympathetic, but it didn't change the fact that the camera was gone. That was my tool for making money. I had planned to use that camera to get work in Hollywood. Now, I was going back to L.A. with nothing. But, as young men do, I brushed it off. The combination of the mushrooms and alcohol helped me compartmentalize it. I wasn't going to let that ruin my night.

Around 1 am, the mushroom high began to wear off. My brother suggested we head down to the cliffs by the beach, and we all agreed. The waning gibbous moon hung low in the sky, casting a soft, eerie glow on the sand and surf. As we walked, it felt like some Hitchcockian noir movie from the fifties.

Sitting on the beach, the cool sand beneath us and the distant crash of the waves, we took turns telling tales of our life's experiences. The darkness of the night was punctuated by our laughter and the occasional comment about how surreal everything felt. But deep down, I knew that every time I dabbled with these mind-altering substances, I was inviting something darker into my life. It was like casting a line in the water, hoping to catch something small and harmless, but instead pulling up a monstrous fish you weren't prepared to face.

The shrooms dissolved in my brain, amplifying certain things yet dulling others. I felt the weight of the spirits surrounding us. We sat there all night, lost in the high, until the sun began to rise. That's when the comedown and hangover hit. The crash after the high is something you just don't forget. The mood shifted from euphoric to volatile in an instant. We were all cranky, short-tempered, and agitated.

When the sun rose fully, I realized two things: First, I didn't have my camera anymore. Second, I had no idea how I was going to explain the loss of it to Jack.

Before I left I sat with my brother drinking a little coffee, trying to shake off the remnants of the night before. The ideas in my head started to form as I tried to figure out my next move. My brother's apartment was quiet, the calm after the storm. I looked through the papers Jack had given me, the ones he used to scam people, and I wondered if there was a way to turn that into something useful.

Maybe I could get a job with one of those casting agencies. Or, if not that, maybe I could become a security guard. The possibilities seemed endless—at least in my mind. I hugged my brother and his friends goodbye, thanked them for the weekend, and hopped in the T-bird, heading back to Hollywood.

Chapter Eighteen

Tin Badge And American Idols

Jonathan Edwards

"Pride is the worst viper in the human heart. It lies lowest of all sins in the foundation of our soul and is the most secret and deceitful."

I rolled into Hollywood around 6:30, exhausted from the long drive and the chaotic weekend. I wasn't in the mood to talk to Jack just yet. The thought of facing him after the camera incident made me uneasy, so I decided to hang out for the night and talk to him in the morning. I grabbed some dinner and parked in the alley, settling in to crash for the night. The weariness from the previous day's events—both physical and spiritual—was weighing heavily on me. I could feel the accumulation of dark energy that had been with me for a while.

Monday came, and I woke up early, feeling like I was dragging myself through a fog. I had a quick breakfast, then headed over to Jack's office. I was relieved when I walked in and saw that it was empty—no clients, no Gabrielle. I didn't want an audience for what I had to say. I sat down across from Jack, and with a fake smile, I launched into my story. I left out the part about the altercation, of course—the part about being inebriated, high, and the gang member smashing my camera into the ground. Instead, I told Jack that my car had been broken into while I was at my brother's house. The camera had been stolen. I gave him the story with a straight face, lying with such ease that it didn't even feel like a lie.

Lying came so naturally back then. It was a defense mechanism, an easy way out when things got tough. Back then, I didn't have the Holy Spirit guiding me, and so deception felt like a safety net. I'm grateful to say that now, the idea of lying makes me feel nauseous. But in that moment, lying seemed like the best option.

Jack didn't seem thrilled, but he nodded sympathetically. "I understand," he said, though I could see the frustration in his eyes. "Not much I can do about it now."

I shrugged. "Look, I get it. Without the camera, there's not much use for me at your agency. But I appreciate everything you've done."

We shook hands, and I left his office, feeling a sense of relief mixed with uncertainty. What was next? I didn't know, but I was determined to keep moving forward.

The week dragged on, and my funds were dwindling. I was rationing my food to one meal a day, surviving on ketchup packets from fast food joints and water. I felt like I was sinking deeper into some dark pit of desperation, and I knew I had to do something. I needed work. I still had that glimmer of hope for the extra casting jobs, but I wasn't sure how much they'd really pay. I needed a place to stay—a real apartment, not my uncomfortable car.

On Thursday afternoon, I decided to take action. I grabbed a newspaper from a nearby stand and flipped through the "Help Wanted" section. Most of the listings were for typical, low-paying jobs—coffee shops, restaurants, and retail positions. But then something caught my eye: a job for Pinkerton Security. The ad was bold, confident, and seemed like the kind of thing that could offer me the flexibility I needed.

By 3 p.m., I was walking into their office, nervous but hopeful. The process was surprisingly simple. They asked for my driver's license and handed me a psychological test. I was a little worried about the test. I thought who knows—maybe I was crazy? But deep down I knew I wasn't. And later down the road as I learned more about spiritual oppression and possession, I realized that I wasn't crazy—I was spiritually oppressed, or worse, possessed. But I still had no clue how deeply those forces were entwined in my life.

The interviewer took my application and then asked, "Can you work on Sunday?"

I was a little stunned. "Of course," I replied, eager for any work. He smiled, pleased with my response.

"I think you'll enjoy this position. I'm going to have you and a female officer working the Emmys. You'll be in charge of taking tickets from the attendees."

My jaw dropped. "The Emmys? Really?"

He laughed. "Yep, you'll see everyone."

He asked for my shirt and pants size, and I awkwardly gave him the numbers. I had to check my clothes in the bathroom to make sure I had the right measurements, and when I came back, he handed me two sets of a uniform, complete with a shirt, pants, and a hat with a badge. Yes, a badge. It felt surreal. A badge!

He gave me the address for the job, and I walked out feeling energized, even though I hadn't known what to expect just a few hours earlier. I felt like I was finally headed in the right direction, even if I didn't realize then that God had been orchestrating the events in my life to protect me from going down a dangerous path.

I stopped at Tommy's Burgers to treat myself—something simple but a small victory in a day filled with uncertainty. Afterward, I returned to my car in the alley, played a little guitar, read a bit, and fell asleep.

The next day, my shift didn't start until 4 p.m. because the Emmys didn't begin until 5, so I took the chance to freshen up. I went to the YMCA for a shower, put on my uniform, badge proudly on display, then got a haircut at a nearby barbershop called Rocky's, across from Universal Studios. It was a great little shop. I guess you could call it a hole in the wall. The owner of the barbershop was a Big, muscular, effeminate gay man who was clearly flirting with me. I felt awkward, especially when he started telling me how much he liked men in uniforms. I was actually repulsed, but I politely thanked him and left with a decent haircut, of course.

At 3:30, I headed to the Pasadena Civic Auditorium, where the Emmys were being held. I was pumped. This was a big deal for me. I parked and headed to the massive building, found the entrance and there, at the top of a flight of stairs, I spotted another officer in the same uniform. I walked up to her and introduced myself. Her name was Carla, and she was young and attractive. I guessed they'd put us together for the image, but I didn't mind.

She explained the job—two lines would be at the entrance, one for her and one for me. Our job was simple: take tickets from the guests.

They had special ticket stubs that were tough to duplicate, so no one could sneak in.

The line outside the door was growing, and my nerves started kicking in. I'd watched hours and hours of TV, movies, and game shows. I knew every famous face by heart, but now I was about to be in the middle of it all. My heart raced as the excitement and terror swirled together. This was it—the beginning of something new. And yet, deep down, I felt the pull of something dark following me, waiting. We watched in awe as the doors to the auditorium opened, and the massive line of guests began to flood in. It was as if a wave of glitter and glamour crashed upon the steps. People began to choose their line, and I couldn't believe it. I was seeing all the actors and actresses I had watched growing up—icons I had admired from afar—walking right past me, heading to the red carpet, each one taking their ticket. The whole scene felt surreal, almost like a dream. It was like stepping into a world that seemed to exist only in my childhood fantasies.

Looking back, though, I couldn't help but see the deeper truth that I had missed in the moment. This was idol worship, plain and simple, something the Bible warns against. But at the time, all I could focus on were the faces of the famous, the flashing cameras, and the buzz of the event. Each star walked by, eyes locked ahead, fixated on the prize they might win or the adoration they would receive once they took their seat. Not once did they glance at me or acknowledge the other security guard. It was as if we were invisible, mere obstacles in their path.

I saw Woody Harrelson, James Woods, Robert Altman, Tony Danza, Bob Barker, Tracey Ullman, Billy Crystal, Robin Williams, Jay Leno—the list goes on. There were so many that I couldn't even list them all. It was like a quarter of a mile of nothing but celebrities. The line lasted over 20 minutes, and when the last one passed through, I turned to the other guard and said, "Not many smiles in this group."

She laughed softly, nodding in agreement. We both knew the world we had just witnessed wasn't as glamorous as it appeared.

The ceremony would last two hours, so we had a bit of time to kill. Our job was done for the moment, and we were left standing by the doors, watching the construction crew work behind us, tearing down the event space as the stars enjoyed their evening inside. Time dragged on, and we stood there, saying nothing, as the buzz from the event simmered down. But an hour later, something unexpected happened.

A man burst out of one of the hall doors, looking flustered and upset. It was none other than Phil Donahue, the legendary talk show host. He seemed like he was in a rush, his face twisted in frustration. He looked right at me and demanded, "Do you have a dime?" I was taken aback but reached into my pocket and handed him the coin. He snatched it without so much as a word of thanks and headed straight for the payphone just a few feet away.

No acknowledgment—not even a glance in my direction. It was as if I were nothing more than a desk with a dime sitting on it, waiting to be used. After finishing his call, he rushed past me back into the hall, disappearing into the crowd, leaving me standing there, stunned by the sheer lack of courtesy. The other guard smiled and shrugged her shoulders. This was a new experience for me. The arrogance and indifference of these celebrities was something I had never encountered back in Colfax. I chuckled to myself, thinking, *These are not my people. But then again, who are my people?*

The night passed, and the last of the attendees began to file out of the auditorium. By 8pm, most had left, chatting about the ceremony and the winners they had seen. It was a relief to see the event winding down, and I felt grateful for the job.

As the last of the crowd trickled out, the other guard and I stood at the doors, watching the night unfold. We stayed there until 11pm, making sure no one tried to sneak in after hours. Once we were done, we walked to our cars, exhausted. I asked her about pay and she said they mail out the checks every week.

I thanked her, wishing her a good night, but as I walked to my car, I thought: I *don't have a permanent address.* How could they mail me a check if I didn't have one? So, I did what I always did—took action. I drove to the alley where I was parked and went to sleep, knowing I would figure it out in the morning.

The next day, I woke up, went to the post office, and rented a P.O. Box. I then called Pinkerton Security to update them with my new address.

"This is Alex, the young guy from yesterday, right?" the man on the other end asked.

"Yeah, that's me," I replied.

He told me they needed me to work the next day and asked if I could do a shift on Tuesday as well. Of course, I agreed. But then he hit me with some unexpected news: after tomorrow, I'd be placed in a more stable position that would last about three months.

"Can you handle that?" he asked.

"Absolutely," I said, my excitement growing.

He gave me the details for my job at the ABC lot in Hollywood, and then, as if to blow my mind even further, he mentioned something that made my heart skip a beat:

"After the ABC job, you'll be working on *The Tonight Show* for Johnny Carson and Jay Leno over at NBC."

My mind was officially blown. I went to bed that night feeling like my life was finally on track. There was a sense of relief that I hadn't felt in months. Life was looking up.

The next day, I woke up early, showered at the Y, and spent some time playing guitar and reading. By the time I got to the ABC lot, I was ready for whatever the day held. The job was 4 to 11:00pm, and I arrived around 3:45. A fellow Pinkerton guard was manning the gate, and he directed me to the security office.

Inside, the Sergeant handed me a list of instructions. I was assigned to patrol the entire studio complex. I was to check every office, soundstage, and even the cafe. My job was to make sure grown adults didn't forget to turn their coffee pots off when they went home for the night. I couldn't help but laugh. "Really? That's it?"

The Sergeant didn't laugh. He was dead serious, his face impassive. "You'll be logging everything in on a DAR(Daily Activity Report) so make sure you're thorough."

I grabbed the notepad, pen, keys, and flashlight and set out on my rounds. The studios were massive and impressive, and I found myself walking through sets for *America's Funniest Home Videos* and *Family Matters*. It was all so surreal. I was walking through the same hallways where stars I had grown up watching had worked.

As I exited one of the buildings, I noticed a familiar figure standing by one of the sound stages. It was Timothy Leary—the infamous psychologist and advocate for psychedelics. He looked exactly as I remembered from his tv, magazines, and interviews.

I walked up to him and couldn't help but quote, "Turn on, tune in, drop out."

He smiled and sparked up a conversation. I told him how I had discovered his work through music and literature—especially *The Electric Kool-Aid Acid Test*. He spoke about his fascination with cryogenics, casually mentioning that when he dies, he intended to freeze his head.

I couldn't help but be intrigued by the man—*and* unsettled at the same time. He had that eerie, otherworldly presence that comes from someone who has pushed their mind to the limits. The more we spoke, the more I realized that I wasn't just talking to a historical figure. I was talking to someone who had lived a life far beyond anything I could imagine. And it was only then that I truly understood how the world of fame and celebrity could warp someone's soul. you could see it in his eyes—the way Timothy Leary spoke, the distant, almost otherworldly glint in his gaze. There was something strange about him, something darker lurking beneath the surface. It wasn't just his words or his presence. It was as though an unclean and ancient spirit had taken residence within him, one that seemed to whisper at the edges of his thoughts, urging him onward.

But like so many people I encountered in Hollywood, there was always a strange undercurrent. Behind the polished smiles and friendly handshakes, there was something unsettling. Something not quite human. I couldn't explain it, but I could feel it deep in my gut. Maybe I was too naïve to fully understand it, but I wasn't the only one who noticed. The way people behaved, the way they carried themselves—it was different. It wasn't the openness or kindness I had expected. It was cold, calculated, and driven by something more primal.

I snapped back to the present when I noticed the Sergeant from across the lot staring in my direction. Realizing I had dawdled for too long, I quickly thanked Timothy for the conversation and inspiration in my life. I turned and headed toward my next task: checking the coffee pots.

I made my way to the far side of the lot and noticed a smaller section with a gate on the other side. Curiosity piqued, I approached, and my attention was immediately drawn to a sleek jaguar parked nearby. It looked like a beauty—a symbol of wealth and status. My fingers instinctively ran along the smooth front fender, the glossy finish reflecting the faint light of the lot.

Suddenly, the air around me seemed to shift. The jaguar let out a deep, ominous voice, a sound that wasn't quite mechanical but eerily human, commanding me to back away.

I froze, bewildered. I had never heard an alarm like that before. A moment later, a large, foreboding black man in a suit appeared from behind a corner, his presence almost as imposing as the car. He eyed me, and with a sharp tone, he barked, "Hey, step away from the car."

I quickly apologized, realizing I must have brushed up against it. As I stepped back, I couldn't resist chuckling under my breath. *Paula Abdul's car?* I thought. Honestly, I wasn't much of a fan. But I didn't say that out loud. The man informed me it was her car, and I nodded, doing my best to show respect, though the situation struck me as somewhat absurd.

Continuing my rounds, I came across the last sound stage I needed to check: *Mama's Family*. The cast had already wrapped for the night, and the set was eerily quiet. As I walked around, I noticed an untouched stash of food—bagels, cream cheese, deli meats, and cheese. I also noticed a refrigerator full of drinks. It was the mother load. My stomach growled in response. I couldn't resist; my money was nearly gone, and I was starving.

I quickly made myself a bagel sandwich, wrapping another bagel in a paper towel and stuffing it into my pants to save for later. The simple act of satisfying my hunger felt like a small victory in the midst of an overwhelming situation.

After I finished, I checked the last few offices on the top floor. As I entered one office, the coffee pot was off, and I noticed a nameplate on the desk. This was a name I definitely recognized—one of the big players in the industry. Curiosity clawed at me. Should I snoop? Or should I just mind my own business? I knew I shouldn't, but my feet moved before my mind could stop them. I stepped closer to the desk, a sense of unease growing in the pit of my stomach.

That's when I saw it. A small mirror, a rolled-up $100 bill, and a brown vial. I opened the vial without thinking, unscrewing the cap. Inside, I saw the unmistakable white powder—cocaine. I wasn't shocked, given who the man was, but a part of me was repulsed. I didn't intend to take anything, but the temptation was too great. *Just a little bit,* I told myself. I chipped off a small piece and wrapped it in a piece of paper. I slid it into my pocket and quickly replaced everything exactly as it had been.

I didn't want to lose my job, but curiosity had gotten the best of me. As I left the office and made my way to the security office, I couldn't shake the feeling that I had crossed a line.

After handing in my DAR and keys, I clocked out and headed to my car, ready to crash for the night. Tomorrow was a big day—I was set to work on *The Tonight Show,* and I wanted to be fully rested for it. So, I resisted the urge to use the cocaine, knowing it would keep me awake all night and leave me jittery. I needed sleep.

The next morning, I woke up early, feeling surprisingly refreshed. While browsing the offices the night before, I noticed that nearly every employee had a copy of *Variety,* A large local LA entertainment magazine, in their office. So I figured it was a good idea to pick one up, so I grabbed a copy from a shop nearby and settled down to read it. Breakfast was small—my funds were running low, and I knew I needed to stretch it as far as possible. But even with that small breakfast, there was a sense of anticipation building in my chest. I had a few days until my check would arrive, and I couldn't wait. I was desperate for more than just money—I longed for a place to call home, a bed to sleep in.

After breakfast, I showered and shaved at the Y. At 19, I didn't have much facial hair, but enough to feel uncomfortable with how it looked. I wasn't going to let my first encounter with Johnny Carson be with me looking like a ragged mess. I made sure I was looking sharp.

With a few hours to kill, I decided to see a movie at the Mann's Chinese Theater. *Dead Poets Society* with Robin Williams. It was a fantastic film, and I left the theater moved by his performance.

But time was tight. I had to get to NBC Studios at 3000 W. Alameda Ave, for my shift at *The Tonight Show*. I quickly changed into my uniform and made my way to Burbank. I parked at the gate of NBC Studios, where another Pinkerton guard was stationed. He directed me to my parking spot, and I could feel the excitement rising in my chest.

This was it the Tonight Show. I was about to be a part of history, in a way. As the show progressed, I couldn't help but notice the stars coming through the tunnel, one by one. Doc Severinsen, in his sparkly gray jacket, walked right past me, his bulldog Tulip tugging at the leash as he ignored my presence entirely. I had to fight the urge to bend down and pet the dog. But I hesitated—what if Doc got mad? What if he thought I was intruding? So I just stood there, watching them all move like a blur of fleeting greatness.

It wasn't long before Bob, the Tonight Show's guitarist, spotted me standing there looking a bit out of place. He came over with a friendly smile and struck up a conversation. What a nice guy. He noticed I was new, and his first question was how long I'd been working security. I told him just a couple of days, and he nodded knowingly. "You've got a great gig," he said. "You're gonna see some fascinating people." His words were warm, encouraging. He asked me about myself, and I told him that I wasn't really sure why I was here, but I played guitar, wrote some songs, and was interested in entertainment in general.

He smiled again, his eyes gleaming with an understanding that only someone who'd been in the industry for years could have. "You're in the right place," he said. "Keep your ears and eyes open. You never know what could happen." Then, he excused himself to get ready for the show, leaving me standing there with his words still ringing in my ears.

I couldn't help but wonder what kind of guy Johnny Carson was. Would he be approachable? Would he be a typical celebrity, surrounded by walls that no one could get past? I didn't know, but my curiosity was piqued.

Then, it happened. Ed McMahon came through the tunnel, his broad frame casting a shadow as he walked past me without even acknowledging my presence. He didn't look at me, didn't even give me a second glance. It was like I was invisible. And then, there he was, Johnny.

He came around the corner, walking with a certain swagger, exuding an air of confidence that made everyone else seem smaller in comparison. He didn't look at me either, just walked past, pausing for a brief moment to work out his shoulders and neck before continuing down the tunnel toward the stage. Over the sound system, I heard Ed McMahon's familiar voice booming through the speakers. "Heeeeeeerrrrrrrrrrr's JOHNNY!" The audience erupted into cheers, clapping and whistling. Johnny rubbed his nose before stepping onto the stage, a natural part of his ritual, and the crowd went wild.

The show began, Johnny delivering his monologue with ease, as he always did, while Ed and Johnny bantered back and forth for the first 16 minutes or so. It was amazing to watch, even if I wasn't able to fully appreciate the magnitude of the moment at the time. But it was then that something strange happened.

Out of the corner of my eye, I saw a man standing at the entrance of the hallway. I thought I was seeing things. The figure looked eerily familiar. I could have sworn it was John Lennon. But no—when I focused more closely, I realized it wasn't John Lennon. It was his son, Julian Lennon.

He caught my gaze, a slight smile curling on his lips as he walked toward me. "Hello, mate," he said, his voice carrying a warmth that instantly put me at ease. I was dumbfounded. I wanted to say something, but the words didn't come. I stood there, awestruck, unable to believe this was actually happening. I wasn't a Christian then, and stars like Julian seemed larger than life. A young man from the lineage of quite possibly one of the greatest songwriters of all time. Julian was almost royalty. I didn't understand the significance of what I was witnessing.

But Julian, being the kind soul he was, smiled again before he was called to the stage. Johnny introduced him, and Julian went on to perform, captivating the audience with his talent and charisma. I stood there, trying to process the surrealness of the moment, when the next wave of guests started to trickle in. Comedian Kevin Pollak, followed by actress Darlanne Fluegel.

That's when the PA approached me, his voice sharp but not unkind. "The show's ending soon. When Johnny comes out, you're to walk him straight to his car. Don't look at him. Don't talk to him. Just walk him to his car. He might stop at his dressing room first. If he does, follow him wherever he goes."

I nodded, a bit dazed by the instructions. I had been here for a couple of months now, but this was a new level of responsibility. Soon enough, the show wrapped, and I could hear the familiar outro music playing.

Johnny came through the door, and I followed him, keeping my distance as instructed. We walked around the corner, and he didn't stop at his dressing room. Instead, we went straight outside. A small crowd of people gathered—mostly photographers shouting, "Johnny! Johnny!"

He smiled, waved at the crowd, and then made his way down the steps toward a brand-new Corvette. I watched, almost hypnotized, as he slid into the car and reached behind the seat. And then, Johnny Carson, the legendary talk-show host, pulled out a long blonde wig. He threw it on, adjusting it carefully in the rear view mirror, as if this was just part of his regular routine. And then, with a roar of the engine, he drove off the lot.

I was left standing there, my mind racing, trying to make sense of what I had just seen. I walked back inside, my brain buzzing with questions.

"Why did Johnny put on a wig?" I asked the PA, the confusion obvious in my voice.

The PA sighed and explained, "Johnny received a few letters by stalkers threatening to shoot him." So that is why I was there, and that's why he wears the wig. It's a precaution-a disguise.

I nodded, understanding now, but also feeling unsettled by the strangeness of it all.

As I finished my shift and headed back to the park, I couldn't shake the strange feeling I had. There was something magnetic about this place—the celebrities, the energy. It was intoxicating in a way. But it wasn't the kind of high that comes from God. No, this was something far more human. Something that spoke to a deeper, darker part of me.

The next few months went by, and I continued to work on *The Tonight Show*. I saw a lot of big names—Randy Travis, Patti LaBelle, and many more. But there was one person who stood out, and that was Jay Leno.

Jay was the kind of guy you never forget. He was driven, sure, but he was also kind. Every time he passed me in the hallway, he'd grab my head and mess up my hair, and say, "What's up, kid?" before running on to the stage. Johnny Carson never acknowledged me, never looked my way. And I couldn't help but notice the differences in them.

Johnny—there was something darker in him. Anger, fear, sadness, and a deep loneliness colored his presence. Rumors swirled about his alleged cocaine addiction, and after seeing his behavior firsthand, I couldn't help but wonder if there was some truth to them. If you watch old clips of Carson, there's hardly an episode where he doesn't rub his nose. And from what I had heard, the rumors seemed to fit. But that was all it was—rumors. Still, I couldn't shake the feeling that there was something deeply broken inside of him.

And me? I was just a kid, caught up in a world I didn't fully understand, surrounded by lights, cameras, and a lot of brokenness.

Chapter Nineteen

Skid Row

John Wesley

"Do not seek riches, but be content with what God has provided, for even a humble home with peace is greater than a mansion with strife."

The next day rolled around, and I found myself heading to the post office to check my PO Box. To my surprise, there was a check from Pinkerton Security waiting for me. A check for $150. For just three days of work. I couldn't believe it. I thought to myself, this was my golden ticket. It wasn't much, but it was more than I had in a long while, and it felt like a jackpot. With that, I started considering my next step. I had been thinking about getting an apartment, but with my limited funds, I figured I'd never be able to come up with enough for a down payment and the first and last month's rent.

So, I opened up the newspaper, scanning for alternatives. And then, it caught my eye—$15 a night for a hotel. It sounded too good to be true. I thought, well, what's the worst that could happen? I could always bail if it didn't work out. I headed in that direction, and surprisingly, it wasn't too far from the Hollywood Hotel, just up a couple of streets up. In fact, when I got there, I was a bit taken aback—it was directly across from Hollywood Billiards, where I had spent an unforgettable night shooting pool with Gabrielle and Gina .

I pulled up to the hotel, and the reality of it hit me like a slap in the face. This place was a dump. Scratch that—it was downright scary. The building looked like it hadn't seen a coat of paint in decades, the kind of place where homeless people dream of living someday. Then it dawned on me, I was that homeless guy. But, desperate times and all that required desperate measures. I walked into the lobby, and I immediately noticed the grated window in front of the desk. It reminded me of a prison, not exactly the welcoming vibe I was hoping for.

A tired-looking old guy, seemingly more interested in the TV than anything else, looked up at me. I asked him if I could get a room for the night. Seeming bothered, he took my money and handed me a key—room 207. No questions, no credit checks, just a key. I was in. I took it, walked outside to my car, grabbed my bag and guitar, made sure it was locked up tight, and headed toward the stairs. No elevator. I had to trudge up to the second floor with all of my worldly possessions, and let me tell you, this place wasn't exactly in tip-top shape. There were cracks in the walls, remnants of earthquakes long past, and the smell...oh, the smell.

It was a strange mix of Chinese food from the office downstairs, TV dinners, old carpet, layers of paint, and a faint, lingering smell of body odor. The kind of odor that just lingers.

I finally found room 207 at the end of the hall. I pushed open the door, and it creaked in protest as I entered. It wasn't much of a room—more like a closet. The carpet was thick and brown, flecked with yellow stains, and the wallpaper looked like it belonged in a haunted house. The bedspread was straight out of the sixties, and the bed itself was tiny and squeaky. And the faded mustard yellow bed spread was abhorrent. The room was probably about fifty square feet. I felt like a rat in a cage. But hey, it had a bed, a sink, and a toilet that leaned back at a forty five degree angle. I couldn't complain. At least I wasn't sleeping in my car.

I took a quick shower to rinse off the grime of the day, played a little guitar to soothe my mind, and read for a bit. The silence of the room was deafening. After a while, I decided to go downstairs and call my parents. I walked down to the dingy lobby where a payphone sat in the corner. The handset was chipped and stained with graffiti. I rubbed it with my shirt before putting it to my ear. I wasn't sure who had used it last, but I didn't want to think too much about it.

It was around 6 on Saturday evening, so I knew my parents would be home. My mom answered, as usual. She was the talkative one, my dad more the silent type. But I could tell he was listening in the background, as he always did. My mom greeted me with her usual cheerfulness, talking about the dogs and how my dad had just started a new job building Diamond Lumber stores. It was good to hear that things were going well for them. They always seemed to make it work, no matter the circumstances.

She asked how I was doing, and like I always did, I told her I had a place to stay. I never mentioned the rough conditions, never went into detail about the hotel, because I knew she'd worry. She'd probably faint if she knew I was staying in a place that could easily double as a whorehouse. And I wasn't about to tell her that. No way. I didn't want her to send money that they didn't have. Besides, I was too proud to admit it. I wasn't ready to face the reality of how far I'd fallen. So, I kept my stories vague and my pride intact.

After a short chat, I told her I loved them both and promised I'd talk to them soon. Hopefully, I'd be able to visit them sometime this year, but I wasn't so sure anymore.

As the sun set, I figured I should grab something to eat. I walked down the street and found a small burger joint, ate a quick meal, and then decided to go shoot some pool. I would have called Gabrielle and her friend, but I didn't have their number. I was on my own for this one.

I had to do some quick math to make sure I could stretch the $200 I had. The hotel was $15 a night, and I needed food. I figured that I could last the week with what I had, but it was going to be tight. I had enough for about seven days at the hotel, which would cost me around $100, and I'd need to eat, so that left me with just enough to scrape by.

It was about 8 o'clock by the time I crossed the street to Hollywood Billiards. The pool hall was just a stone's throw away, literally 60 feet or so. I grabbed a couple of beers at the bar, then found a table and hoped someone would want to play. The place was full of old guys, the kind you'd call barflies. And, as always, they were game. No one turned down a challenge, and I was ready to shoot. And I know this is gonna sound absolutely ridiculous and I have no idea why, maybe it was the booze in me but as the night went on, and I was about four beers in, I decided to use a silly southern accent, which I did not actually have. I'm sure it was fake phony and terrible, but nobody ever called me on it. By around 11:30, I was pretty toasted. The booze had worked its magic, and I figured it was time to call it a night. I stumbled back to the hotel, still chuckling at my own ridiculousness. As I walked up the stairs, things took a turn for the weird. Right outside the hotel, girls were lined up, wearing short revealing outfits, offering their "services," and I had to be brutally honest—they were not the prettiest flowers in the flower pot. I was trying to sneak by but I could tell that one of them was fixated on me and was approaching me. She blocked my entering the hotel and asked if I wanted some company. I smiled politely and told her, "Appreciate the offer, but not tonight." I was thinking in my head, or tomorrow, the next day, or forever. I was truly repulsed by the whole proposition.

I went upstairs, opened the door to my room, and immediately noticed a faint glow coming from the tiny window by the bed. Curious, I walked over, pulled the 1970s curtains back, and—well, I kid you not—there it was. A neon adult bookstore sign, flashing just 30 feet outside my window. The whole thing felt like a scene straight out of a gritty early sixties noir film. I stood there for a moment, half-smiling, half-shaking my head. This place... this hotel... it was something else. There was also the fact that I'm sure just about every single room in that hotel was visited by those girls outside and there John's, So I decided to replace the sheets with ones my mom put in my bag. Thanks mom!

For the next couple of months, I worked on the *Carson* show, collected my weekly checks, played a lot of pool and drank a lot of beer. Life was a blur of late-night gigs, early-morning calls, and the chaotic hustle of surviving on next to nothing. After the *Carson* show wrapped up, I found myself working on several other studio lots, including ABC, CBS, NBC, and Fox.

The best part? I had the keys to every office and studio I worked at. It was a strange sense of power—knowing I could walk into any studio I wanted. But instead of stealing anything of value, besides food, which, let's be real, in a Godless sinners mind was necessary. I just went about my business. The food was always a big help because I couldn't afford to eat much else.

One studio I enjoyed working at was Fox. It wasn't glamorous, but there were memories. I remember napping on the Arsenio Hall set and drinking his Heineken beer in his dressing room. Not that I cared for Heineken, but it was beer, and beer was something I could get behind at the time. Graveyard shifts on the movie lots were usually staffed with two guards, one sitting in a booth at the gate and one roving. Curtis, the other guard I worked with during the graveyard shift, was a huge part of those long, quiet nights. We both had aspirations of things more significant than being security guards. So we needed to be able to do things during the day. Being awake all night long made it almost impossible to get daily tasks done because you needed your sleep. However, if we could catch an hour here or an hour there of sleep on our graveyard shift, we had enough energy during the day to get a few things accomplished. So Curtis and myself devised a sleeping schedule on the lot during our shifts. He'd take his hour of sleep; then I'd take mine. If anyone came onto the lot and posed a threat, we had a code word to send over our walkie-talkies to wake each other up. It was a good system. And Curtis? He became a close friend.

Sadly, Curtis's story didn't have the happy ending I had hoped for. Nearly ten years later, in 1999, he took his life. I never really saw it coming, but in hindsight, there were signs. Curtis was a man haunted by demons, both real and imagined. Towards the end, he got deeply involved in some strange stuff—meditation, new-age practices, and a bizarre band. He was looking for something, anything, that could quiet the voices and spirits that taunted him.

A couple of years before his death, Curtis even started a business called "Oh Heavenly Tours." His company offered tours around the city, showing tourists the sites where famous celebrities, actors, and musicians had died or taken their own lives. It's darkly ironic, isn't it?

The man who ran a tour of celebrity death spots ultimately became part of that grim narrative.

I often think about what the Bible says about murder being a commandment. And I have to wonder—does suicide fall under that category? I don't know. It's a question I've wrestled with, but I just pray that Curtis found peace, and that our Lord finds mercy in his actions.

He was a talented musician and a decent songwriter, someone I could talk to for hours about music, movies, and life. He even helped me out with some things I never would have figured out on my own. This might sound totally insane, but we'd borrow wigs from the movie sets and drive the golf cart around with the wigs blowing in the wind, terrorizing the cleaning staff. We figured they wouldn't rat us out—they were from Mexico and, I think, illegal, so we assumed they wouldn't snitch. And they always laughed, so we thought we were in the clear.

One night, Curtis showed me his headshots, and I couldn't help but laugh. I had head shots too. He was amazed I didn't have an agent, and when I told him I didn't even know what that was, he was floored. He asked me to turn his head shot around, and when I did, I saw that stapled to the back was a list of his acting accomplishments: skills like skateboarding, bicycling, karate, and more. I had no idea this was the kind of thing you needed to do to make it in the industry. Curtis sat down with me, helped me craft a resume for the back of my head shot, and even told me to make up experiences if I didn't have any. So, with his guidance, I fabricated a resume. I just hoped I did not get called to ride a bull because that was now on my resume.

It felt like I was living a lie, but Curtis assured me that I'd be fine. He said whenever I was ready, I could submit my head shot and resume to talent agencies. So, I did. I sent out a bunch hoping for a response.

Then Curtis asked where I was living, and I told him about the $15-a-night hotel, stepping over bums and fending off prostitutes every night. He wasn't surprised, but he suggested I try to become an extra in movies. "You're young. You'll get a lot of work," he said. I told him about the scam agency I'd worked with, and he mentioned Central Casting. "That's the best agency," he said. "Go there, and you'll work right away. We'll try to get on the same shows."

He also mentioned that he was a regular on *Saved By The Bell*. I couldn't believe it—*Saved By The Bell* was a huge show. The wheels started turning in my head.

I liked my job at Pinkerton, but I knew it wasn't what I wanted for a career. The next day, I decided I'd go to Central Casting. It felt like the beginning of something new. And maybe, just maybe, it was.

Chapter Twenty

15 Seconds Of Fame

D.L. Moody

"Be humble or you'll stumble."

The next day, I found myself back at my car, clutching the sheet of paper with the circled name of Central Casting. I pulled out my trusty Thomas guide and charted a route to Burbank, to W. Olive Ave. My heart raced with anticipation. This was it. I was on my way to my first real shot in the world of acting, and I was feeling confident. It was a little absurd, honestly, but the thrill of possibility was undeniable.

I parked and walked into the office, where the girl at the front desk greeted me. I told her I was interested in signing up with the extra agency, filled out some paperwork, and handed them one of my head shots. Just as I was about to leave when a very effeminate guy stepped out from the back, eyed me up and down and asked if I could work tomorrow. I froze. Was this real? "Absolutely," I said, trying not to sound too eager. He told me there was a commercial shoot and that I was a perfect fit. Perfect fit? I'd only been in town for a hot minute, but here was my first opportunity, and I was thrilled.

I was just about to leave when the girl at the front desk asked, "Hey, do you have a pager? I noticed you didn't leave a phone number." I didn't have one. "You need to get a number so we can reach you," she explained. I hadn't even thought about it, but she was right. "Is there a place around here where I can get one?" I asked. She gave me an address, and I made a mental note to pick it up. "When you get it, call us back today," she said.

The guy, still in the back, pointed me in the direction of the commercial shoot, but I knew I'd find it on my Thomas Guide. It was happening at eight in the morning. I left the office, headed to a nearby store, and grabbed a pager for about $10 a month. The purple pager clipped to my belt made me feel connected to the world, like I was officially part of something bigger. Little did I know, I was unknowingly stepping into a much darker spiritual world, one that would have its own surprises in store for me.

The next morning, I left the hotel early, still half-excited and half-nervous. I was headed to Universal Studios, to the back lot where they shot scenes from *Jaws*, *Back to the Future*, and *Psycho*. It felt surreal to even be there. When I arrived at the set, the crew was already moving people into place. I quickly realized I might be a little late, but there was no turning back now.

A guy with a headset spotted me and pointed me in the right direction. He asked for my name, then sent me over to hang out with a group of young late teens and twenty-somethings. We gathered around as the Director briefed us on the scene. It was a café scene in "anywhere USA." Two couples would be sitting at a café on a bustling city sidewalk, laughing, talking, and just generally having a good time. We were told to walk past the table as if it were any normal day, and not to look into the camera. Simple, right?

That's when she walked onto the set. It was Britney Murphy. At the time, she was just starting out and was unknown, but I remember thinking she had something special. Little did I know, she'd later star in iconic roles in *Clueless, 8 Mile, Girl, Interrupted, Happy Feet*, and more. I remember being starstruck seeing her glide onto the set. But just as fast as I was infatuated with her after seeing her, oh man, she was as conceited as they come. She was young at the time and might have grown up down the road, but wow, she was the antithesis of self-adornment that day on the set. But I had to respect that she was the lead actress on the commercial. There were 3 other main characters, but Britney was getting the big paycheck.

As we filmed, everything felt canned and stiff. We walked past the table, where Britney and the others interacted—laughing, smiling, being flirtatious. After a few takes in, the Director called for a stop. He wasn't happy with something in the scene. His frustration was palpable, and I could see him directing his attention to one of the lead males. The guy just wasn't doing it for the Director. He wasn't getting it right. Maybe it was his look, maybe something else. Regardless, the Director called for a "Take 5."

During the break, I noticed the Assistant Director, or AD, was giving me a peculiar look. A moment later, he approached me, looked me up and down, and said, "You've got the part." I was dumbfounded. "What?" I asked, not understanding. He explained that the Director wasn't satisfied with the male lead and wanted me to take his place. I couldn't believe it. I was ecstatic but also devastated for the guy who had just been replaced. I knew he'd probably worked a lot harder to get that spot than I had, and now here I was, taking his role. Curtis had always said, "Sometimes you gotta take your shot," and this was mine, but it felt strange. What if this guy had been working for years to get this opportunity?

Still, I couldn't pass it up. The Director wasn't a nice guy—he was rude and crass—but there was no way I could turn down the money. The actor who had been replaced walked off the set, and I caught his eye. He saw the look on my face, and I could tell he knew I felt bad. But there was no time for that now.

The AD handed me a form to sign. I asked what it was, and he assured me it was just a formality. I signed it, naïve and unaware of what I was agreeing to. I didn't know it at the time, but if I hadn't signed it, I would've had royalties from the national commercial. Instead, I was given a lump sum of $500. Not a bad payout, but it didn't even begin to compare to the $20,000 or $30,000 I could have made with royalties. It was a good lesson in reading the fine print. We did around five takes before we wrapped, but like Johnny Carson, Britney did not even acknowledge me during the scene. Here I was, not two feet away from her, and not even a head nod to recognize my existence. I had never experienced this.

When the shoot wrapped, I grabbed some free food from the catering truck and headed back to Hollywood, my mind racing with thoughts of what had just happened. I'd gotten my big break, but the cost of it lingered. What did it really mean to "make it" in Hollywood? Was this it? Or was there more waiting around the corner? I didn't know, but I was going to find out.

Chapter Twenty-One

A Foot Soldier's Journey

A.W. Tozer

"Success is dangerous. The higher a man climbs, the farther he has to fall. If God is not the foundation, the whole structure will collapse."

I had the check from the commercial coming in, so I decided it was time to settle down and find myself a proper apartment. The idea of living in a cramped motel room any longer was starting to wear thin. I opened a bank account, feeling like an adult for the first time in my life, and began scanning the apartment listings in the LA Times. The evening was already falling, but I was determined to find something decent before the day slipped away. A listing caught my eye—a place just a mile south of where I was staying, only $450 a month. The price was not too steep, it was affordable, and that was the most important thing right then.

The neighborhood wasn't ideal, but it was livable. You could tell by the beat-up cars and the old, cracked sidewalks that this wasn't the high-end part of town. It was south on Hollywood Blvd, a left onto N. Edgemont St., and a little ways into Los Feliz. When I arrived, I filled out a month-to-month lease and handed over the first and last months' rent. It set me back a bit, but it was worth it. I knew I'd earn it back quickly from the film and tv work, or my security gigs.

What I found most fascinating about the apartment was the elevator. The building was only three stories tall, but it was a feature I hadn't expected. My place was a small one-bedroom with a cozy living room and a compact kitchen. It was a massive upgrade from the rundown motel I had been holed up in. That day was spent hauling what little stuff I had to the UN-furnished apartment with used pieces from the classifieds. The fridge was empty but I could fill that later.

Then, as I was setting up my place, my pager went off. The only two people who had my pager number were my parents and Central Casting, so I knew exactly who it was. I found a gas station, pulled over, and called them back. They told me they had a gig for tomorrow on a new movie that was shooting it was none other than the *Teenage Mutant Ninja Turtles*. I was going to be a Foot Soldier. I'd never been into the show, but I knew enough to recognize the turtles. The bottom line was that I had bills to pay, and I was more than willing to take the job.

Looking back, I realized something I hadn't fully grasped before: I wasn't the one creating my luck. God had been guiding me the whole time, placing me in these situations to test me, to see how I would act and or respond. He wasn't tempting me, but He was challenging me, especially with the decision to leave my security guard job and venture into the entertainment world. I enjoyed the simplicity of the security work, but it wasn't fulfilling that intellectual part of the human mind. The extra gigs were pulling me in, offering more opportunities to make money with less effort. But there was something else tugging at my other sleeve. I wanted to play my music and I knew LA, and especially Hollywood, had open mics on every corner. And the casting calls mostly happened during the day, leaving my evenings open for other pursuits. It was clear which direction I was meant to go.

I picked up the phone and dialed Curtis. He didn't have my pager number, but I had his home phone, so I gave him a call. He picked up, and I asked how he was doing. He said everything was good. I asked if he had any security gigs lined up, and he said he did. I told him about the Noxzema commercial and the *Teenage Mutant Ninja Turtles* shoot. Curtis had read about the Ninja shoot in *Variety* and was eager to join. He told me he wanted to work on it too. I suggested he call Central Casting to see if he could get in. I told him they had me playing a Foot Soldier, and he said he would try his luck.

It was late in the workday, so I told him to call the casting company and then call me back. I waited at a payphone for only a few minutes before he called me back, excited. He'd gotten in, and just like that we were both slated to play Foot Soldiers in the morning. I couldn't help but laugh. We were going to be working together again, and I couldn't wait to see him on set.

The next morning, I headed to the shoot, arriving around 7:30. The crew was still setting things up, and all the extras were gathered in a holding area near an alley between Hollywood Boulevard and Sunset Boulevard on Vine Street. That's when I saw Curtis strolling up, a big smile on his face. We greeted each other, and I told him how grateful I was for him pushing me in the direction of TV and film. Without his encouragement, I might still be stuck behind a security desk.

Curtis and I met with the Production Assistant, or PA, and told him that we were the Foot Soldiers. He led us to wardrobe, where we got fitted for our skin-tight Foot Soldier outfits. The costume was bizarre—grey and strange, with the kind of design you'd expect from a cartoon. We looked more like aliens. I felt both ridiculous and cool at the same time. The director Steve Barron explained what our scene was and what we'd be doing.

As we waited for the shoot to start, I couldn't help but reflect on how far I'd come. Just a short time ago, I was still working security and living in that dingy motel. Now, I was an actor in a *Teenage Mutant Ninja Turtles* movie, playing a Foot Soldier. Life had a funny way of changing in unexpected ways. And as the cameras started rolling, I felt a new sense of purpose. Maybe this was just the beginning. The day on set was bizarre, to say the least. Curtis and I were briefed on what our role was going to be. We'd be positioned in the back of a white delivery van with double doors, loading up stolen goods from a group of young neighborhood criminals—TVs, stereos, and other stolen items. The kids would rush up to the van, handing us their loot as we tossed it in the back. Once everything was loaded, we'd slam the doors shut and the van would take off, speeding around the corner.

We shot the scene, and it felt like a blur. It was quick, no real action or danger, just a simple exchange of stolen goods and a van driving away. I couldn't tell you how far into the movie the scene is, but if you watch *Teenage Mutant Ninja Turtles*, it's there. I never actually sat down to watch the entire film, but I've seen our scene So I know it's there.

When we finished, I caught up with Curtis. I was curious about what he thought was more fulfilling Film and TV or security work?

He smiled and told me he much preferred the film work. He said it was a great way to pay the bills, and I felt the same way. I had to admit I was getting more and more hooked on the idea of this new life. What did I have to lose? My rent was low, and I was starting to make enough from these gigs to cover my expenses with ease. This could be my future.

Then Curtis dropped a bombshell on me. He'd just been cast in a show called *Tribes*. He said it was a test run for the a new show that was going to start a year down the road called *Beverly Hills 90210*. I couldn't believe it. He was making $300 a day! That was the kind of money I could only dream about. My mind raced with the possibilities. I had to get in on this. So, on my way home, I called Central Casting to see if they had anything available. The guy on the phone had a couple of shows lined up for me, and I was eager to jump on board. For the next couple of months, I worked on some pretty big shows: Tribes, Who's the Boss?, Mr. Belvedere, Family Matters, Quantum Leap, Chucky, Arachnophobia, and The Outsiders. And it didn't stop there. I found myself working on the set with legends—Bruce Willis, Meryl Streep, Goldie Hawn, Jeff Daniels, John Goodman, Harrison Ford, Brad Pitt, Joe Pesci, Mel Gibson, Danny Glover, Matt LeBlanc, and so many others. It was surreal.

But it wasn't just about being in the background anymore. They were putting me in scenes where I actually interacted with the lead characters. In fact, I was getting paid double or triple what your typical extra made. I couldn't believe it. Things were happening fast, and I was starting to feel like I was in the right place at the right time.

Then, came the *Tribes* gig. The casting agency actually called me and said the casting directors wanted to meet with me for a part. They wanted to cast me as a prominent character, not just some extra. But here's the catch: they wanted me to wear a speedo. I had never worn one in my life, and I wasn't about to make my debut on national TV in a speedo. It wasn't my thing. As much as I liked the idea of the extra cash, I couldn't bring myself to do it. So, I turned down the role. Then much to my surprise they still wanted to use me even after I turned down the roll. Instead, I was stuck as a regular background artist, earning that steady $300 a day.

The gigs just kept rolling in. I wasn't the main star, but that was ok I was in a lot of memorable scenes. Like the time I was cast as a high school bully on *Family Matters*, storming out of a diner with my fictitious high school jocks, and pushing Jaleel White—aka Urkel—through a bunch of chairs. It was small, but it was my moment, and I felt like I was building something.

I had one speaking role in a movie called *Vision Quest* with Matthew Modine, but they cut the scene. I didn't mind. I wasn't in Hollywood to be an actor. That was never the goal. I wasn't interested in pursuing fame or a career in acting. In fact, I didn't really care for the whole Hollywood scene. The narcissism, the self-importance—it all made me uneasy. It wasn't just the actors; it was everyone on set. Craft services, wardrobe, the camera crew— the cast had this air about them. It was a world of inflated egos, and I wasn't here for it. Looking back, I thought my time on all of these movie sets was about my own confidence. But now, I wonder if there was more to it. Maybe the casting and film directors saw something in me—something that wasn't just about my outward confidence. It's strange, but I think the spirits within me were somehow connecting with the unclean spirits of the people around me. They were drawn to each other, like some unseen force linking us all together.

I started to see the industry for what it really was. It was a dark place, a place full of people fighting battles I could feel but couldn't fully understand. I saw the hunger for fame and validation in the eyes of the actors and crew, and I realized that something was deeply wrong. The whole industry was steeped in darkness.

At that time in my life, I didn't care about the people I worked with. I wasn't interested in fitting in or making friends. But I knew something was happening inside me. I could feel the internal battle. I could see the nature of mankind, the way we all long for attention, for recognition. God created us to be social beings, but without the guidance of His word, we're left to navigate the world on our own, lost.

And so, I kept going, taking each gig as it came. I wasn't seeking fame, but I couldn't help but notice the allure it had on so many around me. Everyone on set seemed consumed by it, even if they didn't realize it. I was just trying to find my way, trying to get through the darkness, searching for something real in a world that often seemed so fake.

I saw it in their eyes—the spirits. I knew what they were, and I knew what I was carrying inside of me. The unclean spirits that followed me, that had followed many of us, they were drawn to the spirits around me, just as the actors and crew were drawn to their fame. It was a strange and terrifying realization. But the more I worked in the industry, the more I saw it for what it truly was. The lights, the cameras, the actors—they were all part of a bigger, darker story. And I was just trying to find my way out.

What is an unclean spirit? It's a disembodied soul, an entity that latches onto a human host, quietly observing and studying. Much like the fictional Dracula, inspired by Vlad the Impaler, you typically have to invite a demon into your life. There are countless ways to open the door to these parasitic spirits—through music, books, symbols, rituals, spells, and even jewelry. Fear and pornography are common entry points, allowing these entities to creep in unnoticed.

I've encountered many people carrying these unclean spirits, and I've always made it a point to tell them what they're dealing with. It's not always easy to confront someone with this truth—some are ready to hear it, and some are not. They can choose to accept it or reject it, and when I can see the spirit inside them, it gives me a sense of relief to name it, to shed light on what's hidden in the darkness.

I believe God calls us to be bold, to fight for the souls of the people around us, even for strangers. If someone is willing to seek deliverance, I will do whatever I can to help. If they choose to stay in the darkness, it saddens me, but I accept their decision. However, in those chaotic days on film sets, things weren't always so clear-cut. Many of the extras would bring Tarot cards for readings while waiting in between scenes. While I never took part in the readings, I did have an encounter with a street witch years later—a warlock who was disturbingly accurate in his predictions. But that's a story in a few chapters.

I also got engaged to a girl whose mother claimed to be a witch. That's also another chapter of my life that we'll get to later, but suffice to say, the more I lived in this strange world, the more I was pulled into things I never thought I'd experience. Despite all of that, I kept getting work, and the bills were covered.

Chapter Twenty-Two

Double Vision

C.S. Lewis

"When we find that the people we admired have feet of clay, we should not be surprised. Every human is fallen. Our hope was never meant to rest in man, but in God."

Saturdays came around, and I found myself craving music, a release from the tension of the week. I remembered a hip coffee shop on Vine Street, near where we shot *Teenage Mutant Ninja Turtles*. I'd heard they had an open mic, so I figured I'd drop by around 7.

When I arrived, the place was small, with a piano and a couple of microphones set up. Most people were leaving, and only a couple of musicians remained. A girl at the mic called up the first performer, a guy with a guitar. He played and sang, and honestly, it was awful. The next guy wasn't much better, just a little less painful. But just as I was about to throw in the towel and head south, the third guy stood up—a frail fellow with John Lennon-style glasses and messy shoulder-length hair. He sat at the piano, and frankly, I expected more of the same garbage. What I wasn't prepared for, though, was a performance that would absolutely blow my mind.

This unassuming guy was a virtuoso, pure and simple. I've been to my fair share of concerts, but I've never, in my life, heard anyone play like this. His music wasn't just good—it was transcendent. Three songs, and the entire room was silent, captivated by his raw talent. I honestly didn't want him to stop, but as fate would have it, more terrible acts were streaming in with guitars in hand, and his time was up.

He got up to leave, and that's when I knew I had to meet him. Who was this guy, and why was he playing at a corner coffee shop when he could easily be selling out arenas? I approached him, introduced myself, and asked if I could buy him a coffee and hear more about his story. He looked a little startled but agreed.

We found a quiet table, and he started telling me his life story. His name was Peter, born in the late fifties and raised in LA. He began playing the piano at age six, and as he grew older, he dove into a music career. As we spoke, he casually dropped the names of some pretty big bands—Foreigner, Gary Wright, Seals & Crofts, and the Strand. I recognized three of those bands, but Foreigner caught my attention immediately.

Peter told me he played keyboards on Foreigner's *Double Vision* album and toured with them for two years. But his journey with Foreigner ended on a sour note. In the 1980s, during a European tour, Peter allegedly had a bit too much to drink at a high-end hotel. And in an alleged drunken state, he took a valuable painting, something worth thousands of dollars, and allegedly stuffed it into his suitcase. He thought nothing of it until customs in Italy discovered it while the band was going through security. The band allegedly had to pay a hefty fine to get Peter out of jail. That was the moment that allegedly cost him his spot with the band.

As he told me the story, I could feel the weight of it—how one reckless decision in a drunken haze could change the course of someone's life. Peter wasn't the kind of guy who wore his past like a badge of shame, though. He spoke about it with a kind of resigned humor, as if it was just part of the story.

But there was something more to Peter than just the rock 'n roll drama. As he spoke, I could see the depth of his soul—the way he carried himself, the weight of experience in his words. There was a darkness to his past, sure, but there was also a light. A part of him, I realized, was still searching. Searching for something that would give his life meaning. I didn't know what it was yet, but I knew that meeting him wasn't just a coincidence.

So we sat there, talking about life, music, and the strange path that had brought him to that tiny coffee shop. There was a certain resonance to his story, a lesson in it about the choices we make, the demons we invite in. And as I listened to Peter, I couldn't help but wonder if he, too, was carrying an unclean spirit, one that had influenced his decisions and led him to a crossroads in his life, where he made a deal with a demon or the devil.

Little did I know, our meeting was just the beginning of a series of strange and unexpected events that would take me even deeper into the world of unclean spirits, rock 'n roll, and the tangled web of fate. The band Foreigner allegedly liked Peter but saw him as a liability, someone too unpredictable to keep around. After the incident with the painting, they cut ties, and just like that, his time with Foreigner was over. It was a harsh reality, but that's the way the industry worked. But Peter, ever the storyteller, didn't dwell too long on that chapter.

Instead, he shifted to another story—one about his time with Gary Wright before Foreigner.

It was a great gig, Peter told me, but it ended in betrayal. Gary Wright allegedly took one of Peter's songs, a song Peter had been working on for months. You might know it, *Dream Weaver*. Peter was devastated when he found out that Wright had allegedly stolen the tune, taking credit for it without so much as a nod to Peter. At the time, Peter was young, new to the business, and hadn't recorded the song himself. So, there was no real recourse. It was his word against Gary's, and in the music world, that's usually a losing battle.

We spent hours talking—Peter spilling his life story while I mostly listened. My life didn't seem nearly as interesting; after all, I was just a guy who had been on a few movie sets. So, I stayed quiet, taking in the incredible stories Peter shared. One story that stood out to me was about Peter Criss, best known as the original drummer and co-founder of the iconic rock band KISS. Peter told me that there was a time when Criss was homeless and living on the streets, an alcoholic struggling to find his way. I was shocked. How could a guy from one of the most famous rock bands of the seventies end up on the streets? But it made sense when Peter went on to explain that Criss had been taken in by him, that Peter had shared what little he had, offering Criss a place to stay during those dark days.

Hearing that made me even more disillusioned with the whole *KISS* crew, especially Gene Simmons. Stories of Simmons hoarding all the royalties while other members of the band struggled didn't sit well with me. It was heartbreaking and selfish. But we were in Hollywood, and considering *KISS* had always dressed like demons, I couldn't help but wonder if they had attracted more than just bad press—maybe they had invited these unclean spirits into their lives.

As our conversation continued, I asked Peter where he was staying. He told me he was bouncing from place to place, staying with friends but eventually being asked to leave. His friends had told him there wasn't enough room, and Peter was once again out of a home. I understood that. I had been homeless for a few months myself, and it was a miserable experience. It broke my heart to see someone as talented as Peter in such a situation.

So, without thinking twice, I offered him a place to stay. He was grateful, and just like that, I ended up with the keyboardist from Foreigner living with me for a few months. The first couple of weeks were good. Peter had a few gigs—recording demos and playing small shows. One evening, he asked if I wanted to join him in watching a personal recording session with some of his friends. I was intrigued. Why not? So, we hopped in my car, and Peter directed me up through the Hollywood Hills.

The house was beautiful—large, single-story, and hidden among the winding streets of the Hills. We knocked on the door, and an Asian woman answered. I wasn't sure if she was a maid or the wife of one of the musicians, but she welcomed us in. She directed us to the back, where two men were recording a flutist. I noticed they were using a Mac computer to record the flute player, which was a first for me. I had never seen a setup like that. It wasn't the most exciting session, but we stayed for about an hour and a half, watching and listening to the recording process.

When we left and got back in the car, Peter asked me if I knew who the two men were. I admitted that I didn't. Peter smiled and told me "that was Donald Fagen and Walter Becker of Steely Dan." I couldn't believe it. Back then, Steely Dan was one of my favorite groups, but I had no idea what they looked like. Their album covers never showed their faces. I was blown away by how casually Peter spoke about them, as if he bumped into rock legends like they were just regular guys.

One thing that constantly amazed me about Peter was his ability to compose music in his head. He didn't need an instrument—he would oddly sit in the bathroom, in his pants on the toilet, writing music on a notepad. he'd be in there for hours. But the question kept nagging me: With all this talent, why was Peter struggling so much to find steady work?

Weeks passed, and I began to notice something troubling. Peter seemed content to drift. He was waiting for the phone to ring not calling to find work. He didn't seem eager to find a real job, and as much as I respected him as a musician, I couldn't ignore that he wasn't contributing. He was an able-bodied man, and yet he was unwilling to do the work necessary to support himself. I decided to confront him. I asked Peter if he had any plans to look for work, and that's when he told me something that made everything click.

He started to tell me that an artist, someone like him, shouldn't have to work. He saw himself as above the need for a regular job. Instead, he subscribed to the Zendik Farm philosophy, a lifestyle he believed in with all his heart.

Now, if you look up the definition of *Zendik*, you'll find that it contradicts everything I now believe in as a Christian. But back then, I just viewed it as crazy. It's an atheistic, heretical philosophy that rejects faith, the very thing that now sustains me. Zendik, according to its teachings, is about living without regard for God or morality. It's a mindset that frees the individual from responsibility, which seemed to explain Peter's inability to settle into any stable work.

He would often bring up Karl Marx and the ideals of the hippie commune movement. It all became clear—I wasn't just offering a place to stay to a gifted musician. I had unwittingly invited a Neo

Marxist Egalitarian Atheist Hippie into my home. Peter's refusal to contribute, to be productive, and his reliance on others to provide for him was becoming too much.

It was hard to watch someone so talented slip further into the abyss, especially when I knew he was searching for something, but he just didn't know what. He was lonely, confused, and lost. It was clear to me that Peter needed Christ, but I couldn't share that with him because I wasn't saved and wasn't a believer in anything, let alone Jesus.

Twenty five years later, I found some old cassette recordings of Peter and a female singer he had been working with when he was living with me. I transferred them from cassette tape to digital format, connected with him on Facebook, and sent him the files. He was very thankful and even invited me down to Los Angeles for a visit. I guess he became a piano teacher and he was actually making a living and doing OK. He invited me down to play with some of his friends from the band Toto. I guess they jam with the drummer Jeff Porcaro in his garage. That all fell through when PETER noticed on my social media page that I had become a Christian and he didn't care for my political stance or religious philosophy of being a Christ follower. PETER was a non religious Jew. I could tell his mind was still captured by the world. We were on different paths now, and that was the last time we spoke.

Back when Peter lived with me, I had tried everything to help him find work. I even suggested security work and extra work on film sets. He gave film and television extra work a try, but after a couple of weeks, the reality set in that he had to put some effort into it so he abandoned that. Living with me without contributing wasn't an option anymore. I gave him an ultimatum find steady work or living with me wasn't going to work. So one morning, I woke up, and Peter was gone.

It was a bittersweet ending. If Peter would have accepted Christ, along with his talent and drive, he could have avoided much of his pain, but somewhere along the way, he'd gotten lost in the world. I only hope that one day, he finds the peace that only Christ can offer.

Chapter Twenty-Three

Neverland

Psalm 91:5-7

*"You will not fear the terror of night, nor the arrow that flies by day,
nor the pestilence that stalks in the darkness, nor the plague that destroys at midday.
A thousand may fall at your side, ten thousand at your right hand, but it will not come near you."*

God.

Later that week, I found myself involved in a few memorable shoots. One of them was a wine-tasting video for Wolfgang

Puck, featuring the legendary Dudley Moore. The shoot took place at Michael Jackson's iconic Neverland Ranch, in his wine cellar. I woke up before at the crack of dawn, ready for the shoot. The drive to the Malibu canyons loomed ahead, and I wanted to leave by 4:30 am to make it a little earlier than expected. This wasn't just any gig—it was a rare privilege to work at the home of the world's biggest pop star. I fired the T-bird up and headed to the shoot.

The streets of Hollywood were nearly deserted at that hour, only the occasional city vehicle or service truck rolling past under the glow of scattered streetlights. I decided to take Santa Monica Boulevard all the way down to the ocean. The darkened streets felt eerie but calm, the kind of stillness that felt loaded, as if something was about to happen.

I stopped at a red light, the ocean breeze starting to roll in, faint but distinct. The streetlights cast faint halos on the wet asphalt, and I knew I must be close to the beach. That's when I noticed a car pull up beside me on the left. It was packed—four guys, all Asian, their faces barely lit by the glow of their dashboard.

They were staring at me.

The passenger in the front seat rolled his window down and gestured for me to do the same. My gut hesitated, but I figured they might need directions. Maybe they were lost, and I wanted to be courteous despite the early hour. I rolled my window down just enough to hear them.

The passenger leaned out, motioning me closer, like he wanted to say something quietly. I obliged, leaning slightly toward the open window, thinking he might struggle with English and I'd need to hear him clearly.

And that's when it happened.

The guy spit in my face.

The shock hit me like a slap. My head jerked back, and I instinctively wiped my face, repulsed. "What the—" I yelled, unleashing a string of expletives. But before I could process what was happening, the guy reached into his jacket, pulled out a knife, and waved it at me through the window.

He didn't say a word, but the message was clear.

My pulse rocketed, and my fight-or-flight response kicked in. The light was still red, but I wasn't waiting around to see what these guys wanted. I slammed my foot on the gas, tires screeching as I shot through the intersection.

They followed.

I glanced in the rear view mirror and saw their headlights whip around the corner as they gave chase. My heart pounded like a war drum. I didn't care about running lights or breaking traffic laws; I figured I'd have a good excuse if a cop stopped me. The problem was there were no cops.

I turned left. They turned left. I turned right. They turned right.

Every move I made, they stayed on me. The streets were barren, amplifying the terror as I weaved through intersections and backstreets, trying to lose them. My breaths came fast, shallow. My hands gripped the wheel so tightly that my knuckles turned white.

For twenty agonizing minutes, the chase continued. My headlights cut through the darkness, but every time I thought I had shaken them, their car appeared again in my mirror. It felt like a nightmare, one where no matter how fast you run, the danger is always right behind you.

And then, just as suddenly as it started, it was over.

I made another sharp turn, expecting them to follow, but their headlights disappeared. I kept driving, zigzagging through side streets just to be sure. By the time I returned to Santa Monica Boulevard, the adrenaline was still coursing through me, my body shaking from the near-death encounter.

Miraculously, I was still on schedule. I merged onto Pacific Coast Highway, the ocean now fully visible under the faint glow of dawn, and headed toward Neverland.

When I finally turned into the driveway of the Jackson estate, the first thing that hit me was the silence. No carnival or amusement park, no laughter echoing from amusement park rides—just the hum of my engine. It struck me that all the stories I'd heard about this place—the rumors of lights and attractions—must've been added later on.

What I saw instead was something different, something more grounded in reality. It was just dry dirt, but it wasn't the circus-like atmosphere I had imagined. The mansion itself was a sprawling structure, nestled perfectly into the landscape. The driveway seemed endless, winding through an empty non manicured landscape. The gates however whispered wealth and exclusivity.

This place wasn't built for spectacle, but for someone who craved solitude and grandeur in equal measure. It was impressive, though, in its own right. When I got there the first AD directed me to where the cellar was. I was to play one of two waiters in the scene, but I thought being on such hallowed ground was surreal. The mansion was more impressive than I had imagined, with its grandiose, whimsical design and lavish decor. There was something magical about the place, though there was an underlying sadness too. Sadly, the project would never be seen by the public, It was created for the wine industry for hotel services. But the shoot was a masterclass in acting. Dudley Moore was a classy English man who gave you an air of an actor from the days of silent films. He was very physically funny. I've looked for the shoot and have seen still images of Dudley Moore on that very set but no actual video footage of the shoot. The day wrapped, and though I never met Michael, I was fortunate enough to have experienced a little bit of his world. After the shoot, which took most of the day, I was beat so I cautiously drove back through Santa Monica getting back home and sleeping earlier than usual.

A couple of days later, I worked on a Miller Lite commercial up in the same hills of Malibu. The shoot featured a group of familiar sports faces from the seventies and eighties—Bob Uecker, Mike Ditka, and Bubba Smith. The scene was simple enough: twenty extras holding a massive Miller Lite T-shirt in the middle of a meadow, with the sun shining down on us. As we waited for the director to call action, we all fluffed up the shirt, much like when you fluff up a colored parachute for toddlers as they run underneath it, waiting for it to settle on them. Everyone was in a good mood, laughing and joking.

Then, I heard it—someone screaming, followed by frantic shouts of "Snake!" Panic spread like wildfire as everyone froze for a second before rushing to get out of the way. It wasn't just a garden-variety snake. It was a rattlesnake, a massive one, and it was slithering right toward the set. The extras scattered in all directions. The ginormous shirt fell to the dirty ground and over the snake.

Everyone seemed to be losing their minds, and the situation was escalating quickly. At that moment, something clicked inside me. Growing up in Colfax and Applegate, I'd spent years around rattlesnakes. In fact, there was a time when I used to catch rattlesnakes, skin them, and then tack the skins onto wood. I'd oil and cure them for various crafts—headbands, boots, you name it. I knew exactly what to do.

While everyone else was running around in a panic, I calmly walked over fond the snake under the parachute. It was a beautiful creature, its scales glistening in the sunlight, its tail rattling with warning. But I wasn't afraid. In fact, I felt a sense of control. I reached down, grabbed the snake firmly by the head, and, with one swift motion, walked away from the set. The extras were watching me with wide eyes, completely dumbfounded. I tossed the rattlesnake far from the shoot into the brush and returned to the set as if nothing had happened. I felt like Clint Eastwood on the set of High Noon or some other spaghetti Western masterpiece.

As I walked back, I could feel all eyes on me. The cast and crew were stunned, many of them still frozen in place. Bob Uecker, Mike Ditka, Bubba Smith, and the director all came over to thank me. Their gratitude was palpable, and I could tell how much of a liability that snake had been. With so many people on set, if that rattlesnake had struck, it would have been a disaster. But for me, it was just another day in the life—no fear, no hesitation.

I had grown up with rattlesnakes. I understood them. And more importantly, I wasn't afraid of them. People often talk about fear, but I've learned that fear is something you conquer, not something you let control you. I fear no demon, no devil, and certainly no rattlesnake. After all, I've had my share of experience slaying things much darker than a serpent on his belly.

The crew seemed to appreciate the calm I had displayed as if they were witnessing something extraordinary. I wasn't just some random Background artist—today, I was the hero, the one who saved the day by doing something so simple yet so necessary. But for me, it wasn't about being a hero. It was about knowing my limits, knowing my abilities, and understanding that when you face down fear, you come out stronger.

That rattlesnake was just another challenge. It could've been a disaster, but in the end, it was nothing more than another day in the life of someone who had faced far worse. It reminded me that we often fear the things we don't understand, but once you conquer that fear, the world opens up in ways you never thought possible.

And in Hollywood, when you're dealing with larger-than-life stars, ridiculous stunts, and unpredictable situations, sometimes the only thing that can save the day is a steady hand and a clear mind.

Chapter Twenty-Four

Lost Luggage

Charles Spurgeon

"If you are a child of God, why would you seek to unite yourself with one who is still a child of wrath? Light and darkness cannot walk together."

It was Friday night, and I was feeling adventurous. After having already explored Hollywood Boulevard, I figured it was time to check out Sunset Boulevard. I had heard a lot about the nightlife there and was eager to see for myself. I pulled out the Recycler, hoping to find some live music to check out. Scanning through the listings, I came across a bar called Club Lingerie, which was hosting several bands that night with no cover charge. That sounded perfect to me. I grabbed my Thomas guide, charted the route, and made my way over to 6507 Sunset Blvd.

When I arrived, the place was buzzing with energy. The marquee outside read "Lost Luggage" as the headliner. The name struck me as strange, but in a way, it was also kind of intriguing. I figured it would be worth sticking around to see what kind of music they were playing.

The bar was packed, the air thick with the scent of cigarettes and the low hum of conversation. I grabbed a beer from the bar, settled into a spot, and took in the scene. The band was setting up, and they had a very distinct look. The lead singer had poofy, curly blonde hair that screamed eighties new wave,' and the rest of the band looked equally stuck in that era. It was clear they weren't quite ready to let go of the style and sound of the mid-eighties, even as the nineties loomed on the horizon.

The new wave era was winding down, and you could feel the shift in the air. Grunge bands like Guns N' Roses and Alice In Chains were taking over the airwaves, while the glam and big hair bands were struggling to maintain relevance. Some musicians embraced the changing tide, but others, like Lost Luggage, stubbornly clung to the past. I couldn't help but admire their conviction. They were clearly holding onto the era that had shaped them, even though the music landscape was quickly changing.

When the band started playing, I was surprised by how tight they were. There was a definite ska influence in their sound, which was not what I expected at all. The lead singer's voice wasn't anything extraordinary, but it fit well with the music. The crowd was enjoying themselves, dancing, drinking, and smoking, caught up in the carefree vibe of the night.

As I nursed my beer at the bar, I couldn't help but notice a couple of girls on the dance floor. One had curly blonde hair, while the other had dark brown almost black hair that cascaded down her back. They were both dancing, but every so often, their eyes would meet mine across the room. It was subtle at first, but it didn't take long for me to realize they were staring. Not just glances, but real stares, like they were sizing me up or deciding if I was worth talking to.

The longer I watched them, the more intrigued I became. There was a certain energy in the air, something unspoken but electric, as if the night had a life of its own. I felt a strange pull, like I was being drawn toward them without even realizing it. Maybe it was the fact that they seemed just as out of place in the scene as I did. We were all kind of holding on to something that was slipping away—the music, the vibe, the era. And yet, here we were, in this bar, in this moment.

As the band continued to play, the crowd got livelier, and the girls' glances became more frequent. Finally, after what seemed like an eternity, the curly-haired blonde gave me a small, playful smile. The brunette followed suit, her lips curving into a subtle but confident grin. It was clear they were interested, but I wasn't entirely sure what to do about it.

I took a deep breath, finished my beer, and decided to make my move. I wasn't one to sit idly by and wait for things to happen. As I approached the dance floor, I couldn't help but feel a rush of excitement. I wasn't sure what was going to happen next, but I knew this was a moment that could change everything. It was funny how one chance encounter could lead to a new relationship, a new connection. Sometimes, life just had a way of surprising you, even when you weren't looking for it. After a song or two, the girls made their way over to me, their curiosity piqued by our earlier exchanges. They began chatting with me, asking where I was from and if I actually lived in the city. I told them I did, but that my story was a little different. I explained how I had moved from Northern California to Hollywood on a whim, with no real plans in mind—just curious to see what would unfold in the entertainment capital of the world. It was a vague answer, but it was honest. I didn't know what I was doing yet, but I was ready to see where this would take me.

Just as we were talking, the bar had a large TV playing in the background. Something caught my eye. I saw the Noxzema commercial that I worked on flash across the screen. Without thinking, I pointed at the TV and said, "Hey, that's me!" they both looked up, and sure enough, there I was, a split second on screen in that commercial. They looked at me, impressed, and I could tell right then that I had struck gold. This was my ticket to earn their attention, but I wasn't about to push it. I'd wait for the right time.

I smiled, then asked them about themselves, turning the spotlight on them. The blonde girl, Laura, introduced herself first and then, without missing a beat, rushed over to some guy across the room. I shrugged it off and focused on the brunette. She told me her name was Danielle, and as we spoke, she revealed that she was attending the Fashion Institute downtown, with dreams of becoming a fashion designer. I found that intriguing. She was passionate, driven, and had a clear vision for her future.

What caught my attention, though, were her eyes. They were so strikingly blue, an electric blue that was almost unnatural. I remember thinking I'd never seen someone with hair that dark and sharp blue eyes. It wasn't until later that she admitted to wearing blue contacts, which I didn't even know existed at the time. It was another layer to the mystery of Danielle.

As the band wrapped up their set, the three of us decided to head to Canter's Deli on Fairfax. They told me it was a popular late-night spot and the perfect place to grab a bite after a show. We spent a good hour there, sipping iced tea and talking about everything and nothing at all.

I felt at ease with Danielle—there was something about her energy that made me feel comfortable, like we were just two people talking about life.

Eventually, it was time to part ways. Before they left, I worked up the courage to ask Danielle for her number. She smiled, then said, "Well, if you give me yours, I'll give you mine." "All I've got is a pager," I said, half-laughing. She chuckled, then wrote her number on the receipt from Canter's. It felt like a small victory in my otherwise uncertain world.

After they left, I sat in my car for a moment, feeling a sense of satisfaction. I hadn't had a real connection with a girl in years. The last time I had an actual girlfriend was back in eighth grade. Her name was Josie . Josie was an attractive sweet girl, and years later, after college, she'd gain notoriety as a news reporter for NBC. Josie's big break was an interview with the infamous Gary Condit, who gained national attention after the disappearance of Chandra Levy, an intern at the FBI with whom he was having an affair. That was all years later, though. Back in those days, Josie and I were just kids, and I was an awkward, introverted guy. Growing up in the mountains, with a population of only around 1,000 people within a 20-mile radius, didn't exactly offer much opportunity for dating.

Now, here I was, talking to a woman like Danielle. Smart, attractive, and six years older than me, with a sense of culture and a passion for fashion that made me feel like I was out of my league. I was still wearing my brother's hand-me-downs, and I knew they didn't fit my growing sense of self or style. I was a far cry from the sophisticated, fashionable woman sitting across from me. Yet, I didn't let that stop me. I had no idea at the time that she might not think I was much of a catch, but it didn't matter. In that moment, I felt seen, and for the first time in a long time, that was enough.

Chapter Twenty-Five

Broken Cars And Big Stars

Charles Spurgeon

"Trials are the way God refines our faith. Even a broken-down car can be a reminder that our true destination is not on this earth, but in heaven."

As I left Canter's and drove back to my apartment, I noticed something was wrong. After about a mile, a strange clunking sound started coming from the engine, and I could feel a grinding through the gas pedal. I tried to ignore it, but the more I drove, the worse it seemed to get. The grind was almost like a warning, a vibrating message from my car telling me something was about to break. By some stroke of luck, I made it back to my place, finding a parking spot just before the car started to overheat. I barely had time to put it in park when steam began pouring out from under the hood.

I sat there for a second, watching the steam billow up like smoke from a campfire. My heart sank. I couldn't afford a major car repair. I had barely enough money for the basics, let alone fixing whatever catastrophe was happening under the hood. This couldn't be happening. But there it was: the unmistakable sound of my car's final last breath.

The next morning, I walked around the corner to the local gas station, hoping someone could help me figure out what was wrong. The attendant behind the counter directed me to the mechanic who worked in the service area. "you can go around back, and talk to the mechanic," he said, almost without looking up from his newspaper.

I went around the back and talked to a man there and he said he could have it towed And he could look at it. I told him it's literally just around the block would there be anyway he could swing by to just look at it. He could see the desperation in my face. He said that he got off at around five and could come and check it out on his way home. I wrote down my address, and thanked him

He gave me his word, and I headed back to my apartment, still unsure of what was going to happen. But my thoughts were interrupted when I got a page from Pinkerton Security. I had barely walked 100 yards from the gas station, so I turned around found a payphone and called them back. They asked me if I could work a security job at a gallery exhibit opening on Wilshire Blvd. That was a big deal, a high-profile event, and I knew it could help me cover my expenses—especially the car repair. There was just one problem: I didn't have a car. It hit me, I now had to rely on Los Angeles's notoriously unreliable bus system to get there.

The job was supposed to start at 7 pm, and the mechanic was coming around 5, so there should be enough time to get both tasks done. I agreed to take the job, though it was on short notice, and made my way back to the gas station. I asked the attendant where I could find the bus schedules, and he handed me a folded pamphlet that looked like something you'd get at Disneyland—except it was for LA's bus system. I got a bad feeling the moment it was in my hands. I unfolded the paper, looked at the route numbers and schedules, and groaned inwardly. But there was no turning back now.

I went home, showered, worked on some music for a bit, and read through a book I had started weeks ago. The clock ticked closer to 5, and I went outside to wait for the mechanic. He pulled up right on time, driving a rusty old seventies Chevy Love. I couldn't help but chuckle to myself. This guy was every bit the mechanic I had imagined—covered in grease and carrying a toolbox that looked like it had been through a dozen oil changes. He was kind enough to bring paper to sit on so he wouldn't stain my car with grease, though.

He started the engine, and the clunking sound came back almost immediately. It sounded worse now—like something was about to give. The mechanic revved the engine a few times, stepping out of the car and telling me to hop in. He asked me to step on the gas, and I did you could hear the dreaded knocking and soon the blue smoke from the tailpipe. He said. "Shut it off," he ordered, his face grim. "This is bad," he said flatly. "You're looking at a serious repair bill, kid. Probably a rebuild or a new engine" My stomach dropped. The last thing I needed was a massive expense. I felt like the world had just caved in. I could see Joe noticed my reaction, but he didn't sugarcoat it. I asked him how much it would cost to fix it, and he told me the price would be more than what the car was worth. His words hit me like a punch in the gut. I had no savings. I barely had enough to make it from day to day. I wasn't even sure how I'd get to work the next day.

Joe continued, "I've got a buddy who might buy it from you as is for $400." It wasn't much, but it was better than nothing. I had no other options. I didn't know anyone who could help. I didn't know how to get a new engine or even where to begin. "If your friend's willing, I'll take it," I said, defeated. Joe gave me a nod and said he'd check with his friend the next day.

In hindsight, thirty-plus years later, I would've found a way to fix that car. Maybe I would've put in the effort to rebuild it and then sold it for a profit. But when you're nineteen, clueless, and scraping by, you make choices that don't always make sense. It's part of the journey, though. And it's those very decisions that led me to where I am today—where I found wisdom, grace, and ultimately, Christ. But at the time, I had no idea.

Joe told me he'd come back Sunday with his friend to take the car. I thanked him for his help and headed inside to get changed into my guard's uniform. I needed to make money to get by, and the job with Pinkerton was the only thing I had going. I pulled on the uniform, left my apartment, and walked to the bus stop on Western and Beverly. The bus pulled up, the door swooshing open as hydraulics hissed. The bus was decorated in white, black, orange, and red stripes, and I could feel my heart sink a little. This was it. The bus was now my only means of transportation.

"$2.25 to Wilshire and Doheny," the driver said as I stepped on. I dug out a few dollars and quarters and loaded them in the change machine. The ride was only about twenty minutes, but that didn't make it any less awkward. The bus was my new reality, and while I didn't love it, I wasn't about to complain. It was part of the grind now.

When I got to the gallery, a guard handed me a map of the premises and informed me I'd be patrolling the parking garage. I couldn't believe it. This was a high-end, boujee event, and instead of mingling with the elite guests, I was stuck walking around a smog-filled parking garage. As exotic cars rolled in, I was trying to imagine the scene inside, of what the event might actually be like. I never even saw the artwork; I was too busy pacing the garage. From what I imagined, it was probably just a bunch of abstract nonsense anyway. The kind of stuff that I always thought could be made by an 8-year-old with finger paints.

For two and a half hours, I circled the garage, scribbling in my DAR report, which, in hindsight, was not the best idea since it made me distracted and less aware of my surroundings. The lights in the garage weren't great, and I found myself walking around one of the massive concrete pillars when, out of nowhere, a small woman barreled right into me, knocking me back. I stumbled, caught off guard, but quickly gathered myself, apologizing.

"Hi there, honey," she said, startled but friendly.

I looked down at her and froze. No way this was happening. It was Dolly Parton—right there in front of me. I blinked in disbelief and stammered, "You're Dolly Parton?"

She chuckled and said, "Well, the last time I looked, I was."

I had no words. Dolly Parton was one of my childhood idols. I'd grown up listening to her songs, especially *Jolene*. Her voice had a magical quality that could stop time. When she and Kenny Rogers teamed up, it was pure magic in my world. But seeing her in person was surreal. The woman who had soundtracked so many of my childhood memories was standing in front of me, and two inches shorter than my five foot two inch mother.

We chatted for a moment, and I walked her to her Cadillac. I couldn't help but feel starstruck, even though I wasn't much of a celebrity chaser. I'd had my share of brushes with fame, but this was different. This was Dolly. It felt like the universe had dropped a tiny slice of magic into my dreary day.

By then, it was around 10:45, and I was tired of being stuck in that garage. I'd been stuck in this smoggy underground hell for hours, and my feet were sore. The captain on site finally gave me the option to leave early. "If you want to head out, you can," he said.

I didn't need any more convincing. I said my goodbyes and headed back out to the bus stop, where my trusty ride awaited. It had been a strange, surreal night, and I couldn't help but laugh a little to myself. It wasn't the glamorous night I'd hoped for, but I had a story to tell. And sometimes, that's all you need.

Chapter Twenty-Six

Bus stops And Bullets

Charles Spurgeon

"God is our shield in times of trouble; even in the midst of violence, His hand can deliver."

I looked at the schedule and saw that I'd have to take a more extended route home. It wasn't ideal, but it was the only option I had. I hopped on the bus, which took me up Doheny, all the way to Santa Monica, then down to Western. After a long ride, the driver dropped me off and told me that the transfer bus would take less time. I stepped off, walked over to the bench at Western and Santa Monica, and sat down, waiting for the next bus that would take me to N. Edgemont St. The night was quiet, but there was a slight unease in the air.

It was around 11:30, and the corner felt deserted, the flickering yellow light casting weak shadows. I glanced around, my eyes landing on the empty street, the faint hum of the city surrounding me. Then I saw him: a young Black man crossing the street, making his way toward the bench. He sat next to me, his posture slightly tense. It was just the two of us, waiting for the bus, our figures ghostly in the dim glow of the streetlight.

And then we heard it—a sound that didn't quite fit in with the quiet stillness. Footsteps. A group of men was walking around behind us from the direction of a gas station that was under repair. The place had been chained off, but there was a small parking lot with two hot rods parked in it. Six men, all wearing khakis, white t-shirts, and sporting shaved heads, were talking amongst themselves. They spoke Spanish, and I caught a few words, but mostly it was just noise that faded into the background.

As I turned to glance at them, I saw them drinking beer, laughing, and one of them was even urinating on the fence while the others made jokes. The whole scene was unsettling, but what really got my attention was the sudden shift in atmosphere. Something wasn't right. The man beside me seemed to notice it too, his body stiffening ever so slightly, a slight unease in his eyes.

And then it happened.

A car cruised slowly horizontally directly in front of us, moving at a deliberate pace. I could hear him shout something in Spanish at the men in at the gas station behind us. His voice sharp with aggression. And before we could even process what was happening, the gunfire erupted.

I've never heard anything like it—the deafening crack of bullets piercing the air. The sounds of bullets whizzing past us, close enough that I could feel the wind from them. My heart raced, and instinct kicked in. I didn't think, I just moved. I dropped to the ground, crawling under the bus bench as fast as I could.

We were lying sideways under the bench, one ear pressed to the ground, trying to keep as still as possible, hoping we wouldn't draw attention. The world around us felt like it was moving in slow motion, and every second stretched out longer than it should have. From our position, I could hear the angry voices of the gang members as they yelled at the car driving by. They were furious, but it wasn't over yet.

I watched as the men emptied their pistols in the direction of the car. The gunfire echoed down the empty street, sharp and unforgiving. In the low light, I could see the bullets sparking and skipping down the pavement, ricocheting off the concrete like rocks skipping across a pond. It was an unsettling sight—like watching time unraveling, each bullet a moment that couldn't be undone. They fired until their guns were empty, the anger and disappointment clear on their faces. Then, as quickly as it had started, they turned and started walking back in our direction.

My heart raced, and my stomach tightened. Every part of me wanted to run, but I knew better. Staying still was our only chance. As the men walked by, their presence was overwhelming. I could smell the cheap beer on their breath, the stale scent of cigarette smoke clinging to their clothes. They passed by so close I could feel their anger radiating off them, thick in the air. The six of them, now back at the gas station, resumed their laughter, their conversation in Spanish a reminder of how out of place I felt in that moment.

I didn't know how the guy next to me was feeling, but I could sense the same fear in him. We were sitting there, facing away from them, pretending to be invisible, but in my mind, I couldn't help but wonder if they were angry at their missed target. And if they were, the two of us on the bench were perfect targets for their rage. A rent-a-cop, sitting alone on a bench in the middle of nowhere.

Every second that passed felt like it could be my last. I didn't know how much longer I could keep it together. I kept thinking about those men behind us, thinking about how easily they could turn around and take their anger out on us. In that moment, I was sure that at any moment, I would feel the sharp sting of a bullet, the world would go black, and everything would be over. And after the weed gone wrong incident I knew exactly what the barrel of a gun felt like pressed against my body. I was waiting for the same feeling.

We stayed there for what felt like an eternity, the air thick with tension, neither of us daring to move or speak. Five minutes dragged on like an hour, but then finally, we heard the hydraulics the bus as it turned the corner and rolled into view. Relief hit me like a tidal wave, washing away the fear, the anticipation, and the anxiety that had been building up inside of me. I didn't dare look back. I just stood up, my legs shaking beneath me, and slowly walked onto the bus.

We sat down across from each other, both of us silent. I didn't know what to say. How could I say anything after what we'd just been through? The only thing I could do was look at him, and I could see it in his eyes—the same recognition, the same understanding. We had dodged more than one bullet that night. And not just the ones fired by that gang. I felt a strange sense of camaraderie with this stranger, a bond formed in the shared experience of that fear, that terror.

I didn't say a word to him. I just sat there, trying to calm my racing heart, my mind struggling to comprehend what had just happened. I felt it—something had changed in me. I had felt the brush of death against my skin, and it had left a mark. I wasn't sure what that mark meant, but I knew I wouldn't forget that moment. It wasn't just the fear I would carry with me, but the weight of knowing how close I had come to losing everything.

That moment—the gunshots, the fear,—shaped something inside me. It was like a switch had been flipped, and suddenly, I understood. PTSD wasn't just something soldiers came home with. It wasn't just a result of combat or war. PTSD could come from any trauma, any moment that shatters the way you see the world. It was something I would carry with me for a long time, maybe forever. And in that moment, I had a deep, unsettling understanding of what it must feel like to return from battle, to face the world with a heart forever altered by the horrors you've witnessed.

I didn't know it yet, but I was living with my own form of PTSD, a quiet kind that seeped into my soul and settled there uninvited. It would stay with me for years, quietly shaping my thoughts, my actions, and the way I moved through the world. But that was just one chapter of a much larger story. There was more to come. More experiences, more fear, more pain. But also more healing, more growth, and, eventually, more light. But a spirit of fear most definitely had entered me that night.

Chapter Twenty-Seven

Violation In The Valley

Matthew Henry

"Let me be thankful, first, because he never robbed me before; second, because although he took my purse, he did not take my life; third, because although he took all I possessed, it was not much; and fourth, because it was I` who was robbed, not I who robbed."

The day felt like a roller coaster. First, I lost my car—my lifeline in LA, the thing that gave me freedom to travel at will. Then, I met a childhood legend, Dolly Parton, and to top it off nearly had my life cut short in a hail of bullets. I was exhausted—physically, mentally, and emotionally drained. That night, I'm sure my dreams were as wild as my day had been. The car was towed the next morning, and though it was gone, I managed to sell it for $400. A small victory in a world that felt upside down. I could've dwelled on the loss, I could've seen the glass as half empty, but instead, I chose to see it as half full. After all, at least I had something to show for it. But wait there's more, It gets worse.

I didn't tell my parents about losing the car. It felt too embarrassing, too shameful. I was 19, still figuring out how to navigate life, and the last thing I wanted was to let them down, so I kept it to myself. But I had finally gotten a phone number—a way to contact my parents, my work at Central Casting, Pinkerton, Curtis, and, most importantly, my new girlfriend, Danielle.

I started spending a lot of time with Danielle. She was always at my apartment, and we had become close. We still hadn't had sex, though. Danielle had grown up in a very conservative Christian home. Her parents were both born-again Christians. Looking back you could say that their Christian values shaped just about everything they did. They were very protective of her, and she, in turn, was hesitant to move too quickly in our relationship. We had a couple of close calls, but we always stopped before things went too far. Despite my hormones running wild, I understood, so it was totally fine with me.

Danielle could tell I was from a small town—a place where culture didn't quite reach, where art and fashion were just words on a page to most people. I think she felt it was her duty to elevate me, to expose me to the finer things in life. She took me shopping, buying me fancy outfits I never would've worn outside of hanging out with her. But because she bought them, I wore them. I'm sure I looked out of place in them, but I wore them anyway, hoping I'd blend in or at least not stick out too much.

She also took me to a lot of foreign films, mainly French. There were a few Italian ones, but it was French cinema that she loved. At first, I hated reading subtitles. I'd grown up watching Hollywood blockbusters where the dialogue was the focal point. But after watching a few, I started to get it. I began to understand that watching them in their native language gave me a fuller context for the story. And slowly, I began to appreciate it. Now, I can't stand dubbed films—it feels like something essential gets lost in translation.

I'm thankful to Danielle for exposing me to that world. It opened my eyes to new cultures, new ways of thinking. It broadened my perspective in ways I hadn't expected.

There was one incident with Danielle that I definitely won't forget. One night, I took her out to a restaurant in the Valley. We had a nice dinner. Like I mentioned before, she was into fashion and always made sure we both looked our best. That night, she had just bought me an expensive leather coat, so I wore it proudly along with the new Doc Martens I had picked up a couple of weeks prior.

After spending a good amount of time at the restaurant, we decided it was time to head back to the car. Unfortunately, there hadn't been any parking near the restaurant, so we had to park a couple of blocks away and the neighborhood wasn't exactly the privileged zone. The night air was cool and quiet as we walked, and for a few minutes, everything felt perfectly fine. But then, out of the corner of my eye, I caught movement behind us. Something made me glance back, and that's when I saw them: two guys trailing us about forty yards away.

Immediately, I knew something wasn't right. Their pace, their body language—everything about them screamed trouble. My gut tightened, and I turned back to Danielle, trying to keep my voice steady as I told her, "Don't look back, but we need to pick up the pace." I saw a Denny's up ahead, its neon lights casting a faint glow on the sidewalk.

It was about twenty yards away, and I made a decision: if we could just get inside, we might be safe.

We hurried to the entrance, following the walkway up and around to the doors. I reached for the handle and pulled. Nothing. It was locked. My heart sank. I turned around, and there they were. The two Mexican or Guatemalan men had followed us right to the entrance. They weren't there for English lessons. My mind instantly went to what had happened to me that last week at the bus stop and the Mexican gang members shooting up that passing car.

One of them, the taller of the two, pulled out a long Bowie knife. The shorter one revealed a screwdriver, gripping it tightly in his hand. My fists tightened as the taller man grabbed Danielle's purse, yelling demands in Spanish. I couldn't understand his words, but his intentions were clear. I reached into my pocket, pulled out the small amount of cash I had, and handed it over. He wasn't satisfied. His eyes landed on my leather jacket, and he motioned for me to take it off. Reluctantly, I complied, slipping it off my shoulders and handing it to him. The heavy leather felt like it weighed a thousand pounds in that moment.

But Danielle wouldn't let go of her purse. She clutched it tightly, screaming, "No! No! No!" Her defiance seemed to anger the man with the knife. He pressed the blade to her throat, his intent deadly serious. My heart raced as I tried to think of a way to diffuse the situation. Before I could act, the man with the screwdriver punched me across the face, sending a sharp jolt of pain through my jaw. I staggered but stayed on my feet. Desperate to protect Danielle, I physically pried the purse from her hands and handed it over to them. It was the only way to keep her safe.

And then, as if the humiliation wasn't already complete, the taller man pointed at my shoes. My brand-new Doc Martens. I felt utterly defeated as I knelt down, untied them, and handed them over without a word. By the time they left, we were both mentally and physically drained. I didn't care about the things they had taken. What stung more than anything was the violation—the feeling of being powerless to protect Danielle.

As a man, there is no greater humiliation than failing to shield the people you care for. I stood there, in my socks and bruises, as Danielle sobbed quietly beside me. The weight of that moment crushed me. I wasn't in a good place, and for a long time after that night, the memory lingered. It wasn't just about the loss of material possessions; it was about the loss of security, the helplessness, and the way that moment shook my identity to its core. I hoped that was the last incident or brush with violence and potentially even death.

But after a couple of months we had been spending a lot of time together, so Danielle suggested we head up to Agoura Hills, just 30 miles north of LA, to meet her parents.

I wasn't sure what to expect. When we arrived, it was clear that Danielle came from a different world than I did. Her mom was sweet but a little nervous. Her dad, on the other hand, was intense—very type-A, military-type. He was direct, rigid, and protective. I could feel the weight of his gaze as he sized me up. And honestly, I understood it. I wouldn't want my daughter to date someone like me, either. I could tell that he had certain expectations, and I wasn't sure I was meeting them.

But what I didn't know then was that Danielle was struggling with something much deeper than I had realized. She had been battling bulimia for years. At the time, I didn't even know what that was. All I knew was that there was something strange going on.

When we went out to dinner, Danielle would often want to leave right after eating. I didn't understand it at first. But then I started to notice something else—every time I went to her apartment, the cupboards were packed with canned foods. Not just a few cans but hundreds, maybe more. But I thought to myself, she was so thin. Too thin.

Over the years, after we broke up and went our separate ways, I remained in contact with her sister Laura, and she briefed me on Danielle's situation. It continued to get worse. Her obsession with her appearance spiraled out of control. And I couldn't help but draw the proximity to Los Angeles as a big role in her struggle. The city's influence on beauty standards, the pressure to conform to a certain look, was overwhelming. Danielle was studying fashion, a industry that has a dark, competitive edge. The media told women that they had to weigh a hundred pounds or less to be considered beautiful. And it wasn't just Hollywood that had this effect—it was the magazines, the billboards, the fashion shows. It was everywhere.

Looking back, I now see that the culture Danielle was surrounded by was toxic. It was an impossible standard. Fast forward to now, and the pendulum has swung too far the other way. Today, the media promotes obesity as beauty, completely missing the middle ground. Hollywood has become a mess, pushing one unrealistic standard after another. It's a reflection of the confusion in society, a society that has lost its way. But despite all the dysfunction in the city, I still liked Danielle's parents. They were good people, loving and kind, even if they were a little over protective.

I understand now that their protectiveness came from a place of love, especially after learning about Danielle's struggle. They wanted to shield her from the pressures of the world, to protect her from the very culture that had a stranglehold on her self-worth.

Chapter Twenty-Eight

The Road To Highland Grounds

Bach (Johann Sebastian Bach) –

"The aim and final end of all music should be none other than the glory of God and the refreshment of the soul."

When I wasn't working as a guard on set or hanging out with Danielle, I was writing music. Peter had been the one to inspire me to pick up a pad of paper and my guitar again. I already had three or four songs I'd written, but watching him play, watching him pour his soul into his music—it made me want more. I wanted more material and more depth. Even with his flaws, his worldly gifts were contagious. He made me believe that I could create something that might make a difference.

But as I started to write more and more, I began to see a pattern in the themes of the songs I was crafting. I found myself writing about the world, relationships, the state of things in my life, and current events around me. When I look back at myself thirty five years ago, compared to who I am today, it's almost unbelievable how much has changed. As a musician, singer, artist, and songwriter, the transformation is staggering. Without Jesus Christ in my life, I now see how self-centered my music was back then. It was all about me—the trials, the struggles, the evils of the world. The songs I wrote were focused on despair, on the darker side of things.

If you listen to most secular music, it's all about sex, drugs, alcohol, war, murder, lying, and stealing. Country music, thankfully, still has some decent themes, but the ones that sell the most are the ones that focus on depravity. It's like people crave sex, chaos and destruction, and the industry serves it up without a second thought.

I finally decided it was time to share the songs I had been crafting with actual people. So I started searching the newspapers and magazines, hoping to find a place to showcase my songs. One spot that caught my attention was a place called Highland Grounds. It was a cool, hip coffee shop on Highland Boulevard, just a mile from my place. Convenient for me since I had lost my car. Now, without a car, a quick bus ride was my new mode of transport.

The first time I walked into Highland Grounds, I was immediately struck by the place's atmosphere. It had this laid-back, artistic vibe that I loved. On the wall, there were flyers advertising musicians who would be performing. The more I read, the more I thought, "Maybe this is the place where I can share my music." I had never played in front of anyone before, so I was nervous just thinking about performing. I'd only ever played for myself. Not even Danielle had heard me perform.

I sat at a small table and ordered a ham and cheese sandwich with a bowl of soup. The waitress was young and pretty, with an earthy, hippie vibe. I asked her about the open mic night and how it worked. She smiled and explained that you just show up before or at 7 pm on Wednesdays, sign up, and then wait your turn. She told me they usually get about ten or fifteen people, so it could take a while if you were at the end of the list. If the audience liked your performance, they might even book you for a show on one of the weekends. I felt a rush of excitement and fear. I told her I'd think about it, but I joked that I had the DNA of a chicken, so I wasn't sure I could go through with it.

She laughed, her eyes sparkling. "Don't worry," she said. "Most of the players are horrible." Then, she laughed again and walked away. It was blunt, but it was also kind of funny. And, in a weird way, it made me even more nervous. The idea of performing in front of strangers terrified me. I didn't know if I was any good or if I was just fooling myself. I thought I sounded amazing in my own head, but you never really know until you step in front of an audience. I mean, we've all seen enough episodes of *American Idol* to know that some people genuinely believe they're the best singers in the world, only to get laughed off the stage. Maybe that was me.

As I sat there eating a guy had walked in with a guitar case and a shaved head. He looked a little like Sting but with more hair, a bit skinnier, and a prominent Adam's apple. He set up his gear, and I noticed his guitar was a beauty—so much nicer than mine. And then, he plugged in a Roland amp. I felt a pang of jealousy. I wasn't a Christian yet, so I hadn't learned about how sin works, but I was definitely envious of his setup.

But as soon as he started playing, all that jealousy disappeared. What he played wasn't just music; it was a revelation. He was hammering on the strings with a force I'd never seen before—something like Eddie Van Halen's technique, but on an acoustic guitar. It was raw, it was powerful, and it was beautiful. I stayed for the entire hour that he played. Every note felt like it was telling a story. After he finished, I couldn't help myself—I approached him. I introduced myself, told him I was Alex, and complimented him on his performance. His name was Sean.

He shook my hand, thanked me, and continued packing up his gear. I left shortly after, my mind buzzing with excitement. I couldn't wait for next Wednesday's open mic. I spent all my free time the following days memorizing and polishing a couple of songs I thought might be good enough for Highland Grounds.

But I need to backtrack for a second. While I was working on various TV and film sets, I was introduced to a very different, destructive world—the world of smoking. It happened on the set of *Adam 12*, the updated version of the classic 1968 police drama. The new show starred Ethan Wayne, the actual son of legendary cowboy film star John Wayne, and I found myself drawn into a world of bad habits I hadn't anticipated. I noticed something when I worked on all the sets—it seemed like everyone smoked. It was almost as if it was part of the uniform of the industry, like a badge of coolness. And, to be honest, I thought it looked mighty cool. Now, mind you, I had a bit of asthma. Simple things like dust, dander, pollen, or food preservatives would set it off, causing inflammation in my lungs. But that nasty sin nature? It overrode all the common sense I had left. I knew I shouldn't smoke, but the pressure to fit in, to feel like I belonged, was too strong.

One day, while I was in wardrobe, making sure my outfit and my hair were on point for the scene, the wardrobe coordinator—a very gay man, who I could tell had a certain fondness for me—asked if I'd ever smoked. I told him when I was like six. I told him I chewed tobacco on occasion. His reaction was immediate. "Gross," he said, with a grimace.

Then, he pulled out a cigarette from his pack and handed it to me. "Try it," he said. I hesitated, reluctant but curious, and finally took the cigarette from his hand. A couple of puffs later, I was choking on the smoke, and he was laughing at me. But then—just like that—the nicotine rush hit me, and I was hooked. Instantly. He smiled and said "see".

Only later, as I drove home from the shoot, I realized how far I'd fallen. I purchased a pack of Camel Lights for $1.25. And I guarantee the demons were rejoicing, celebrating my decision to shorten my lifespan with this new addiction. It didn't take long before I was lighting up every couple of hours. I thought I looked cool, but I knew the price was far too high. A price on my health and my pocketbook.

But life went on, and so did my music. I spent time polishing up the couple of tunes I'd been working on—one original and one cover of Cat Stevens' "Trouble." The following Wednesday arrived, and I decided that tonight would be the night. I was going to conquer this fear of performing. I had no choice but to face the dragon, slay it, and prove to myself that I could do this.

By 6:30 pm, I was heading over to Highland Grounds. Abby, the waitress from last time, was there. She smiled when she saw me. "Hey," she said, recognizing me immediately. I returned her greeting. She asked, jokingly, where I was taking my guitar. I didn't catch the humor at first, so I looked at her like a deer caught in headlights, making myself look foolish. She laughed and pointed me to a table in the corner, where the sign up sheet was. Six people were already ahead of me, all hanging out with their guitars, looking like seasoned pros. I scribbled my name down and grabbed a coffee before sitting down to wait.

I'd love to tell you I remember the other musicians' performances, but honestly, I can't. All I remember is how awful most of them were. It was like *American Idol*, where you see the worst auditions that make you cringe. Now that I'm a Christian, I try and avoid shows with the word "idol" in them, but at the time, I couldn't help but notice the painful reality that 95% of the musicians were unbearable. By the time the sixth player came up, I was ready to stuff napkins in my ears just to avoid the torture. The man behind the soundboard, a small guy with dark purple Roy Orbison glasses, was working hard, but all I could think about was how much I wanted to leave. He introduced the performers, and I heard Abby call him Chucky. When my name was called, the camera metaphorically zoomed in on my face. I felt queasy, nervous, and scared. But I told myself, if these people could get up here, then so could I.

I had been raised in the middle of nowhere, surrounded by isolation and far from the social life that most kids experienced growing up. My social skills were lacking, and my stage presence was nonexistent. But I kept telling myself, "You've got this, Alex. You're more than capable."

Chucky signaled for me to plug in my guitar, and I did, feeling the tension build with each second. The PA speakers came alive with my guitar's sound, and I was ready. I strummed an E chord, cleared my throat, and introduced myself. "I'm Alex. I'll be playing an original called '1871,' and then a cover of 'Trouble' by Cat Stevens."

The sound system wasn't perfect, but it was good enough. I wasn't expecting the guitar to sound as good as Sean's did, and it wasn't, but it was better than I had hoped for, given my equipment and the venue. As I played, I noticed a few people listening. Then I saw Chucky, his head slightly tilted, giving me his full attention. When I finished, I was surprised to hear applause. In fact, I was taken aback by how many people clapped. Even the other musicians were applauding.

I smiled, feeling a rush of pride and relief. I thanked everyone and then launched into my cover of "Trouble." When I finished, the same applause followed. I couldn't believe it. I had just played in front of real people—and they liked it. I had never performed for anyone but my dog, who frankly had terrible taste in music. She'd always run out of the room whenever I played, so to have people clap or even stay for me was surreal.

As I packed my guitar back into its case, Abby approached me. She told me she loved my tunes, and I was pleased she liked them. "The owner really enjoyed your music," she added. That's when Chuck E. Weiss, the sound guy and host, came over to introduce himself. Chuck E. had a relaxed demeanor, and he asked if I'd be interested in playing on a Friday night. I was so excited—I agreed immediately.

Chuck E. told me to prepare a thirty—minute set and that I'd be playing first. He mentioned another musician would follow, but I didn't ask who it was. I had a week to prepare, but only six songs memorized. I figured I could do a mixture of originals and covers, maybe fifty-fifty. After all, no one wanted to hear a whole set of songs from some unknown artist.

As I left Highland Grounds, I felt a mixture of excitement and nervousness. One week to prepare for my first real gig—it was overwhelming, but I was ready.

And then, Monday came, and with it, a new experience. I had been cast in *Who's The Boss* as one of the students in a classroom scene. The set was lively, filled with energy. Tony Danza was everything I expected—full of energy, commanding attention at every turn. Judith Light seemed nervous, almost fragile, but Alyssa Milano came across as entitled and self-absorbed. I wasn't trying to throw anyone under the bus, just sharing what I saw. But my favorite person on set was Kathrine Helmond. She was nurturing, kind, and funny—exactly the kind of person who made you feel at ease.

But through all of this—the gig, the set life, and everything in between—Tony Danza was also a walking, breathing comedy show. The man had an infectious energy and a sense of humor that could light up the whole room. One of his favorite things to do was let out a big fart and then blame it on someone else on the set. Usually an unsuspecting grip, gaffer, or sound guy. He'd point at the cast or crew, and everyone would burst into laughter. He had this natural charm about him, effortlessly bringing everyone a smile. But, as much as I enjoyed my time on set with him, the real challenge was waiting for me on Friday night. The gig I had been working toward, the one I had been practicing for all week, was drawing closer, and my nerves were absolutely on fire.

The enemy was loud that day, whispering lies in my ear. "You're a no-talent loser. No one wants to hear your music." It was a constant barrage of negativity, and it was working. For a moment, I actually started to believe those lies. The doubts were suffocating, but I pushed through. I reminded myself that I had made it this far and wasn't about to back down now. I had no choice but to persevere. So, by 6:30, nerves and all, I walked into the coffee shop.

The room was thinly populated—only about seven people, not counting Danielle and her sister, which added another layer of stress. I set up my gear, plugged in, tossed the strap over my neck, and began my set.

As I started, I couldn't help but notice the sea of self-absorption around me. I couldn't explain it, but the more I observed, the more it became clear—those who didn't have Christ were wrapped up in their own insecurities, their own fears. It was like they were carrying around an invisible weight, trying to keep up with the world while not even realizing how trapped they were. And I could see it now, clearly.

To the nonbelievers reading this, it may sound strange, but once you accept Christ and receive the Holy Spirit, your eyes are opened to a world that was always there but invisible before. It's a reality that can't be understood until you experience it. If you haven't yet, I encourage you to seek Him. Until you do, you may not see what I'm saying here. But trust me, once you do, you'll understand.

The nerves started to loosen up after a few songs. Slowly but surely, people began to pay attention. The energy in the room shifted. I noticed Danielle and her sister Laura, sitting at a table nearby, watching me with interest. As I looked up, I saw Shawn, the guy who had played at the coffee shop the other day, walk in with his guitar. It dawned on me—he must be the headliner after me. I gave him a nod, and he acknowledged me with a quick, subtle nod in return. He grabbed a seat at the bar, sipping his coffee while I continued my set.

The nerves never fully went away. Between songs, I stumbled over what to say, fumbling for words, trying to connect with the audience. I had written a few notes on what I might say, topics on current events, but it wasn't easy. My set wasn't flawless, but I did my best. I was trying to give them something real, something from the heart.

When I finished my set, the response from the crowd was better than I expected. Shawn walked up to me, shook my hand, and told me he really enjoyed my performance. That meant the world to me. I unplugged my guitar, packed it up, and walked over to an empty table to sit with Danielle and Laura. They complimented me, saying they had no idea I could play so well. I was floored by their kindness.

"Would you mind listening to Shawn's set?" I asked them. They agreed, and we stuck around for his performance. As he set up, I noticed a group of well-dressed business types entering the coffee shop. They chose a table near where Shawn was performing. I didn't think much of it at first, but then, as Shawn began to play, they started talking loudly, carrying on their own conversation, ignoring him completely. Their conversation wasn't just loud; it was offensive. And the craziest part is they were from a prominent record label talking about an artist they were representing. And how did I know know that? They made sure we all heard them. Just arrogance times ten. And yet they proved how much they actually cared about musicians and artists because there was Shawn playing right in front of them. They were insulting everyone and being downright despicable.

I wanted to say something, to stand up for Shawn, but I didn't know how to respond. I could tell he was getting frustrated, and his performance started to reflect that. The business guys carried on for about thirty minutes, and during that time, Shawn's focus seemed to waver. But then, just as they left, something clicked. The room opened up. The last fifteen minutes of his set was pure magic. Shawn played with rhythm and precision, his fingers hammering down on the strings, sliding to different frets; his sound was crisp and rhythmic, almost like he was drumming on the guitar.

The crowd finally settled into a comfortable silence, genuinely listening. He received an enthusiastic response when he finished. I was glad to have stuck around to hear him. We said our goodbyes, and I headed out into the night, still buzzing from the adrenaline, both from my performance and Shawn's.

But as I walked out of that coffee shop, something inside me had shifted. It wasn't just about the gig anymore. It wasn't just about playing for an audience. It was about stepping into who I was meant to be—fearful and flawed but growing, evolving, and constantly pursuing what God had in store for me. This was just the beginning.

Chapter Twenty-Nine

Bigger Dreams

St. Teresa of Calcutta (Mother Teresa)

"I can do things you cannot, you can do things I cannot; together we can do great things."

I was playing open mics, writing songs, and generally figuring out the next steps in my journey. Chuck E. Weiss had been booking me to open for a lot of smaller up-and-coming acoustic artists, which was cool, but I had bigger dreams. I wasn't content with just the coffee shops. I wanted the clubs—the Roxy, the Whisky, the Troubadour, Viper Room, and the rest of those legendary venues that had seen so many greats pass through their doors.

But for that kind of music, I'd need a real band, something I didn't have yet. So, I grabbed an LA Recycler and started combing through ads, hoping to find the right fit. My first thought was a bass player. That seemed like the logical starting point, so I circled a few options. Eventually, I settled on a guy named Louis Ventaloro, a bass player from New Jersey. His ad spoke to me, and when we connected, the conversation went smoothly. We had similar influences, and the vibe seemed right, so we decided to meet up.

I took the bus over to his place, and when I arrived, I couldn't help but laugh. His apartment was at the mouth of Runyon Canyon, just a block up from the famous Man Chinese Theater. This is where I had spent countless hours my first month wandering around during my time in LA. His apartment was a cool little place—slightly smaller than mine, but I liked the neighborhood better. Louis had that unmistakable New Jersey accent, a little like New York but with a bit more of a drawl. He seemed like a solid guy, and I immediately clicked with him.

We chatted about the place, and I asked him how much the rent was. He told me it was $450 a month. And then came the million-dollar question: "Does it have cockroaches?" Louis laughed and said, "Maybe, but I haven't seen one yet." That was all I needed to hear. It was a sign. Time to make a move.

I had my guitar with me, and Louis had one of his own. I played a few songs for him, and he played me some of his that he had recorded on a Tascam 4-track recorder. To my surprise, they sounded really good—well-produced, clear, and authentic. We agreed that we should play a small show together just to see if we meshed well musically. Before I left, I asked if there were any open spots in his building. He handed me the landlord's number, and I thanked him, grabbed my guitar, and headed out.

The bus dropped me off a couple hundred yards from my place, and as I walked home, my mind was buzzing with ideas about the future. That was when things took a strange turn. As I walked, I heard a whistling sound, and suddenly—WHAM! A beer bottle exploded against a telephone pole, just inches from my head. I froze, my heart racing, as the car packed with gang types sped by yelling something at me in Spanish. I didn't know what they said, but I didn't hear amigo in his incoherent ramblings.

I finally reached my place crawled up the small flight of stairs trying to shake off the last 5 minutes of my life. It was plain and simple I had bigger things to focus on, but my nerves were rattled. I fumbled for my keys, unlocked the door and wandered to the couch. Pulling out a sheet of paper, I glanced over the list of songs that Louis and myself had planned to play.

It was a mix of his cover choices and my originals. We decided to get together the next day to rehearse. Louis suggested recording us on his 4-track, which seemed like a brilliant idea—he'd have a reference to practice with, and we'd have something to listen to afterward.

But as I was getting ready to sleep, I heard something that made my blood run cold. At first, I thought it was fireworks—until I realized it was gunfire. Not pistols. This was machine gun fire. The sound of hundreds of rounds being fired off, echoing through the streets, probably just one or two blocks over. I couldn't believe it. The reality of my situation hit me like a punch to the gut. This wasn't the life I was looking for. I had my brief stints with gross violence and I did not want to have to experience it around my home. This was strike three in my book—the gang incident, the beer bottle that barely missed me, and now this: machine gun fire right outside my window. A resounding no!

I lay awake for hours that night, staring at the ceiling, unable to ignore the growing sense of dread. There was no way I could keep living like this. I couldn't ignore the signs. Change had to happen. And it had to happen fast.

The next morning, I called Louis's landlord. I called the landlady, and to my surprise, she picked up. She said yes, there was a single available, and I jumped at the opportunity. But there was a catch—I had to go through a credit check. No big deal. I hopped on the bus, filled out the application, and asked her to get back to me as soon as possible. I explained my story, and she, surprisingly, knew the neighborhood well. She agreed things weren't exactly great around there, which only made me more determined to get out.

I decided to stop by Louis's place to share the news with him. He opened the door, his eyes wide with surprise. I explained everything—the potential new place, my story, and how the situation around my current home had gotten unbearable. He was genuinely happy for me and seemed excited about the idea of me moving into the building. He asked what I was doing for work, and I mentioned the odd jobs—TV, film, and security work. That piqued his interest, and I gave him the address of the extra casting company. He said that he wouldn't mind working as an extra.

As we talked, the landlady happened to return from getting her mail. She greeted Louis and, noticing me standing there, asked, "Are you guys friends?" Louis nodded and replied, "Yeah, we're friends." The landlady then looked at me and, almost as an afterthought, said, "Bring the first and last rent, and I'll get you a key." I couldn't help but smile, feeling the weight of this new chapter ahead. I thanked her and immediately felt a sense of relief.

Before leaving, I asked Louis if we could swing by my bank after registering with Central Casting. I needed a cashier's check, and honestly, I couldn't spend another day in that old place. Louis was on board, agreeing to help me grab some of my things once we were finished with the errands.

The first stop was Central Casting, then the bank, and after that, we headed over to my place. I knocked on my landlady's door and let her know I was moving out. I didn't give her much of an explanation—just that I was leaving. I didn't want to make her feel like the place wasn't good enough for me. I couldn't bear the thought of that. Once Louis and I packed my things into his '89 Suzuki Samurai—everything from my clothes to my guitar, I handed my key to the apartment manager and we were off.

We headed to my new place, which was just down the hall from Louis's. It was a little smaller than the place I'd been in, but it felt right. I couldn't quite shake the heavy feeling that came with moving in, though. Every time I moved, I carried the weight of the demons I'd picked up along the way, and I was certain there were also dark forces in the new area. It was the kind of weight that just hung over the city.

But as I moved in, something inside me began to click into place. At the time, I didn't understand divine providence. I thought it was all just some weird system of destiny, the universe guiding my every move. I had almost a New Age perspective on life. Now, though, I know it wasn't just some cosmic coincidence. God was with me. Even though I had not accepted Him.

Christ, I believe, was steering me in the right direction, even if I didn't always see it. It's like how God might shift the angle of a president's head just enough for a bullet to miss but graze his ear. Maybe the bullet's close enough to make him stop and think about the Creator. In my own life, I can see how God worked in mysterious ways—angels intervening to save me from countless dangerous situations.

As I settled into the new apartment, my mind was filled with gratitude and a strange sense of peace. Louis and I started practicing for nearly two hours every day. We began booking small shows at coffee shops around town. It felt like the beginning of something bigger, a real partnership. We even wrote a couple of songs together, and they sounded decent. I was impressed with Louis's musicianship. He was and is a talented man.

Our collaboration wasn't just musical, we worked on some film and TV shows together. I vividly remember the time we did a commercial for Nissin, not the car company, Nissin is a Japanese soup company. The production company drove us up to the desert at the crack of dawn, around 5:30 am We were wearing nothing but loincloths, covered in mud and prosthetics. It was freezing cold, probably around 45°F, and Louis and I could barely keep warm between takes. But we laughed through it all, joking about how ridiculous we looked and how miserable we were. Louis ended up with a nasty cold.

In the end, it was a funny shoot, and according to Louis, the commercial is still floating around. It became one of those little memories that made everything seem a bit more bearable. Life in LA wasn't easy, but moments like these made the grind worthwhile. I was starting to find my groove, and in that, I found some hope.

Chapter Thirty

A Small Town Soul In A Big-City Show

William Shakespeare

"All the world's a stage, and all the men and women merely players."

Like me, Lou moved to Los Angeles just out of curiosity. There was no grand scheme or specific reason. He wasn't chasing fame or fortune. He simply wanted to experience the city, soak it in for a couple of years, and then return to New Jersey. I didn't blame him. If I could use a metaphor; if California was the human body you can take a wild guess on what part I think LA would most be. there is the glitz and the glamour, but also the grime, the emptiness, and the unsettling energy that so many people walk around with. For some, it's a dream, but for others, it's a bona fide nightmare. I was fairly new to the city so it was a little bit of all of it.

Louis had a group of guys, who were also East Coasters, that moved out to LA for the entertainment business: Music, TV, and film. They all arrived with that same hope and youthful energy, ready to conquer the city. One of Lou's closest friends, Michael, was an actor and the lead on a TV show called *California Dreams*. The NBC show featured a group of teenagers who form a rock band. Michael played the bands high energy manager. The program aired once a week and right before the highest rated teen show at the time, Saved By The Bell. Michael had that rare quality in Hollywood: extreme self-confidence. Not the arrogant confidence, but more like "Hey, over here, lets get this thing moving." It was an unshakable aura of self-confidence, and quite frankly more positive.

And from what I was learning, that's exactly what it took to make it in this city. If you wanted to be in front of the camera, you had to have a healthy heaping of self love. And like I said It wasn't arrogance. It was survival. I never really brought up the shows I had worked on or some of the scenes I'd been in when I was around Michael or his friends. I didn't want to sound like I was bragging. He was already an established actor with solid credits under his belt, and here I was, a guy who'd dipped his toe into the entertainment world but never quite got in the pool.

One night, Lou invited me to go out with him, Michael, Punky Brewster (yes, the actress), and a few other actors to some clubs in Hollywood. I knew right away I wasn't going to fit in. I was from the mountains—isolated, away from the noise of the city. I grew up surrounded by trees, and the closest thing to a "night out" was packing the car with my brothers and sister and driving 30 miles down the hill to the town of Auburn, and it was also a small town but just a tiny bit bigger than Colfax. Lets face it my personality didn't fit the fast pace of New York or New Jersey, where these guys were from. They thrived on that rhythm, that city buzz, but I couldn't help but feel like a fish out of water.

It wasn't that I minded. I just felt like a drag on their clubbing adventures. The club scene wasn't for me. I wasn't into the flashing lights or the music so loud it rattled your bones. The whole vibe just wasn't my style. A couple of his friends in this group reminded me of Steve Martin and Dan Aykroyd in the famous *Saturday Night Live* skit—two wild and crazy guys. But they weren't bad guys. They just weren't my speed.

But I watched as Michael and his crew reveled in the chaos of Hollywood's nightlife that it was a world I was growing more and more distant from, and that night, it became clearer than ever. LA, for all its shiny exterior, was starting to feel a little more like an outhouse to me. There was something suffocating and foul about it all—something unnerving. Maybe it was the constant chase, or maybe it was the way people would step on each other to climb higher.

I couldn't blame Michael for being so self-assured. In a city where everyone is trying to stand out, it's not only necessary, it's probably the only way to survive. And maybe that's why I didn't quite fit in with the Hollywood crowd. I couldn't pretend to be something I wasn't, and in a city full of people who made a career out of pretending, that didn't always go over well for me.

As I stood there in the club, watching the scene unfold around me, I couldn't shake the feeling that I was a small-town guy in a big town show. I wasn't sure if I was ever going to make it here, or if I even wanted to. The lights, the music, the people—it was all starting to feel like too much.

I definitely had a feeling like I should just pack up and head back north. Sometimes, I wondered if I had made a mistake coming to LA. But then I considered the other possibilities, the mountain life, the peaceful life.

It was appealing, but it also felt like something I had to leave behind to truly know what I was capable of. So, for now, I stayed. But every time I looked around at the people who had made LA their home, I wondered if I would ever truly fit in. Or if maybe I was just built to be different in a city where everyone tried to be the same.

And yet, through all of it—the noise, the fake smiles, the egos—I knew one thing for sure: I had gotten this far so I needed to see it to its conclusion.

Chapter Thirty-One

You Can't Handle The Truth, Or Can You?

Dietrich Bonhoeffer

"The more you struggle to make something last, the less lasting it becomes. The world does not have a lasting foundation. Only God's word remains."

Later that week, I worked a few days on *Who's The Boss* again. The studio was a short walking distance from Jack's Faux Casting Company. After we wrapped up for the day, I decided to walk over to say hey.

When I got there, Jack was talking to an older, grey-haired man. I walked in and greeted them both. Jack smiled warmly and introduced me to the man. His name was Hank. Jack explained that Hank and he were partners in a casting company called Telecast, the same one from the '70s and early 80's that did all the extra casting for the blockbuster movies Jack had mentioned to me during his sales speal when I first met him. Jack told Hank that I had been helping him in the office with video and client management. Hank, getting ready to leave, handed me his business card. He mentioned that if I ever wanted to help him, he had a casting office on Sunset Boulevard, right across from the Chinese Theater. I told him I lived just a block away. He smiled, said goodbye, and left.

I lingered with Jack for a few more minutes, catching up. I asked how he was doing, and he reassured me that things were good. He mentioned the new clients he had been working with, and I shared stories of the films and shows I had worked on. Then I left and headed back to my place.

But honestly, Hank intrigued me. I wasn't sure what his operation was all about, but I figured it might be something worth checking out. I suspected it was similar to Jack's setup, but there was always the chance it could be more legitimate. So, I put on a nice shirt, some decent pants, and walked over to Hank's office the next day.

When I arrived, I was surprised to find that his office was directly across the street from the Chinese Theater. The building wasn't exactly beautiful, but it had an office on the third floor, which certainly couldn't have been cheap.

Hank seemed a little surprised to see me but welcomed me inside. He gave me a quick tour of the operation and explained what he was working on. It was a small operation, but it looked pretty legit. He showed me some of his clients and how he managed to pick the right actors for various roles. Hank kept large photo albums full of 8x10 headshots. Each album was categorized by age range, race, and gender.

One album he showed me had women aged eighteen to twenty five. He chuckled and said, "These girls can do more than act." I smiled, but it struck me as a strange comment.

Hank asked if I wanted to help him out. I said I could swing it a couple of days a week. He explained that he did things similarly to Jack, registering people to keep the business running, but that he had other projects in the works. I couldn't help but feel suspicious—there was no way he was paying rent in this prime area without pulling some shady moves.

Then Hank told me something that caught my attention. He said he had an interview the following week for extra casting and under-fives, for a movie that was in pre-production called *A Few Good Men*. He briefly told me the plot, and it sounded interesting enough. He mentioned that he needed to submit a bid for the extras and under-fives, and I asked if I could help him break it down. Hank agreed, and I told him that I had a lot of experience working on film sets, TV shows, and commercials. I felt confident I could give him an accurate breakdown of the extras and how many would be needed for each scene.

Hank seemed impressed by my eagerness. He leaned back in his chair, opened his desk drawer, and handed me a second draft of *A Few Good Men*. He didn't say much, but his quiet confidence spoke volumes. He told me to read it that night.

When I got home, I immediately opened the first page of the script. As soon as I saw the cast list, I was floored. Jack Nicholson, Kevin Bacon, Demi Moore, Tom Cruise, Kiefer Sutherland, Cuba Gooding Jr.—the list of actors was one of the most impressive I had ever seen. On top of that, the script was incredibly well-written. The plot was gripping, the characters were complex, and the dialogue was sharp.

It was a story that had all the potential to become one of the most talked-about films in Hollywood.

As I read on, I could feel the intensity building. I was hooked. This wasn't just any movie—it was a game-changer. The kind of film that could define a generation.

But what really hit me was that I was about to become part of something huge. Not just as a spectator, but as someone who could influence the outcome. I knew this wasn't just another film or TV show. This was something that could leave a lasting impact.

I sat there, stunned by the script in my hands, realizing that I was standing on the precipice of a life-altering experience. It popped in my mind that if I got this right, this could be the start of something good. I read the script from cover to cover, the words jumping off the page like they were alive. By the time I finished it, I dropped the script and just sat there, dazed. This movie—this story—was going to win an Academy Award. I could feel it in my bones. And now, more than ever, I was determined to get the breakdown of each scene just right.

I spent the next few days reading, re-reading, and analyzing the script. Every detail mattered. I dug out my old typewriter from the back of the closet, dusted it off, and began typing out the costs per scene for every background artist (extra) I thought each scene required. I didn't rush it. Hours passed, but I didn't mind—I was too invested.

By the time I finished, I felt confident in my calculations. Every extra, every detail, every cost was accounted for. I showed the breakdown to my girlfriend, Danielle, and she was intrigued. After looking it over, she surprised me. "I went to CSUN Northridge University for accounting," she said with a smile. I had no idea! I was impressed, and she offered to help. She said she'd go over the numbers and bring it back to me in the morning.

I agreed, knowing that I didn't want to hand over a single mistake. She took it with her, and I anxiously waited.

The next day, Danielle came by in the afternoon, and I could immediately see the difference. It looked polished, professional—like it had come straight out of a MGM's financial department. "It should be mostly correct." She smiled and added, "My mom also retyped it." And wow—her mom did a fantastic job. It was perfect.

I hugged Danielle, feeling a sense of pride swelling in my chest. It was all coming together. I grabbed the finalized breakdown and headed to the printers to make four copies: one for Hank, one for me, and two for the people we were meeting with. The next day was the big meeting with Castle Rock Entertainment, and I needed to be prepared.

That night, I rehearsed with Louis then went over the proposal again making sure every detail was worked out. I crashed early to make sure I'd be sharp. The phone rang early the next morning—it was Hank. "I'll meet you at Castle Rock," he said. "We're meeting with Rob Reiner and Steve Nicolaides." My stomach did a little flip at the mention of Reiner. "I hope your breakdown is good," Hank added. I assured him it would be.

As I hung up, the reality of it hit me. I was going to meet *Meathead* from *All In The Family*. I grabbed the four copies of the breakdown, jumped on the bus, and headed to the studio.

When I got to Castle Rock, I found Hank waiting for me outside. He stood out in a canary yellow jacket, which, surprisingly, looked sharp on him. He motioned for me to hurry up, and I did. I handed him one of the printed breakdowns, and he glanced at it. "Looks good," he said, and that was all.

The front gate checked us in, making sure we were who we said we were, and handed us guest passes. We followed the signs and made our way to the office. Rob Reiner's secretary greeted us and told us to wait. We sat for just a minute before she called us in.

The room was smaller than I had imagined. Rob Reiner was sitting behind a desk, looking as casual as you'd expect—like someone who had been through this hundreds of times before. Steve Nicolaides stood next to him, and they both rose to shake our hands when we entered. I had to admit, Hank and I made a curious pair—me, a youthful 20, and Hank, looking like he'd been in the business for decades.

I handed them each a breakdown, and I stayed quiet while Hank did most of the talking. Nicolaides was friendly, though a little reserved. Reiner, on the other hand, didn't seem too thrilled to be there. He barely said a word. The whole meeting lasted maybe ten minutes—definitely the shortest meeting I'd ever been in.

As we left, Hank looked pleased. "That went well," he said with a grin, clapping me on the back. "Thanks for the work on that breakdown."

I hopped on my bus, reflecting on the meeting, but I honestly don't remember how Frank got there or how he left. My mind was still reeling from being in the same room as Rob Reiner. When I got home, I immediately called Danielle. I told her about the meeting and thanked her for helping make the breakdown so professional. I also asked her to thank her mom for her hard work—apparently, her mom had really done an excellent job.

And when the producer complimented it, I couldn't help but feel a deep sense of accomplishment. For the first time, I realized that this could be the start of something big. Something that could change everything. Later that night, Louis and I played a small bar inside a restaurant down near LAX Airport. We had a set of covers with a few originals mixed in. There were only about 10 people in the bar, but they seemed to appreciate our music. The intimate setting gave our songs a special kind of energy. Afterward, we packed up and called it a night. When I got home from the gig I was still buzzing from the meeting at Castle Rock with Reiner and Nicolaides. I was for sure it would take a week or more till we heard back. I slept as well as I could that night. The next day I rolled into the casting office and Frank looked at me and raised his shoulders and his hands in the air and said " they went with Jackie Brown." I said what? "Ya, they went with another casting outfit." I was floored. Now I understood what it means to have the wind take out of your sail. It felt worse then the death of my T-bird. I sat down and just stared at the wall. Hank said "Don't take it so hard". I honestly do not think Hank understood the impact that movie was going to have. But there wasn't much I could do. The door was shut. I didn't do or say much that day and headed home early.

Chapter Thirty-Two

Five Lines For A Faustian Bargain

John Piper

"Sexual sin is a serious matter, not because God is a cosmic killjoy, but because sin destroys us and the people around us."

The next day, I went into the casting office. Hank said he was meeting with a producer for a pre-production film. I asked if there were any well-known actors attached to the project, and he told me William Hurt, Mandy Patinkin, Elizabeth Perkins, and Christine Lahti. I was impressed. "What's the name of the film?" I asked. "The Doctor," he replied. I raised an eyebrow. "Interesting," I said.

Curious, I asked Hank how he had landed the casting. He told me that in the '70s, he had supplied extras and under fives for *The*

Godfather Part II for a producer named Mike. This same producer had reappeared years later, asking Hank to help with the casting of *The Doctor*. He explained that this producer, Mike, was coming by around 11 AM to go through the headshots in order to pick an under-five for this very movie.

I was eager to learn more. "What's an 'under-five'?" I asked.

"It's a role where an actor has five lines or less in a film," Hank explained. "But if you get a speaking part, even a small one, you're eligible to join Hollywood's prestigious actors' union—SAG. You pay the fee, get your card, and suddenly you're part of the union. It's a golden ticket. And that's what every actor in Hollywood is fighting for: a chance at those five lines, a chance to join SAG."

The odds, he said, were brutal. "Less than 5% of actors in Hollywood even get their SAG card. And less than 2% actually make a living from it. Just because you land a role doesn't guarantee you'll keep landing them," Hank added, his voice tinged with experience.

An hour passed, and then Mike walked into the office. He was a slight, balding Jewish man in his mid-fifties, wearing a nice suit. He didn't say much—just walked in, sat at Hank's desk, and waited.

Hank greeted him, and they exchanged a few words. Then Hank opened a photo album and laid it on the desk in front of Mike. It was a collection of headshots: young actresses, all in the eighteen to twenty five range. Mike began flipping through the pages, his eyes scanning each photo, turning the pages slowly as he methodically looked over every potential candidate.

He flipped back a few pages, stopped, and tapped on a photo of a young blonde-haired girl. Hank nodded, pulled the photo from the album, and flipped it over to reveal a pager number. He called the number, and within five minutes, the girl called us back.

Hank told us she was a waitress working a shift but that she'd leave right away to come to the office. She'd be there in ten minutes.

As I sat there, I wondered what exactly was going on. I assumed she was coming down to audition for a role in *The Doctor*. But I couldn't have been more naïve.

I had heard the rumors growing up about the infamous casting couch. I had always thought they were exaggerated, maybe even mythicized, by people who wanted to dramatize the industry. But now, having lived in Hollywood for a while, I started to see the truth—there were dark undercurrents running through the town. The casting couch wasn't just some legendary tale—it was real.

I knew something was off when Hank called me into the other room. I could feel the tension in the air, thick and heavy. It was as if something sinister was brewing.

Hank sat me down and explained, in a quiet voice, that this fifty-something-year-old man—Mike—was allegedly about to have sex with this young actress on the couch in Hank's office. In exchange for her body, she would get her five lines in *The Doctor*.

The transaction was clear. Hank, Mike, and the young woman were all allegedly consenting to it. But as I sat there, listening to Hank explain, I felt the bile rise in my throat. I was disgusted—repulsed by what I was hearing. This was a deal made out of desperation, coercion, and sin. It was nothing short of a Faustian bargain.

I knew deep down that I wanted no part of it. I told Hank I was leaving. I didn't have to say much—he could see it in my face, in my body language, that I wanted nothing to do with this depravity. I didn't say another word. I just left.

I knew I was never coming back when I walked out of that office. And I never did. Hank didn't try to reach out to me either. He got the picture.

At that point in my life, I didn't know Christ—I didn't know what it meant to be saved. But I did know that what was happening in that office was a form of human degradation. Selling your body for a few lines in a movie, for fame, for an opportunity—it was one of the lowest things a person could do.

To be fair, I never watched *The Doctor*. I don't know if that young waitress ended up rattling off five lines or less in the movie. Maybe she did. Maybe she didn't. But if she had a change of heart on her way to Hank's office and didn't show up, I'm sure they would have just kept flipping through the pages of the album until they found someone else to satisfy their sinful desires.

Chapter Thirty-Three

Vanity And Vultures

Francis Schaeffer

"Modern man's need is not for more information but for a new mind—a new way of thinking that can evaluate life's priorities rightly. When we stop seeking outward approval and start looking for God's approval, we begin to understand what is truly valuable."

As I left Hank's building, I found myself pausing, curious about what other businesses shared the building with Hank. On a whim, I stopped at the directory in the lobby. I scanned the list of offices and was surprised to see so many casting and talent agencies.

I shook my head, wondering how many were on the up and up. One name jumped out at me: *Vanity Models/Talent*. It was located on the top floor, and something about it sparked my curiosity. Instead of heading out the door, I turned around and pressed the elevator button, deciding to investigate.

Vanity occupied half of the top floor and was impressively set up. The decor was sleek and modern, giving off an air of legitimacy. I stepped inside, feeling both excited and cautious. Through a bit of schmoozing—let's call it embellishment—I managed to get my foot in the door and started working there. The owner, a man named Arman, was an Iranian with an air of authority. The operation was divided into two sections: the modeling agency, run by a jittery, tall, skinny Frenchman whose name escapes me, and the acting agency, overseen by a sharp-tongued Englishwoman named Kim. I had no interest in the modeling side, so I gravitated toward Kim and began working in the acting/agency department.

The casting process operated through a system called *Breakdowns*. Agencies like Vanity paid a monthly subscription to receive detailed descriptions of characters needed for film and TV projects. Every morning, we'd get a fax listing of roles for every demographic imaginable: men, women, children, old, young, Black, white, Hispanic, Asian—everyone. Vanity had a large roster of clients that fit these descriptions. Many of them landed small roles, generating a steady stream of income for the agency. It was rewarding, in a way, to see these hopefuls get a shot at their dreams.

But as I soon discovered, the real money didn't come from booking actors in roles. It came from selling photo packages. Vanity preyed on the dreams of aspiring actors and models, offering expensive headshots and *ZED cards* to anyone who walked through the door, no matter how unrealistic their prospects were. The realization left a sour taste in my mouth, but I didn't dwell on it—at least, not yet.

One day, Kim asked if I could start delivering headshots to studios. I told her my car had recently died and that I was relying on the bus. She seemed unimpressed, so I added, "But I'll figure something out."

That's when I decided to buy a motorcycle. It wasn't flashy—a Kawasaki 1200, an old police bike I picked up for $600. It wasn't the fastest or the prettiest, but it ran, and that's all I needed. I'd only ever ridden dirt bikes before, but I was confident I could figure it out. Within a day or two, I was comfortable on the road, zipping around town and delivering headshots like a seasoned pro.

Riding around the city gave me a sense of freedom. By now, I'd worked on nearly every major studio lot as an extra, a security guard, or in some other small capacity. It was funny how often people on the lots would recognize me but couldn't quite place where they'd seen me before. I let them wonder—it added a bit of mystery to my otherwise mundane tasks.

One day, a breakdown came in for a role that required a "large, menacing black gang member." We didn't have anyone on our roster who fit the bill, but I immediately thought of someone: George Sharpeson. I called him and asked him to bring in some headshots. George came by within the hour, grateful for the opportunity. I submitted him for a few auditions. I can't remember if he landed anything, but he was a good guy, and it felt good to help him out.

Despite the occasional moments of satisfaction, it didn't take long for me to see Vanity for what it really was: another scam. It wasn't as overtly sleazy as Hank's operation, but the tactics were the same. Vanity lured in untrained, often unattractive hopefuls, dangling the dream of Hollywood success in front of them. Whether or not they had the talent or the look didn't matter—what mattered was selling them expensive photo packages. And while it's possible that some clients went on to achieve success, the agency was primarily designed to profit from their aspirations.

I can't remember the exact moment I decided to leave Vanity, but I do remember how it ended. I had a falling out with Arman, the owner. He was a Middle Eastern man, likely from a Muslim background, though he didn't seem particularly religious. I can't recall what we fought about, but I think it had something to do with how he treated the models. At some point, in a fit of frustration, I told him I'd throw him off the top of the building. Not my proudest moment. My temper got the best of me, as it often did back then.

After that, I was done. Like Hank and Jack before him, Arman and Vanity became a part of my past. I walked away from the agency and the slimy underbelly of Hollywood's dream factory. I didn't have all the answers, but I knew one thing: I couldn't keep participating in an industry that exploited the hopes and vulnerabilities of others just to make a buck.

God had other plans for me, though the Devil seemed determined to derail them. But I was learning, slowly but surely, that every closed door was leading me closer to where I was meant to be.

Chapter Thirty-Four

Roads Less Traveled

Augustine of Hippo

"The world is a book, and those who do not travel read only one page."

We had recently added a bass player named Chris to our duo, moving Louis to guitar, turning us into a trio. Between the three of us, we were hustling to book as many gigs as possible. Danielle, was still in the picture quite a bit, but Louis was showing signs of Hollywood fatigue. One night, over beers and half-hearted laughs, he confessed to me that the city had disillusioned him. "It's not what I thought it would be," he said, shaking his head.

I nodded. I knew exactly what he meant. Los Angeles had a way of eating people alive, especially the dreamers. He went on to tell me he was thinking about moving back to his hometown of Elmwood Park, New Jersey. "You should come with me," he said suddenly, catching me off guard.

I was taken aback. The idea hadn't even crossed my mind, but the more he talked about the music scene in New York—the clubs, the opportunities—it started to sound like an adventure. My life in LA wasn't exactly tethered to anything solid. I could always come back if things didn't pan out. So, in the spirit of spontaneity that had defined my life for the past few years, I said, "Sure. Let's do it."

Of course, agreeing to move meant facing the reality of leaving Danielle. That's when it hit me: I wasn't truly in love with her. I was in love with the idea of being in love, the fantasy of it all. But she deserved better than that, and I knew I had to tell her.

We planned to leave in a couple of weeks. Notices were given to the landlord, and preparations began. Fitting all our belongings into Louis' tiny Suzuki Samurai was going to be a challenge, to say the least. Later that day, I called our bass player Chris to let him know we were moving to New Jersey, then I called Danielle and asked her to come over. She arrived that evening, and I broke the news to her. She took it hard, leaving angry and confused, which I had expected. Still, it didn't make it any easier.

That night, Louis invited a few friends over to celebrate his departure. Mike dropped by to say goodbye. I had a few things I wanted to sell before we left, including a stereo. Mike asked what I planned to do with the stereo, and when I told him I was selling it, he offered to trade it for some weed. It had been quite some time before I had smoked any marijuana, but the idea of having some for the road trip sounded like a good addition. I agreed, even though he didn't have the weed with him at the time. As it turned out, he failed to deliver the weed on his end, and you'll see how that plays into the story later.

That year of 1992 was a year of upheaval, especially in Los Angeles. By April, the city was a racial powder keg. Rodney Glen King was an African-American man who was brutally beaten by Los Angeles police officers for suspicion of alcohol drugs. The police officers stood trial for their unjustified attack, and the Rodney King case quickly gripped the nation. Everyone understood that an acquittal could ignite the city in unrest.

On April 29th, at 3:15 PM, the verdict came in: not guilty. We watched the news that night as chaos erupted. Rioting and looting spread like wildfire. It was pure mayhem.

We had planned to leave early the next morning, and the riots cemented our decision. "The rioters will probably be asleep," Louis joked nervously. He wasn't wrong. When we woke up, the streets were eerily quiet, as though the city itself was catching its breath after a night of rage. Luckily I sold the motorcycle and had an extra $500 in cash for the trip.

We loaded up the Suzuki Samurai, cramming our guitars, keyboards, and clothes into the tiny backseat. The seats were pushed upright to accommodate everything, leaving us little room to breathe. Then, we hit the highway.

We decided to take the southern route, making a slight detour heading toward Florida to visit Louis's friend, Jason Metnik. I'd never been to Florida and was excited at the prospect. Plus, the most southern route that is along Highway 10 would take us through some of the most iconic blues and country music areas in the country. And blues music was by far the catalyst to rock music and rock music, like I said earlier is a conduit to the unclean realm. The deals that these men and women made early on in blues music reverberate to this very day. It's a powerful tool used by Satan and demons to influence anyone at any age. But I did not know this back then and couldn't wait to see and experience some of these iconic cities and towns. We made markings on our map on where we wanted to stop. And we planed on a red eye drive…"no sleep till Brooklyn", or Florida.

We marked our map with stops we wanted to make, though we knew money would limit us. Gas and food had to take priority over sightseeing. With the Suzuki's broken air conditioning, the warm April air wasn't exactly pleasant, but we made do.

Our first major stop was Phoenix, Arizona, about five and a half hours into the trip. By then, the heat was starting to wear on us, and the novelty of the road trip was already giving way to the realities of discomfort. But we pressed on, two restless souls chasing something we couldn't quite name, leaving the smoldering chaos of Los Angeles behind us. The windshield was a mess of squashed bugs, their remains smeared across the glass like an abstract painting. We pulled over to do a quick scrub and grab some snacks. Louis filled the tank while I wandered over to a nearby payphone. It felt good to hear my parents' voices as I gave them an update on the trip.

But as I chatted, I noticed something out of the corner of my eye—a group of young black men walking toward me, their expressions cold and intense. They were about twenty yards away, but their energy was undeniable. It hit me then: the riots weren't just a Los Angeles phenomenon; they were a wave of anger sweeping across the country. And here I was, a lone white guy at a payphone in the middle of nowhere. I hurriedly told my parents I'd call them later, hung up the phone, and bolted back to the car.

Louis barely had time to react before I jumped in, and we sped off. Neither of us spoke for a moment, the tension sitting heavy between us. Finally, Lou broke the silence. "What happened back there?"

"Let's just say we're not in LA anymore," I replied, trying to play it cool.

By noon, we were back on the road, with Louis behind the wheel and me navigating. The map showed we'd be skimming the Mexican border as we entered Texas at El Paso. I pointed out the name Ciudad Juárez and mentioned it would technically be my second time in Mexico, the first being a chaotic trip to Tijuana with Curtis. This time, it would be a brief stop—just long enough to say we'd been there and maybe take a shot of tequila.

The drive to El Paso was long, nearly seven hours, and by the time we reached the border, the sun was setting, painting the sky in fiery oranges and purples. Crossing the Rio Grande, we entered Juárez, and just like Tijuana, it felt like stepping into another world. The streets were alive with a kind of energy that was both fascinating and sobering.

"I get why people cross into the U.S.," I said to Louis as we drove through the town. "The quality of life is night and day."

We didn't feel like braving any of the bars, so when we spotted a small store, I asked Louis to pull over. I went inside to grab a bottle of tequila—one of those iconic ones with a worm at the bottom—and a bag of pork rinds. The cashier didn't speak English, and I didn't speak Spanish, but $5 seemed to do the trick. Her smile was a mix of relief and amusement as she handed me my change.

Back in the Samurai, we headed toward the border crossing, but the line to re-enter the U.S. was slow-moving. After 20 minutes of creeping forward, we finally reached the gate. A female border patrol agent leaned into the window, her sharp eyes scanning us and the packed to the gills backseat.

"Carrying any drugs?" she asked, her tone more skeptical than curious.

"No, ma'am," Louis replied, his voice steady.

Her gaze lingered on our tightly packed belongings before she gestured for us to step out. A German Shepherd, sleek and intense, sniffed around the car while we unpacked every single item. It felt like hours before they finally cleared us, and we were left to repack everything—a tedious game of Tetris with all of our worldly possessions.

As we loaded the last of it, Lou tossed me the keys. "Your turn," he said with a smirk.

I wasn't thrilled about driving at midnight, but I took the wheel. The events at the border lingered in my mind, and that's when it hit me: Mike never gave me the weed for the stereo. A chill ran down my spine. If he had, that dog would've found it, and we'd be in a world of trouble. Thank you Mike! I chalked it up to fate, not knowing that it was a gift from God.

We stopped for gas, smoked a cigarette, and grabbed a pack of No-Doze. I'd never tried the caffeine tablets before, but I figured they'd help me stay awake. The label warned against taking too many, but exhaustion clouded my judgment. Around 11:00 PM, as Louis slept soundly beside me, I popped four tablets, hoping for a quick boost.

At first, nothing happened. I kept driving, the hum of the engine and the darkness of Highway 10 stretching endlessly before me. But a couple of hours later, the effects hit me like a freight train. My heart raced, my hands gripped the steering wheel like a lifeline, and the road seemed to blur and ripple under the dim glow of the headlights.

Adrenaline coursed through me, but it wasn't the good kind. It was the kind that made you feel like the universe was folding in on itself. I glanced at Louis, still asleep, oblivious that his co-pilot was starting to spiral.

The car sped forward, the speedometer creeping higher as my foot pressed harder on the gas. Somewhere in the back of my mind, a small, rational voice whispered that I needed to slow down, but the thundering rush of caffeine-induced chaos drowned it out. The night stretched on, each mile feeling more surreal than the last. The Texas highway stretched endlessly ahead, a dark ribbon illuminated only by the glow of our headlights. The night was quiet, but somewhere around the Trans-Pecos region, my peace was shattered. In the rear view mirror, a semi-truck appeared, barreling toward us with alarming speed. At first, I thought nothing of it, but then it got closer. Too close.

8 tons Ten feet from our bumper, the truck loomed like a beast, its massive grille filling my rear view mirror. I hadn't seen another car for 30 miles, but this guy—this maniac—was right on top of us. I couldn't understand why. The second lane was wide open, but instead of passing, he clung to my tail as if we were in some twisted game of cat and mouse.

I gripped the wheel tighter, adrenaline coursing through me. My mind raced through a hundred scenarios. Maybe he was angry about something? Maybe he thought I was in the fast lane too long? Maybe he saw our California plates. Then I remembered our plates weren't even Californian—they were New Jersey. What could this guy possibly want?

I flicked on my blinker and moved into the right lane, hoping he'd pass. But instead, he followed me into the right lane, inch for inch. The caffeine from the four No-Doze pills I'd taken earlier amplified every nerve, every heartbeat, every thought. My palms were slick on the steering wheel as the truck edged even closer, his headlights almost blinding me in the mirror.

I glanced at Louis. He was sound asleep, completely oblivious to the unfolding nightmare. It's like he could sleep through a hurricane if he wanted to.

I had to think fast. An overpass loomed in the distance, and an idea formed in my mind. I called it "Operation Overpass." As we approached, I signaled to exit the highway. The truck mirrored my move, staying glued to my bumper. My heart pounded as I climbed the ramp. At the last second, I jerked the wheel and swerved back onto the highway. The trucker didn't have time to correct. He was stuck on the ramp, his massive rig too slow to recover.

I floored it, pushing the Samurai to its limits. My speedometer needle trembled near its max as I raced down the highway, putting as much distance between us as possible. The highway was empty again, but my nerves were fried. I didn't slow down until another 30 miles had passed, and even then, it was only because we needed gas.

Pulling into a small truck stop, I cut the engine and exhaled deeply. My hands shook as I gripped the gas pump. Louis stirred awake, yawning and stretching like he'd had the most peaceful nap in history.

"Snacks?" he mumbled groggily as he headed inside.

When he returned, I mentioned the trucker incident, but I downplayed it. No sense in freaking him out, especially when there was nothing he could do about it now. He shrugged, munched on a bag of chips, and promptly fell back asleep as we hit the road again.

The caffeine was still surging through my veins, and now exhaustion mixed with a bizarre, jittery energy. My vision began to blur at the edges, and strange things started happening. I swore I saw deer darting across the highway, but when I blinked, they vanished. My pulse quickened. I knew there were no deer out here.

And then, like something out of a horror movie, I spotted the semi-truck's headlights in the rearview mirror again. My stomach dropped.

No. No way.

I couldn't believe it. Where had he come from? Was he waiting for me at the gas station? Had he been hiding somewhere along the highway? The truck's headlights grew brighter, and soon he was on my bumper again.

I didn't wake Louis. My heart pounded as the truck stalked us for another five miles before pulling alongside. The driver laid on his horn, the sound deafening in the stillness of the night. Then, as suddenly as he appeared, he hit the gas and roared ahead, disappearing into the darkness. Louis stirred, looked up, then crashed again.

I slowed down, letting him gain as much distance as possible. I wasn't taking any chances. For the next ten minutes, I stayed well below the speed limit, my eyes scanning every shadow for signs of the truck.

By the time we reached Houston, I was done-drained, burnt toast. We stopped for gas again, and I told Louis I needed sleep. The caffeine crash was hitting hard, but the lingering effects of the No-Doze kept me too wired to relax completely.

As the first rays of sunlight crept over the horizon, we left Texas behind and entered Louisiana, the land of mystery and history. The swampy beauty of the bayous caught my attention, and for a moment, the terror of the night faded. Louis, wide awake now, was buzzing about our upcoming stop in New Orleans.

"Cafe Du Monde," he said with a grin. "Beignets. You'll love it."

The thought of sugary, pillowy fried dough was enough to keep me going. Only three more hours. We'd make it. After about an hour and a half on the road, I couldn't hold it any longer—I had to pee. Louis and I spotted a secluded area off the side of the road, surrounded by water and swamp. Perfect. He pulled over, and I headed down an embankment to relieve myself. The humid air clung to my skin, and the thick, swampy smell mixed with the earthy scent of wet vegetation.

As I stood there, I noticed what I thought was a massive log floating about ten feet out in the water. Something about it seemed off, though—it moved slightly against the gentle ripples of the swamp. Curiosity got the best of me.

"Louis! Come down here!" I called, motioning for him to join me.

Louis sauntered over curious. I grabbed a heavy branch from the ground, pointed at the log, and said, "Watch this." With all the grace of a middle school pitcher, I hurled the stick at the "log."

The reaction was instant and terrifying. The "log" whipped around, revealing itself to be an alligator. Its tail thrashed, it might have been a small one but it was an alligator.

"Run!" I shouted, scrambling up the embankment as fast as my legs could carry me. My heart raced, and adrenaline surged through my veins.

Louis, still standing at a safe distance, burst into laughter. "Man, you run faster than a French man from a cap gun" he said, half-amused, half-amazed.

"Laugh all you want," I huffed, catching my breath. "Im not about to be dragged into the swamp!"

We climbed back into the car, the gator encounter now a funny story we'd tell for years. The surreal beauty of Louisiana's bayous surrounded us as we drove along Highway 10, the thick humidity pressing in like a damp blanket. It was my first time seeing this part of the country, and while movies had given me a glimpse, they didn't come close to capturing the strange, enchanting atmosphere of the swampy landscape.

Highway 10 took us along the western edge of Lake Pontchartrain before leading us straight into the heart of New Orleans. The moment we entered the city, the smell hit us like a punch to the nose. It was a mix of dead fish, rot, and dampness, and it woke me up faster than any smelling salt ever could.

"Welcome to New Orleans," I muttered, wrinkling my nose.

But the smell wasn't the only thing that hit me. A dark, oppressive feeling settled over me, one I couldn't shake. Years of spiritual sensitivity to the demonic and occult had honed my instincts, and New Orleans practically radiated with dark energy. The city's long history with voodoo and witchcraft only amplified the unease.

We navigated the narrow, cobblestone streets that looked like they belonged in a scene from *Pirates of the Caribbean*. After finding a parking spot near the Pontchartrain Expressway, we walked to Café Du Monde. Louis had been raving about their beignets, and I was eager to try them.

When the powdered-sugar-dusted treats arrived, I took a bite and... well, they were fine. Just fine. Maybe I'd hyped them up too much in my mind, but they didn't blow me away.

We didn't linger long in New Orleans. After about thirty minutes, we were back on the road. As the city faded in the rear view mirror, I felt a sense of relief. I know New Orleans has its fans, but for me, the oppressive energy and the overpowering smell made it hard pass.

The journey to Florida was long—about eight and a half hours—but the promise of Jason Metnick's place in Pembroke Pines kept us motivated. The humidity intensified as we crossed the state line, and after driving over 2,700 miles from Los Angeles to Florida, we were desperate for showers and a bit of relaxation.

Jason's apartment was a dream, right by the ocean. The sand was impossibly white and fine, like powdered sugar, and the water was a stunning green-blue. It was the kind of beauty you cant escape, it's all around you.

There's something deeply spiritual about the ocean. Standing on the shore, watching the waves roll in, I can't help but think back about the connection between water and cleansing. Christ's command to be baptized in water makes so much sense. Water washes us clean, just as

His blood does spiritually. But I would not understand this till many years later.

We spent a day lounging at the beach, swimming, and Louis catching up with Jason. But I quickly discovered something new about myself: I'd become allergic to the sun. Where I used to bask for hours as a kid, now the sun cooked me within an hour, leaving me nauseous and miserable. I was officially the pale white guy in the big straw hat and long sleeves, slathered in sunscreen.

The next morning, we thanked Jason for his immense hospitality and set out early for the next leg of our journey. Driving through Georgia, South Carolina, and North Carolina, we eventually crossed into Virginia and the outskirts of Washington, D.C.

When we reached D.C., I was in awe. The city practically dripped with history, its streets and monuments telling stories of America's past. As we drove through, I couldn't wait to explore the landmarks and soak in the weight of everything this city represented. Washington, D.C. greeted us with its remarkable architecture and a sense of weight that felt both historical and spiritual. The early American designers left a legacy of carefully preserved monuments, each structure seemingly imbued with stories of triumph and turmoil. The Washington Monument stood tall and timeless, its stone construction a testament to the ingenuity of the era. The foundation, laid with large blocks of genesis rock set into lime and cement mortar, seemed as steadfast as the ideals this country was founded upon—or so we like to believe.

But as I stared at these impressive structures, my thoughts wandered to the movements calling for their removal, claiming they symbolize oppression and the sins of a bygone era. The idea troubled me. If we erase the past, how can future generations learn from it? History, no matter how flawed, is a teacher, and to dissolve it is to risk repeating its mistakes.

Our drive through scenic highways led us to yet another destination steeped in significance. Much like New Orleans, Washington, D.C. carried a heaviness. The city seemed shrouded in darkness as though an unseen battle raged between forces of good and evil.

Washington's founding fathers, many influenced by Freemasonry, had undoubtedly left their mark on the city. The more I learned about Freemasonry, the more it unsettled me. Most of the early founders were Masons, and their Masonic Bibles, oddly enough, included portions of scripture. But I've always believed this inclusion was meant to confuse Christians into joining the secretive group—a society I could only describe as misguided, if not outright deceptive.

The Bible is unequivocal in its guidance:

"You shall not swear falsely but shall perform your oaths to the Lord." – Matthew 5:33

"For there is nothing hidden which will not be revealed, nor has anything been kept secret, but it should come to light." – Mark 4:22-23

With its secretive nature and layered oaths, Freemasonry raised too many questions. Some say it's a pathway to Satan, where only at the highest degrees, such as the thirty third degrees are members confronted with a choice to follow the devil or abandon their progress. While I can't definitively confirm such claims, the Bible's clarity on exposing darkness leads me to distrust anything hidden or shrouded in secrecy.

Still, I couldn't deny that Christ-centered men and women are in every branch of government. Yet, this world belongs to the "Prince of the Air," and D.C., with its influence over much of the world's "airwaves," seemed a natural stronghold for the enemy. If the devil had an office, I wouldn't be surprised if it were in D.C., with perhaps a vacation home in New Orleans, and maybe a condo in Hollywood.

Our visit to the city was short—a single hour—but in that time, we managed to see the Lincoln Memorial, the White House, and the Washington Monument. Each structure stood as a symbol, not just of a nation's history, but of the spiritual and moral struggles that continue to shape it.

By the time we got back on the highway and made our way to New Jersey, the sun was setting.

Chapter Thirty-Five

New Jersey Blues

A.W. Tozer

"A friend is someone who knows the song in your heart and can sing it back to you when you have forgotten the words."

The orange and pink hues painted the sky as we arrived at what I soon learned was Louis's childhood home. His father had passed years earlier, but his mother still lived there, in a modest, single-story house with a basement that seemed to echo with memories.

The exhaustion from our two-day drive hit us like a freight train. My body ached, my mind felt fried, and I gained a newfound respect for truckers. Anyone who's driven 400 miles knows how grueling it can be. Imagine driving 1,000 or even 2,000 miles in a single stretch on a consistent basis—it's enough to make anyone snap. Maybe the trucker who had chased us back in Texas had simply reached his breaking point. Perhaps the stress of the highway made him want to take his frustrations out on two guys in a Suzuki Samurai.

Louis's mom welcomed us with open arms. She had a warmth about her, a motherly kindness that made me feel instantly at home. As I settled into the cozy living room, I thought about how far we'd come—from the gator-filled swamps of Louisiana to the spiritual heaviness of D.C., and now to this little sanctuary in New Jersey.

Sometimes, the road can be terrifying. Sometimes, it can be heartwarming. But every mile of this journey was shaping us, teaching us something new about the trials we all go through to bring us closer to an understanding of who the Creator is and what he desires for us. And for that, I am grateful when looking back. The New Jersey accent was like something straight out of the movies I grew up on—thick, unapologetic, and hilarious. I couldn't help but smirk every time someone opened their mouth. After unloading what little stuff I had brought, Louis showed me to my sleeping quarters. His gaming room, with music equipment scattered around, was like a cozy little nook of creativity. It looked perfect to me. We grabbed a bite to eat, exchanged a few laughs about the trip, and then promptly crashed.

The next morning, Louis suggested we drive into New York City. I didn't need any convincing so off we went. Thirty minutes—that's all it would take from Elmwood Park to the heart of Manhattan. As we zipped down the highway, we found ourselves under the Holland Tunnel and emerged into the bustling city. But parking? Forget about it. Louis told me most New Yorkers didn't even own cars because there were just too many people packed into such a tight space. It became apparent why parking was practically a sport, and we weren't winning.

Seeing New York in person was a bit of a shock. Just like the camera adds ten pounds, it also exaggerates the city's size. In real life, Manhattan wasn't as expansive as I'd imagined, but its energy was something else. Our first stop was Little Italy, where, miraculously, we found a parking spot.

As we walked through the streets, Louis warned me to avoid talking to people. "They're hardcore here," he said, "and you're not ready for it." But I didn't listen. I stopped a random guy to ask for the time. His response? "What do I look like, a f****** watch?" He didn't even break his stride. I stood there, stunned. I'd never had someone be that abrasive over something so trivial. Louis just laughed and shook his head. "Told ya," he said.

It was then I began to understand the characters I'd seen in movies growing up. New Yorkers weren't acting—they were just being themselves.

We explored a few iconic spots, including the Brooklyn Bridge and the Statue of Liberty. Louis even showed me the legendary CBGB club, a grungy relic of the punk rock scene. After a few hours of soaking in the city's grit and grandeur, we headed back to Jersey.

That evening, Louis mentioned a get-together at an old friend's house. I didn't catch the name of whose house it was, but the place screamed 1950s suburbia. About 15 or so people were there, and while Louis caught up with his friends, I ended up on the couch, taking it all in.

A big, burly Italian-looking guy plopped down next to me. His presence was as loud as the room itself. A joint was lit, passed around, and eventually landed in my hand. I hesitated but didn't want to be rude, so I took a quick puff. As I exhaled, I handed it back to the big guy and casually asked, "So, what do you do for a living?"

He took a long drag, exhaled, and said in a thick New Jersey accent, "I'm a cop."

I nearly choked. "You're not worried about a drug test?" I asked, half-joking, half-stunned.

"Nah," he said with a smirk. "Everyone at the department smokes."

I laughed nervously, wondering if this was a joke or just another example of how different life was out here.

The conversation was surprisingly good, and the vibe was relaxed. At some point, I even got a page from Danielle. I didn't call her back since it was 12 midnight where I was in new Jersey and 9 PM back in California. But seeing her number on my pager brought a comforting sense of home.

When we got back to Louis's, we jammed on his music equipment for a bit before crashing again. But as the days passed, I found myself grappling with some serious thoughts.

The East Coast was a whole different beast. The people were sharper, their tempers shorter, and the government seemed to have its hand in everything. It was a culture shock compared to the laid-back vibe of the West Coast. Don't get me wrong, when God shook the tree of life most of the fruits and nuts fell off in California, and the political landscape was rife with socialist and communist overtones, but the East Coast was much more strong-armed about it. You might end up in concrete shoes if you disagree with your government in the Garden State.

As I weighed my options, the prospect of settling down on the East Coast looked less and less appealing. The job market was tight, taxes were steep, and the summer promised to be hot and humid-followed by winter as cold and icy as ever.

I didn't even have winter clothes.

So I told Louis how much I appreciated the adventure but that I couldn't see myself staying there. I missed California—the familiarity and the warmth. He seemed a little bummed, but he got it.

I called my parents to tell them I was coming back. They were thrilled and suggested I stay with them while I figured out my next move. The idea of returning to their cozy home in Loomis, just north of Sacramento, felt like a lifeline.

As much as I'd enjoyed the East Coast adventure, it was time to return to where I belonged. The road had shown me a lot, but it reminded me of what mattered most: home. It felt like a smart idea, heading back to California. There was comfort in the familiar, and something about hearing Danielle's voice solidified my decision. She was thrilled when I called to let her know about my plans. "Come to LA first," she suggested, excitement bubbling in her tone. "Stay with me for a few days before heading to your parents."

The idea sounded perfect—a soft landing before reuniting with family. I told her I'd do it, and we made plans. I'd spend a week in the Valley at her apartment, just catching up and enjoying the simple pleasure of her company. After that, I'd head north to Loomis to stay with my folks and figure out my next steps.

Should I dive back into the film and TV world, or was it time for something entirely new? That question weighed heavily on me as I packed my things. Writing music had become my main focus lately, and part of me wondered if it was a sign to shift gears entirely.

Louis was quiet during the drive to LaGuardia Airport, the weight of our goodbye hanging in the air. The bond we'd built over the past few weeks was unique, forged through long drives, near-death encounters, and shared laughter. When we finally reached the terminal, he gave me a firm handshake.

"Take care of yourself, man," he said, his voice low but sincere.

"You too," I replied, trying to keep the emotion out of my voice.

With that, I grabbed my bag and headed toward the check-in counter.

The airport was its usual mix of chaos and monotony. People rushing to catch flights, others slumped in chairs, waiting for delayed planes. I settled into my seat on the plane, a six-hour journey stretching ahead of me. The city of fallen angels awaited, with all its promises and pitfalls.

The flight felt longer than six hours, maybe because my mind wouldn't stop racing. Memories of New York flashed through my head—its gritty streets, its colorful characters, and that overwhelming energy that seemed to buzz through the air. But I would be in California in 6 hours so I tried to focus what was ahead.

Chapter Thirty-Six

Fiero And The Green Bible

Thomas Guthrie

"The Bible is the most valuable thing that this world affords. It is a message of hope to the world. It is the Word of God, and it is the Word that can change everything."

As the plane descended into Los Angeles, I stared out the window at the sprawling city below. The sight of the endless grid of lights brought a strange mix of nostalgia and unease. LA had always been a city of extremes for me—dreams realized and dreams crushed.

Danielle picked me up from LAX, and we merged onto the 405 heading to the Valley. The familiar rhythm of California traffic surrounded us, with the relentless hum of engines and the occasional impatient honk. Danielle, excited as always, casually mentioned that we'd be meeting her parents the following day.

"For what?" I asked.

"To go to church" she said with a playful smirk, as if I already knew.

I hadn't stepped into a church in 14 years, and the thought seemed strange, almost comical. But I figured it wouldn't kill me to go. That night, we went out to dinner at a local spot. It was a laid-back meal until I noticed something odd about Danielle. As usual, she ate a considerable amount—but as soon as she finished, she wanted to leave immediately.

The bulimia looked like it had its claws in her. it did not look like she was going to give it up any time soon. But I did my best not to reveal that I knew exactly what she was going through and I knew about her disease.

Her apartment was cozy, and since she was a committed Christian, our relationship was strictly platonic. I stayed on the couch that night.

Sunday morning came, and we drove to meet her parents at a church called **The Rock** in the San Fernando Valley. I wasn't exactly thrilled to see them again. They new that I had broken the relationship off with their daughter and moved to the other side of the country. What self-respecting, God-fearing parents would want a guy like me dating their daughter? I was a walking cliché of a loser: twenty years old, no car, no job, no college education, and an impressive resume of sin—smoking, drinking, occasional drug use, and more.

But Danielle had her own struggles, the ones she hid from everyone. Her battle with bulimia was her way of trying to control the chaos in her life, and I knew it wasn't easy for her. In her mind if she could control her weight than the world was in order. But it wasn't.

When we arrived, her parents greeted us politely but cautiously. Her father, Larry, had the kind of stern, protective aura you'd expect from a man sizing up his daughter's boyfriend. I couldn't blame him.

Inside the church, the service began. I don't remember the pastor's name, but his message resonated with me more than I expected. The only problem was my focus kept drifting. Sitting just a row right in front of us was John Stamos and his wife, and I couldn't help but watch their reactions to the sermon.

Looking back, I wish I'd been more present. I wasn't there spiritually, not yet. When the service ended, Danielle's father invited us to lunch. We ended up at a Denny's style restaurant, and as we waited for our food, he reached into his bag and pulled out a green-covered book.

Sliding it across the table, he said, "I'd like you to have this, and I hope you read it."

I hesitated for a moment, unsure how to react. It was a Bible. It felt a little strange, I did not know what to say. I was touched. I picked up the Bible and noticed my initials embossed on the cover. It wasn't cheap—I could tell by its weight and quality.

"I still have it to this day," I'd later reflect, recognizing it as another moment where God was reaching out to me through the people around me. At the time, I didn't fully understand it, but there was something different about born-again Christians. They carried a light in their eyes, a joy and peace I couldn't explain.

As we ate, Larry asked if I'd be interested in buying Danielle's car—a black 1985 Pontiac Fiero. My immediate response was laughter.

"There's no way I can afford that," I said, shaking my head.

The Fiero was undeniably cool and probably worth way more than I could dream of paying. "All I have is $500," I added, half-joking.

Larry leaned forward, extending his hand across the table. "How about this? $1,500 total. You give me $500 now, and the rest in two payments over the next couple of months."

I blinked, stunned. "Seriously?"

"Seriously," he said with a small smile.

This felt like one of those God moments people talked about. I didn't know much about faith back then, but the generosity of Danielle's parents hit me. They could have easily sold that car for more, but instead, they chose to extend grace to a guy like me.

Deep down, I felt a twinge of guilt. I knew I wasn't going to marry Danielle, and part of me felt like I was betraying her family by accepting their kindness. But at the same time, I was grateful.

We left the restaurant, and I handed Larry the $500 I had as a down payment. As Danielle drove us back to her apartment in the Fiero, I couldn't help but feel a small spark of hope.

The car wasn't just a vehicle; it was a symbol of something bigger. I was beginning to see glimpses of God's hand in my life, even when I didn't fully recognize Him.

That day, I walked away with more than a Bible and a Fiero—I walked away with the understanding that genuine Christians lived out their faith through acts of love and generosity. Even in my brokenness, they saw something worth investing in.

As we pulled into Danielle's driveway, I couldn't help but smile. For the first time in a long while, I felt like I had a little wind in my sails, ready to head north and face whatever came next.

Chapter Thirty-Seven

Haircuts And High Notes

Tim Keller

"Work is not just a way to get a paycheck; it's an essential part of human flourishing. Work is a way to love your neighbor."

The week with Danielle flew by, and soon I was driving up north along the great I-5 freeway. Beautiful? Not exactly. Anyone who's been on that stretch of asphalt knows it's anything but scenic. But the drive gave me time to think as I cruised in my newly acquired black Fiero.

When I pulled up to my parents' duplex in Loomis, CA, they were stunned. I hadn't told them about the car, and judging by their expressions, they thought I was hiding some major Hollywood success. I quickly squashed that notion by explaining the generosity of Danielle and her family.

"They're Christians," I added.

My mom, sitting at the kitchen table, responded, "Well, we're Christians too."

I paused. "Are we?"

The truth was, my childhood experience with Christianity didn't extend far beyond celebrating Christmas and Easter. Sure, my mom had a porcelain manger scene she displayed every December, complete with baby Jesus, Mary, and four bearded dudes standing behind them, but beyond that, our faith didn't seem to go much deeper. It felt more like tradition than a relationship with God.

My sister Kimberly stopped by later that evening. She knew I was coming home and wanted to say hello. She was pregnant with Julia, her 2nd of three children, and she radiated that unique glow moms-to-be have. We caught up as she peppered me with questions about my time in LA and on the East Coast.

"It all sounds so exciting," she said with a smile before suddenly shifting gears. "So, what are your plans for the future? What do you want to do with your life?"

Her question caught me off guard. Music immediately popped into my head, but I didn't say it out loud. I knew how risky that dream sounded, and I didn't feel like I had my act together enough to say it confidently. Instead, I shrugged and muttered, "I don't know."

This is when my sister said almost flippantly but carried more weight than could have managed. "Why don't you get your license as a barber or hair stylist? You can still play music while making a decent living."

I blinked. It was such a simple idea, but it made perfect sense. "Wow," I said, genuinely impressed. "Thanks. That's actually great advice."

The very next day—or maybe even that same afternoon—I took my sister's suggestion seriously and started researching how to get licensed. It turned out I needed to complete sixteen hundred hours of training, which would take roughly about a year. I enrolled at Citrus Heights Beauty College, just a few miles from my parents' place in Loomis.

Walking into the school on my first day was like stepping into a completely new world. There were about fifteen women and four men in the class. Of the guys, three of us were straight, and one was either gay or just highly effeminate. Naturally, the three straight guys bonded almost immediately.

Kevin, one of the guys, looked like he'd stepped out of an eighties rock band. Tall, with long, dark, curly hair, and had a quirky class clown personality. Then there was John, who had similar long, curly hair but an entirely different personality—he was type-A high-energy, and full of stories. John and I hit it off quickly, and within days, we were already talking about music.

"You're a singer-songwriter?" he asked one afternoon as we worked through our textbooks on sanitation and basic physiology.

"Yeah," I said casually.

"Let's start a band," he blurted out.

I laughed. "You play an instrument?"

"Not yet," he admitted, "but I'll learn bass. My buddy Eddie is a drummer, and my cousin Darell plays guitar. You sing and write. We've got a band."

The sheer audacity of his plan amused me. "You're going to learn bass just like that?"

"Why not?" he said with a grin.

To my astonishment, John bought a bass that week and started practicing nonstop. I saw that he was actually serious, so we began to get together after school every day, and I would instruct him on the rudiments of the bass guitar. Within days, he was playing with solid timing. I couldn't believe how quickly he picked it up. Before I knew it, we were rehearsing in Eddie's living room. Eddie, a talented drummer, kept us tight, and Darell, John's cousin, was more than proficient on guitar. In fact, Darell was almost a savant with the instrument. I had played with many guitarists throughout the years, and Darell played like no one I had ever known. In fact, when we would finish rehearsing or even a show, Darell put so much into his performance that he had to go off by himself and recharge. People would say that it was his bipolar schizophrenia that gave him his talent. Looking back, I believe it was otherworldly. I think there were unclean spirits involved with his mental disease or infirmity. But Darell was... complicated. Clinicians had given him the diagnosis of schizophrenia. But like I said, watching him play, there was just something deeper going on. His eyes had this ancient, haunted look as if he carried more than just his burden. He was on lithium, a powerful mood stabilizer, and while it helped, it didn't erase the manic episodes that occasionally disrupted our rehearsals.

I remember one moment in particular when Darell's behavior made the hair on my neck stand up. His gaze locked onto me, and I felt a strange, almost tangible darkness. I didn't just see mental illness; I saw spiritual oppression. Maybe even possession.

Through my budding faith, I began to understand that God gives His followers spiritual gifts if we ask for them. One of those gifts is discernment, the ability to see the spiritual forces at work in the world. And in Darell, I saw both torment and potential.

Despite the challenges, the band started to sound pretty good. We had a raw, unpolished energy that felt promising. But I couldn't ignore the feeling that Darell's struggles might hold us back—or worse, put us in harm's way. Looking back, those early days at Citrus Heights Beauty College and in our makeshift band were a whirlwind of change and growth. I was learning not just about cutting hair or playing music but new friendships with a group of guys that I felt I could grow with.

As I drove home from rehearsal one night, the Fiero humming beneath me, I couldn't help but feel a strange mix of excitement and uncertainty. My life was beginning to take shape, but the road ahead was anything but clear. For now, though, I had a plan, a band, and a growing sense that I wasn't walking this journey alone.

Chapter Thirty-Eight

Filling The Void

Charles Spurgeon

"Wisdom is the right use of knowledge. To know is not to be wise. Many men know a great deal and are all the greater fools for it. But to know how to use knowledge is to have wisdom."

Things were going as planned. The music flowed, and beauty school was also going well. I had started talking to a girl in my class—Mildred. She was beautiful in a way that made her stand out. She had moved from Colorado to Sacramento alone, with no family around. I couldn't quite wrap my mind around why she'd leave somewhere like Colorado for a relatively quiet place like Sacramento. But it didn't take long for me to understand why. She followed a minor league baseball player from Colorado to Sacramento where he was playing. I guess they were together for a while, but things didn't work out, so they split. Mildred decided to just stay in Sacramento.

As I got to know Mildred I discovered something else: she was working as a stripper to pay her bills. Now, mind you, I was far from being a follower of Christ at this point. And although I found her job distasteful, I still wanted to pursue her. Looking back, I realize that the spirit of lust had taken root in me long ago. My view of what the "ideal woman" was had been warped since childhood, when I snuck peeks at the Playboys. I could still picture the glossy pages in my head—the images that began shaping my understanding of attraction. Mildred fit that image perfectly.

But as time went on, I came to understand something else: she was broken, just like I was. She wasn't the perfect woman I thought I wanted. She had her own struggles—just as I had mine—and we were both deeply flawed. If I could go back now, I would have understood better. But at the time, I was still trying to figure things out, especially with Danielle back in Southern California. Yes, she was still lingering in my thoughts, even though I was trying to figure out how to make a total and clean break with her.

Danielle was my first real long-term relationship. I didn't know how to end things gracefully. And if I'm being honest, I didn't want to hurt her. I knew I was her only source of support, and the idea of crushing her made me feel guilty. It took me about three months, but eventually, I told her the distance between us was just too much to handle. She was angry. She was sad. I understood all of it. No one wants to be on the receiving end of a breakup, especially when it's someone you care about.

For the first week after the breakup, Danielle called me incessantly. I let the calls go to voicemail, knowing I wasn't ready to talk. But after a while, the calls stopped, and it seemed like she had finally accepted that we were over. That's when I worked up the courage to ask Mildred out.

To my surprise, she said yes.

When I showed up at her place, I felt like I had entered some alternative reality—Standing at her door looking into her apartment, think Stephen Tyler from Aerosmith, only with a New Age twist. Candles, incense, the works. It wasn't exactly my style, but there was something undeniably captivating about her. And looking back, I realize that Mildred, just like me, was struggling with forces beyond our understanding. Her job, her lifestyle, they were all magnets for darkness—an unholy connection I was only beginning to sense.

I didn't realize it at the time, but Mildred was the woman I lost my virginity to. And let me tell you, the spirit world rejoiced that day. There were forces at work, and I had no clue how deep they went.

As our relationship progressed, and after a few more dates, I brought up the idea of us getting a place together. I wasn't sure how she'd react, but I felt like I had to ask if I wanted to keep things going. Mildred had agreed to quit her job at the strip club—though it wasn't easy. The money was good—$400 to $500 a night. But she said she was willing to stop for me. And for that, I was thankful. In hindsight I wished she had actually quit for herself. But if I hadn't been in the picture she most likely wouldn't have.

We found a small one-bedroom apartment just a few blocks from the college. It wasn't much, but it was ours. It felt like the right next step for us. I told her my plans: I wanted to finish beauty school, get my license, and then head back to L.A. to pursue music. She didn't seem too fazed by the idea. "Sounds good," she said, as if it were just another chapter in our story.

When beauty school ended, we both took the state-required Cosmetology test to get our licenses. I finished the test well ahead of everyone else, as I always did, beating the rest by a wide margin. Now I'm not saing I scored 100% I'm just fast. Mildred passed with ease as well. We were both ready to start our new careers, excited about the possibilities ahead.

But Mildred wasn't planning on doing hair. She wanted to do skincare. I thought that sounded great, so she started working as an esthetician at a local spa. She found it fulfilling, and I was glad she was following her passion. I, on the other hand, was all about cutting hair. I wanted to make a name for myself and build a decent clientele, and I was determined to make it happen, no matter what it took.

But deep down, I could feel the darkness creeping in, threatening to swallow us both. Mildred's brokenness, my brokenness, it all felt like too much. Yet, we continued, unaware of the larger spiritual battles happening around us.

Chapter Thirty-Nine

CIA And The Mark Of The Beast

Richard Bauckham

"The perspective of heaven must break into the earthbound delusion of the beast's propaganda. There are clearly only two options: to worship God or to worship the beast."

I landed my very first job cutting hair at a well-known Sacramento salon called Brockway. It wasn't a high-end spot, more like a local chain, similar to Great Clips or Supercuts, but they offered more than just basic cuts. Brockway did everything from color to perms to relaxing treatments. It was the early nineties, and the buzz in the salon was always lively, the air filled with the hum of blow dryers and chatter.

At that point in my life, I had already started to feel a faint stir within me, like a seed being planted. I had met a few people who were Christians, but this one encounter would turn out to be different. One day, while I was idly sitting and waiting for clients to walk in, an old man stepped into the salon. He was a tall man with a thick gray beard, and a pair of worn overalls. At first glance, he didn't look like much—a regular old guy, but his presence was undeniable. There was something about his eyes—a light, a calmness, a love that I couldn't put into words. It was as if he carried a quiet peace with him.

He handed me a small, simple pamphlet with a slight smile and said, "I'm having a gathering at my house nearby. The speaker's a former CIA scientist. He'll be talking about the end times and the technology that's going to be used as the 'mark of the beast."

I hadn't heard the term "mark of the beast" before, but as he explained, he referred to the book of Revelation in the Bible. He started reading Revelation 13:18, and I was taken aback:

"This calls for wisdom; let the one who has understanding calculate the number of the beast, for it is the number of a man, and his number is 666."

I was stunned. This verse sounded eerily familiar—like something straight out of the music I used to listen to when I was younger. Bands like Iron Maiden and Motley Crüe, who often referenced dark, apocalyptic themes in their lyrics, came to mind. But I didn't mention this to the old man; I figured he wouldn't know anything about that kind of music, still what he was saying intrigued me. The idea that there was something beyond what I had known, that maybe there was truth in these cryptic words, was starting to seep into my mind.

I enjoyed my talk with the old guy and said I would try and make it out to his gathering.

When I got home later that afternoon I told Mildred about the meeting, and she wasn't particularly thrilled about the idea. But I decided to go. The gathering took place in the old man's living room—small, intimate, with maybe twelve people there. I had expected it to be packed, but it wasn't. Looking back, I now understand why. There's a truth hidden in Matthew 7:13-14 that I didn't fully grasp at the time:

"Enter by the narrow gate; for wide is the gate and broad is the way that leads to destruction, and there are many who go in by it. Because narrow is the gate and difficult is the way which leads to life, and there are few who find it."

Few find the narrow gate. Few are willing to hear or see what's hidden in plain sight, and at the time, my sin had dulled my perception, making it harder for me to know the truth.

But I was still fascinated, listening intently as an older, balding man in his sixties set up a tripod and a whiteboard. He then displayed a large photograph of a microchip. His voice was calm, measured, and very matter of fact as he began speaking. From what I remember, he introduced himself as one of two scientists who had worked with the CIA to develop a microchip so small it could be injected under the skin, undetected by the human eye.

He explained how this chip could store all your personal information: Social Security number, height, weight, hair color—everything. The idea was to track an individual's movements with satellites, basically giving the government the ability to know where that individual was at any given time. He also mentioned how the chip could be charged with a tiny lithium battery, making it a virtually undetectable device for surveillance. The battery could be charged using the heat from your forehead or in your right hand. This is what makes the book of Revelation a lens into our future. After reading this scripture, I had no doubt that these men may have actually created the Mark of the Beast.

Revelation 13:16-17

"It also forced all people, great and small, rich and poor, free and slave, to receive a mark on their right hands or on their foreheads, so that they could not buy or sell unless they had the mark, which is the name of the beast or the number of its name."

This is where the batteries need to be in your body to receive a charge. He also said that to make the technology more palatable to the public, they would begin by implanting the chip in animals. This way, if a pet ran away, someone could scan the animal and easily find out who it belonged to. He said that a computer in Germany that goes by the name of B.E.A.S.T. would house all of the human races data.

I was stunned. This was 1991, and the concept sounded outlandish. Yet, here we are today—what do they use now to track lost pets? Microchips.

Leaving the meeting, my head was spinning. The whole idea was so deep, so intricate, that it stayed with me for years. I couldn't shake the thought of it. The seed that was planted in me that night would slowly grow, watered by countless other experiences, until one day, it would bloom into something far greater than I could have imagined.

Looking back, I now realize how powerful God's word truly is. It's like a double-edged sword, cutting through the darkness and revealing truths that I wasn't ready to see at the time. But seeds were planted—seeds of understanding, seeds of awakening, and seeds of a truth that would later change my life forever.

Chapter Forty

Whispers In The Dark

Thomas à Kempis

"The devil does not sleep, nor is the flesh yet dead; therefore, cease not to prepare yourself for battle, for on the right and on the left are enemies who never rest."

For years, I had been experiencing sleep paralysis, but at the time, I didn't understand it fully. I had grown accustomed to it, though the sensation of being awake but unable to move—completely paralyzed—was terrifying. I had suppressed the memory of that one night when I was a child, finding myself being carried away from my bed, laid on the ground, unable to scream or resist. I knew something supernatural had happened then, but I buried it deep, pretending it was just a bad dream. But deep down, I understood I was dealing with forces far beyond my comprehension.

The morning after the meeting with the old man and his mysterious guest, I couldn't shake the thought of 666 from my mind. It was a number that had haunted me—something I had heard before, but I didn't really understand. I spent the day with more questions than answers. The words of that old man echoed in my mind as I tried to process the significance of what I had learned. When I mentioned the meeting to some of my clients, they didn't seem to care much. To them, it was just a conspiracy or another odd story. But it wasn't just another odd story to me. Something had been set in motion, and I couldn't ignore the nagging feeling that I was being pulled deeper into something I couldn't control.

That night, after playing a little guitar and watching TV, I decided to turn in for bed. Mildred was already sound asleep when I entered the room. I tried reading for a while to quiet my mind before lying down. It worked—until it didn't. After about twenty minutes of reading, I felt tired enough to drift off. I put the book down, switched off the reading lamp, and sank into the darkness. But just five minutes later, I started hearing low, indistinct chatter.

At first, I thought it was just my imagination playing tricks on me. But when I sat up and listened more closely, I realized the sound wasn't coming from outside the room. I put my ear to the wall, trying to pinpoint the source. No, it wasn't from the neighbors. There was nothing there. So, I crawled back into bed, trying to dismiss it as a figment of my overactive mind.

But as soon as I closed my eyes, I realized the sound was coming from the room itself—right next to my head. The voices were nasally, high-pitched, and foul, like something you might expect from a small creature or a dwarf. They weren't speaking English, or any language I could recognize. The sound was unlike anything I'd ever heard before, and it sent a chill down my spine. There were more than one of them. They seemed to be moving around our bed, from my nightstand to Mildred's side, coming and going, circling us like vultures.

In that moment, if I had known to call out to Jesus, I would have. But I didn't know Jesus at the time. I was terrified, helpless. These things kept me awake for what felt like an eternity—half an hour at least—until, just as suddenly as they appeared, they were gone.

I didn't wake Mildred up. What could I have said? What could she have done? It would have only frightened her, and I didn't want to add to the terror. I lay there, shaken, waiting for them to return. Every creak of the floorboards, every shift in the bed, sent my heart racing. But thankfully, they never came back.

It took me hours to fall asleep, and when I did, it was far from peaceful. The next morning, I woke up exhausted. I hadn't slept nearly enough. I tried to shake off the unease, but it lingered in the back of my mind. My eyes bloodshot and tired.

As Mildred stirred and started making breakfast, I went outside to get the mail. As I sifted through the letters, I noticed a large envelope which I noticed was addressed to a name I didn't know. It was our address so I assumed it was the previous tenant. And I didn't recognize the sender, but curiosity got the best of me, and I opened it. Inside, I found a small booklet, cleanly stapled together, containing illustrations of the most sinister-looking creatures I had ever seen.

They were demons—small, creepy, and utterly unsettling. There were about twenty of them, each with a distinct name, each with a list of strengths and weaknesses. Stocky, skinny, fat, or short—each creature had its own unique look, and each one seemed more terrifying than the last. The images were meticulously detailed, and I could feel a cold, unsettling energy radiating from the pages.

There was also a section that looked like a guide to spells. It was clear to me now that the previous tenant must have been involved with some very dark practices. I didn't know the full story, but this wasn't something that was accidentally mailed to him. I had a feeling that this tenant had been seeking out this kind of knowledge. He must have been involved with the occult.

I didn't show Mildred the pamphlet. I didn't want to frighten her further, and honestly, I didn't want any part of it. I threw the material away, feeling a strong sense of relief as I did so. I wanted to sever any connection to these creatures, to this darkness that had found its way into our lives. I hoped that by getting rid of the pamphlet, I was somehow telling them they weren't welcome in our home.

I couldn't shake the feeling, though, that these demons had come through the previous tenant's involvement with some sort of ritualistic practices. The fact that Mildred and I weren't following Christ at the time—and had no spiritual protection—gave them the freedom to and license to harass us. Looking back, it's clear to me that we were living in a state of vulnerability, which made us easy targets for the supernatural forces lurking in the shadows or even another dimension.

But after that night, I didn't experience another visit from those unclean spirits while we stayed in that apartment. Somehow, those demons seemed to have moved on. Perhaps they had been driven away by my own defiance, or maybe they just found a new place to haunt. Either way, I was thankful. The peace that followed was welcome, but deep down, I knew something much greater was needed to truly rid my life of the darkness I had been flirting with for so long. If I had only called on the name of the most high these Demons would have fled. But as you know I had not yet found the foot of the cross.

And little did I know, that darkness wasn't finished with me yet.

Chapter Forty-One

Back To The Beast

C.S. Lewis

"If we insist on keeping Hell (or even earth) we shall not see Heaven: if we accept Heaven we shall not be able to retain even the smallest and most intimate souvenirs of Hell."

The band was tight and sounded great, my relationship with Mildred wasn't as tight but we were managing. It wasn't the most significant move on my part, but in the throes of ambition, I asked the band mates and Mildred if they'd be interested in moving to Hollywood. To my surprise, they agreed. It was a spontaneous decision, one I made in the heat of the moment, but it felt like the right thing to do at the time. So, just like that, we packed up and headed to LA.

We didn't make it directly to Hollywood. Instead, we relocated about 2 miles from Hollywood, crossing the hills and settling into the valley. Mildred and I found a small place just behind Ventura Boulevard, while the bandmates got an apartment nearby. It was a fresh start—an adventure of sorts, and I was excited about the possibilities. I was the first one in the group to find a job. I quickly landed a job at Piero's, a posh upscale salon on the Third Street Promenade in Santa Monica. It wasn't that far from the apartment, but the traffic on the 405 added an extra 30 minutes to the drive there. The clientele was eclectic, to say the least. The salon catered to actors, models, mobsters, and even madams. Among the regulars were Heidi Fleiss's girls, the owner of Body Glove, and even John Gotti's wife, Victoria. One day, while shampooing Victoria Gotti's hair, she showed me photos of her mob boss husband working out in prison. It was the strangest experience, to say the least. It felt surreal to be in the same room with such high-profile figures, but at the same time, I couldn't help but feel like I was out of my depth.

Mildred soon found a job working at a skincare company closer to our place in Hollywood. She was doing okay, but there was something about her that seemed... distant. I couldn't put my finger on it, but something wasn't quite right. I tried not to worry too much; after all, we were both pursuing our dreams, building our careers. But deep down, I knew something was off.

As for my hair gig, it was going alright, except for one person—Miguel, the owner's boyfriend. Miguel had a dark sense of humor, and he would often refer to me as Jeffrey Dahmer just to get a laugh. It wasn't funny to me, but what could I do? I didn't want to rock the boat. I learned to just smile and nod, even though the nickname made me uncomfortable. Looking back, I realize now that Miguel was most definitely dealing with severe oppression—or possibly even possession. There was something dark about him, something I couldn't quite explain.

Meanwhile, the band was rehearsing regularly in a new space we had found in the valley. We were pushing ourselves hard, writing new songs, and rehearsing for long hours. We also started doing open mics around Hollywood and the valley. We were getting closer to making a name for ourselves, or so I thought. But even though everything was falling into place, I couldn't shake the feeling that something was missing.

Despite the band's progress, despite the fact that Mildred and I had our own little place, despite everything I had worked for, there was this immense void in my soul. At the time, I didn't even know what a soul was. But as I look back now, with the benefit of time and perspective, I realize that there is indeed something inside all of us—something profound, something eternal. And mine was aching, crying out for something I couldn't identify.

I didn't know what it was that was missing. I had all the trappings of success—well, not quite success, but the beginnings of it. The band was getting tighter, we were playing more shows, the gigs were more frequent. Mildred and I were building our life in LA. But no matter how much I achieved, no matter how much I progressed, I was still unfulfilled. The journey felt empty, hollow.

I couldn't explain it, and I couldn't fix it. I was chasing a dream, but somewhere along the way, I had lost my sense of purpose. Even with every milestone completed, the feeling of emptiness lingered. The more I pushed forward, the more I realized that I was spinning my wheels in the mud.

I didn't know where to turn. I didn't have the language to describe what I was feeling, but I could feel it: a sense that there had to be more to life than this. Music, relationships, success—none of it could fill the hole in my heart. And even though I didn't know it yet, the answer wasn't in the hustle or the fame. It wasn't in the bright lights of Hollywood or the promises of success.

No, the answer was something much deeper, and it was a long way off. But I was about to take the first steps toward it. The belly of the beast was waiting for me, and I had no idea how close I was to the revelation that would change everything.

The question was no longer whether I would find it. The question was when.

Chapter Forty-Two

4.7 And The House Of Blues

Thomas Brewer

"The Lord is more powerful than the earthquakes and forces of chaos in your life. The Lord is more powerful than your circumstances, your sin, your mistakes, your losses, and your failures—and He uses His power to accomplish salvation for His people despite the sin and miseries of this life. He is our refuge and strength"

It was January 17, 1994, at 4:29 in the morning when I awoke in a cold sweat, heart pounding, and sat straight up in bed. Something in my gut told me something huge was coming. I turned to Mildred, shaking her awake with urgency. "Something's coming," I said in a foreboding voice, "and it's big." She stared at me, still half-asleep, clearly thinking I had just had a bad dream. But I knew this was different. This is when I hear the phone ring. I'm thinking who's calling at 4 in the AM. And I kid you not it's my father, all the way from Northern California, calling to check in on me. He said he did not know why he felt the urge to call me but he did. I told him everything was Ok and hung up the phone. I crawled back into bed and before either of us could speak further, a low, distant rumble started, like a massive train underground, miles away, slowly heading toward us. The sound deepened, growing louder by the second. I felt the vibrations under my feet. It wasn't just a rumble; the world around us began to shake.

It was like a bull, a massive force clawing its way through the earth. When the quake hit our small brick apartment, we were violently tossed out of our bed as the walls behind us started to crack open, and you could now see outside through our bedroom walls. For a brief moment, I couldn't comprehend what was happening, but then it hit me—this was an earthquake. The floor beneath us rolled like the waves of the ocean, sending everything in its path flying. Our hundred and fifty pound refrigerator was tossed across the kitchen like it was made of cardboard.

We scrambled for clothes, disoriented but driven by the urgency to escape. As we stumbled toward the front door, the door frame cracked, and we could barely get it open. But we made it outside, and that's when we saw the chaos. Women screaming in our complex and echos from others down the street.

Our landlady, bloodied, full of concrete drywall dust, and wearing nothing but her nightgown, was standing in the street, frantically waving her arms. "Get to the street! The building's going to collapse!" she yelled. Half of our ten-unit complex was made of bricks, and now those bricks were scattered all over the ground, no longer on the building. It felt like the very ground beneath us might give way.

I looked around, and tenants—some barely clothed, others in just their underwear—were stumbling out of their apartments. One young woman stood holding a lit candle, and I immediately rushed over to her. "Put that out," I said sharply. "There's gas leaks from all of the buildings. Your candle could spark a massive explosion." She looked startled but complied, blowing out the candle.

As we made our way down the street, I turned to see the apartment building next to ours—just twenty five feet away—had collapsed. It was leaning at a terrifying 45-degree angle, its massive frame threatening to fall on us at any moment. The building had even crushed all of the cars in the carport underneath it. We sprinted even faster, hearts racing, adrenaline flooding our bodies.

Just fifty feet away, a large, furious flame—four feet in diameter and eight feet high—was shooting up from the ground. We all stood in stunned silence as the world around us rumbled, the dust from broken bricks and stucco mortar filling the air. For a moment, it felt like time had stopped, and all we could do was breathe, shaken and overwhelmed.

The fear was palpable. The earthquake had torn through our lives, and we knew, deep down, that we were homeless now. Our apartment, our sense of security, had been reduced to rubble.

With no place to go, we made our way to Ventura Boulevard, where we saw the line for the payphone stretching two hundred feet long. The sun was starting to rise, and the full extent of the damage from the Northridge earthquake—a 6.7 magnitude—was beginning to sink in. Buildings, apartments, businesses, parking garages, and overpasses had been leveled. The city was in chaos, and no one seemed to know what to do.

As we walked along the boulevard, we found no cafes or diners open, only a sense of confusion and uncertainty hanging in the air.

People wandered aimlessly, too stunned to speak, their faces etched with fear of aftershocks. I noticed something strange as we walked: all the clothing stores along the boulevard had been ransacked. The glass on the storefronts had been shattered by the quake, and I watched as a rough looking man wheeled a shopping cart full of Levi's and other expensive clothes in our direction.

I felt my blood boil. I couldn't just stand by while someone took advantage of a disaster like this. I marched up to him and forcefully placed my hands on the front of his cart, stopping him in his tracks. "Take it back," I said, my voice firm. "This is a tragedy. You can't use this to steal." He looked at me, and I saw guilt flash in his eyes. He released the cart with an angry grunt and stormed off. He looked homeless himself, but it didn't matter. What he was doing was wrong.

In that moment, I realized that I wasn't much better than him. I had my own sins, my own flaws, and who was I to judge? But that didn't make his actions right.

We left the boulevard and made our way back to our apartment to gather what we could. The building was too unsafe to stay in, and I knew we had to get out. Mildred mentioned that her aunt lived in Pasadena, a county over, and that we could call her to see if we could stay with her for a while.

We found a payphone, and Mildred called her aunt. Amazingly, her aunt answered. After a brief conversation, Mildred turned to me with relief in her eyes. "We can go. We can stay with her until we figure things out."

I was relieved but still in shock. The world had changed in a matter of hours, and we had no idea what to do next. But one thing was certain: life as we knew it would never be the same.

As I stood there, looking at the devastation around us, I knew that this earthquake wasn't just a natural disaster—it was a wake-up call.

And the road ahead would be full of more unexpected twists, but somehow, we would find our way through it. Our building, on the other hand, was not as fortunate. It had been red-tagged, meaning no one could occupy it. The damage from the earthquake was just too severe. The building would need to be demolished and rebuilt. At that point, the only thing on my mind was making sure that John, Eddie, and Darell were alright. Once I knew they were safe, we piled into the car and drove up to stay with Mildred's aunt and uncle. They lived in the hills of Pasadena, and I had no idea what to expect.

We drove up the winding roads, and when we reached their house, I was taken aback by how charming it was. It was upscale, even by LA standards, and I could immediately tell that Mildred's relatives had done well for themselves. The first thing I noticed was a brand new 1990's Honda NSX parked in the driveway. I couldn't help myself and turned to Mildred. "What does this guy do for a living?" I asked, my curiosity piqued.

"He's a songwriter and owns a blues label," she replied, almost casually, but I was intrigued, and even a little miffed, why wouldn't she have shared that info knowing I was trying to break into songwriting and the music business. Doubt and insecurity started to seep into me thinking she must not like my music.

We walked up to the door and were greeted by Dennis and Lucy. Mildred's aunt was in her fifties, with a bob haircut, and her husband, Dennis, was a slim man with glasses, and short curly graying hair. They invited us in, and after a quick introduction, they asked about our experience during the earthquake. We shared the harrowing time, and then they gave us a tour of the house.

The house was a seventies-era, two thousand square-foot single-story home, very nice and comfortable. The backyard had a fantastic view of the Pasadena area, with a beautiful swimming pool that made the whole place feel like a retreat. I asked them how they had fared in the earthquake, and to my disbelief, they said there was only a little shaking, but no real damage. I couldn't believe it—Pasadena wasn't far from Burbank, and the quake didn't even loosen a shingle. But we were pleased to hear they faired well.

As we wandered through the house, I could sense an underlying tension between Lucy and Dennis. Mildred informed me that they had no children and that Dennis would spend weeks away on music production jobs. I could tell that this had left a void in their lives. I had spoken to many clients in my years as a barber, and countless people, if they had the chance to go back in time, would have made the choice to have children. It was clear to me that their lives lacked a sense of purpose. And I couldn't help but think that kids were a part of God's design—a design that had somehow eluded them.

In the living room, Lucy showed us a painting she had done. She explained that she had gone to art school, but what I saw on that canvas left me speechless. It was a drawing of tiny razor blades and tiny male genitalia, repeated in strange patterns. It was disturbing, to say the least, and as I looked closer, I could sense something dark and sinister in the way it was painted. Later, Mildred confided that her aunt had suffered severe sexual abuse as a child. Seeing her artwork, it was obvious she was still holding onto the pain.

At the back of the house, there was Dennis's studio. Over the course of a month we stayed there, I watched as artists like Robert Cray and Edgar Winter came in and out for meetings. Dennis was definitely a heavy hitter in the blues world. And I couldn't help but feel a sense of awe. The blues had been my first love, musically speaking. I had picked up the harmonica at the age of six, and from there, my love for the genre grew. Muddy Waters, Robert Johnson, John Lee Hooker, T-Bone Walker—these were the artists who shaped my early years of music. The history of the blues ran deep, and here I was, surrounded by it.

I knew I was witnessing something significant, even if I couldn't fully grasp it at the time. I believe that sometimes, demons or the Devil place certain people and experiences in our paths to keep us focused on the darkness, not the light. I know Dennis has passed away now, and I pray he found the Lord before he left this world. The blues industry, with its roots in darkness, is full of stories of deals made at the crossroads—stories of selling one's soul for fame and success. It's an unsettling reality, and it's something that has haunted me throughout my life.

One significant memory stands out from that time: this is when Dan Aykroyd asked Dennis if he wanted to partner with him in a new venture called the House of Blues. Dennis declined the offer. Dennis was a bit of a recluse, a true introvert at heart, so I understood why he would shy away from something so public. It was just the kind of attention he didn't want.

And even though Dennis didn't take the deal with Aykroyd, to partner up, Mildred was able to work at the House Of Blues as a waitress because of her uncle's connection. This is when things between us began to hit rough waters. The strain of our different lifestyles, coupled with the weight of our sin and lack of faith, was taking its toll. I'd be out late playing gigs, thinking I was living the dream, but deep down, I knew something was missing. I had been raised without Jesus, and I felt the absence in every part of my life.

But at that point, I still didn't know where to turn or how to fix it.

Chapter Forty-Three

A House Without Light

John Calvin

"The duty of parents is to bring up their children in the knowledge and fear of God."

There was a time I went to Mildred's house in Colorado to meet her family, and the first thing that hit me when I stepped inside her father and step mothers home was the sight of a Playboy magazine on the living room table and another one in the bathroom. It made sense, in a twisted way, why Mildred was dancing for money at the strip club. When a daughter sees that this is what her father considers acceptable or attractive, it's no surprise she might follow suit.

That night, when I met her father, I was disgusted. The magazines spoke volumes, and I immediately lost all respect for him. I judged him harshly, not considering the fact that maybe he didn't know who Christ was. I didn't know at that time either, but my judgment was clouded by bitterness.

Mildred and I stayed together for about three more months after that trip. What ended it was my own failure. I had contact with Danielle on a couple of occasions. And though there was no actual intimate contact there was a sense of trust that was broke. How it all unfolded was one evening, while Mildred and I were at our apartment, the phone rang, she picked up the phone and put it to her ear, and stared at me. She wasn't saying anything, just listening to the other end and staring at me with a dead, blank look. I knew something was wrong. I didn't know how I knew, but I knew. After a few minutes, she coldly told the caller never to call again and then hung up. Her eyes didn't soften. They were like ice as she said, "I'm moving out."

"Who was that?" I asked, even though I knew the lie was already starting to slip out.

"It was your ex, Danielle," she said, her voice calm but firm. "She said you had been meeting with her."

Now, I don't know if anyone reading this has ever been caught in this situation, but there's a specific kind of cornered hopelessness that you feel when the truth is right there, staring you in the face. You try to deny it, but there's no way to escape the reality of your actions. I told her yes, but nothing happened, and my words rang hollow. She was not accepting my side of the situation.

That's when Mildred hit me. She grabbed the phone and swung it at my head. After that, she tried to hit me with her fists. It was wild, and it hurt—not physically, but emotionally. As if I wasn't already drowning in guilt, the moment's chaos made everything worse. Just days before this fight, O.J. Simpson was all over the world's televisions, driving his white Bronco down the freeway, being chased by the

LAPD on suspicion of having brutally murdered his wife with a long Bowie knife.

It was surreal, and it somehow became part of my tragic moment. After Mildred struck me she stormed into the back bedroom. I walked out back to the laundry room to retrieve some clothes. This is when she irrationally called the police. I had a good five minute smoke out back and when I came back inside the police were at the front door knocking. When they brought me outside, they asked me what had happened, and I told them the truth. I admitted that I hadn't been perfect, but Mildred had assaulted me in her anger. I even told them why. As much shame as I felt, I didn't want to end up in jail for something I didn't do.

The police officer, to my relief, smiled as he listened. He said they had been getting flooded with calls from women ever since the O.J. incident, with accusations of domestic abuse pouring in from all directions. According to him, the bulk of those calls were false. And then he casually said, "Like this one."

I can't even describe how relieved I felt hearing that. I know that abuse is a real and a terrible thing, but in that moment, I had been falsely accused, and for once, the system worked in my favor. I would never, could never, strike a woman—no matter how much I messed up in life. But I understood why Mildred had acted out. She, too, was trapped in sin, just as I was.

When a couple lacks Christ in their relationship, when their home is void of His light, it's like opening the door for darkness to rush in. The devil and unclean spirits love to play their games with those who aren't grounded in faith. And that's exactly what had happened to us. We were like puppets, manipulated by unseen forces.

Mildred moved back in with her aunt and uncle after that. I stayed in the apartment, drowning in shame and regret. It was during this time that I hit an all-time low. I drank myself into oblivion. I called John, my band mate, and he came over and stayed with me for a day or two. I'll never forget his kindness. He looked out for me when I couldn't even look out for myself.

It was a terrible time in my life—utter chaos, emotional destruction, and darkness at every turn. I felt completely out of control as if the unclean spirits were celebrating my misery. That night, a demon of pity seemed to enter my life. I woke up the next morning, my mind foggy from the alcohol. But most of all, I felt empty. I had no idea how to climb out of the pit I was in. It felt like I was being buried alive, and the worst part was—I had no idea how to change.

I couldn't even see how far I had fallen, but I knew I needed something—someone—to save me.

Chapter Forty-Four

Bougie To Snooty

A.W. Tozer

"The man who is proud of his social status or his intellect has no sense of his need of God."

With everything that had happened in my life, I needed a change of pace. My soul was exhausted, and I thought that if I could just change something—anything—about my routine, it might help me feel better about myself and about where I was heading. Piero's was OK, but the drive from Hollywood to Santa Monica was eating up a big part of my day. And after a couple months there, it just felt too pretentious for my taste. I couldn't put my finger on it, but I just didn't feel comfortable there. I needed something different—something that felt real. So, I decided to drive out to the valley to a salon that had been recommended to me by a client who came into Piero's once. The place was called Alan Edwards, and I didn't know it then, but it had a little bit of Hollywood history behind it. There was a film from the 1970's and it was actually inspired by the real life experiences of the owner Alan Edwards.

Here I was, complaining that Piero's was too uptight and pretentious—then I quit and started working at an even more bougie place. But I wanted change so I was making it happen. I put on some trendy clothes to fit in and headed to Edwards to apply. I smooshed my way in and started working there as Alan's assistant, and for about four months, I did my best to fit in. My job was simple enough—shampoo the clients, stand still while Alan cut their hair, and if he dropped a comb, I had another one in his hand within seconds. It was a fast-paced place, but it wasn't the kind of pace I wanted to keep. The clients, to put it mildly, were just as pretentious as Pieros, and so were most of the stylists. I tried to stick it out because I knew that any experience would be valuable, but it wasn't long before I couldn't take it anymore. It wasn't my style. I didn't belong in a world where everyone cared more about their status than their skills.

The roster of clients were the kind of people you'd expect in a salon like that—Motley Crue, the cast of *Friends*, even Tina Louise from *Gilligan's Island*, and Marcia Clark, the prosecuting attorney in the O.J. Simpson trial. There were a lot of celebrity stories that came with those names. Tina Louise, for instance, seemed like she was still processing the years of fame. Vince Neil, the lead singer of Motley Crue, was going through the unimaginable grief of losing his child, and Marcia Clark, well... she was the most self-absorbed out of the bunch.

The OJ trial was under way while I worked there, and news stations camped outside the salon—especially *Hard Copy*, always hanging around because my boss Alan Edward's was changing Marcia Clark's hair weekly. It was all over the news, and it felt like the world was watching us, but I didn't want to be a part of that world.

And funny enough, when I looked in the mirror, it dawned on me that I needed a haircut myself, but I didn't want to get it done at Alan Edwards. Something in me rebelled against the idea of giving any more of myself to that world. So I went back to that barbershop Rocky's. The guy who cut my hair for my limo driver interview. From what I remember, it was a serious hole in the wall, but it had a fantastic location—just a couple hundred yards from Universal Studios. And just like Alan Edwards, it had its share of actors, directors, writers, dancers, producers, and musicians getting their haircuts there. only It wasn't pretentious.

It was the same big gay guy who greeted me before. He remembered me. I asked for another haircut cut so he cut my hair. That's when I asked him if there was a spot open for another cutter. It was a shot in the dark, but I was desperate for a change of scenery. He said, "Well, this isn't that fancy, honey," chuckling at the contrast to the place I had just come from. I laughed too, and told him I liked the vibe of the shop. No pretension, just great clients who appreciated a good haircut.

Rocky asked me to cut his hair to see how I did, so I grabbed my scissors and got to work. It felt good to just be a barber again, not the assistant to someone who was more concerned with their ego than the craft. Rocky was pleased with the cut, and that meant everything to me. He asked if I could come in on Monday, and I was excited to tell him yes. He said, "9 am, and I'll see you here."

And that was it. I had a new job lined up. A fresh start. It wasn't glamorous, but it was real, and it felt like it was where I needed to be. Rocky's was everything I needed at that moment: no frills, no judgment, just a place where I could be myself, do what I loved, and hopefully start piecing my life back together, one haircut at a time.

Chapter Forty-Five

Beneath The Hollywood Sign

Augustine of Hippo

"If you live according to man, you will perish with man. If you live according to God, you will live with God."

This was the point where I made my move. I found a place in the Hollywood Hills, a location I'd always dreamed of. It wasn't the swanky mansion you'd imagine when thinking of Hollywood Hills, but it was affordable, and more importantly, it had the feeling I was craving. It was a room for rent, but it wasn't just any room—it was right directly below the Hollywood sign, deep enough in the hills to give you that sense of being far away from the city, yet close enough to feel like you were living in the heart of it all. That kind of balance was exactly what I was looking for.

I took the plunge and rented the room. The place was month-to-month, so no contract tying me down, and I loved that flexibility. If I didn't like it, or if the roommates were unbearable, I could just leave. Likewise, if they didn't like me, they could kick me out. It was a win-win situation for everyone. The other two roommates were interesting in their own ways. One was a young, pretty girl, about nineteen or twenty, and the other was Yogi, a young guitarist with dreams of making it big in the music biz. I had no idea at the time, but years later, Yogi would go on to record and tour with some major names—The Wallflowers, Fuel, Chris Cornell, Cat Stevens, Melissa Etheridge, Alanis Morissette, and many more.

I lived in that house for about five months, balancing shows with my band and honing my skills as a musician and stylist. As much as I was soaking in the city of angels, I couldn't ignore the darker, more sinister side that seemed to lurk just below the surface. Every place in LA seemed to have that shadow—a demonic presence that hung around, as if it were a necessary part of the scenery. This house didn't have cockroaches, thankfully, but it certainly had demons.

I spent a fair amount of time hanging out with Yogi, and one night he invited me to a friend's house in downtown LA. His friend, Alex, was a bit of a character. He made low-budget horror films but had gotten his start as a child prodigy, designing horror masks and molds. We showed up at his downtown loft a little after 8. We'd smoked a little weed before we got there, so I was already feeling a bit high. Alex's place was in an old warehouse building, and his door—it must have been 12x6—looked like something out of a The Lord Of The Rings. It was massive, like it had been designed for a giant or a Nephilim. It looked... mid evil.

When we reached Alex's door, Yogi told me to put on a blindfold. I was immediately uneasy, but I trusted Yogi, so I complied. After a few knocks, I heard the door unlock and creak open. Yogi guided me inside, and after just a few steps, he stopped me. Then he spun me around, and I could feel my heart rate picking up. I could hear him and Alex trying to stifle their laughter, but I wasn't in the mood for games. I was getting nervous.

Without warning, Yogi pulled the blindfold off, and to my horror, what I saw stopped me dead in my tracks. The corner of the entryway was filled with life-sized replicas of almost every horror character I'd ever seen in my life. These weren't cheap imitations—they were the real deal. Freddy Krueger, Robocop, an alien from *Aliens*, even Stripe from *Gremlins* with his menacing Mohawk, and many more. These characters—these nightmares from my childhood—stood right in front of me, towering and staring with their frozen eyes. I think I actually screamed. Yogi and Alex were in hysterics, laughing at my reaction. This was their initiation for newcomers, I later found out.

I'd spent much of my childhood watching horror films, so standing there in front of these life-size versions of the creatures that had haunted my nightmares was surreal. Once I got past the initial shock and regained my composure, we walked through Alex's loft. The place had an air about it—something dark and worldly, almost satanic. The whole atmosphere felt heavy like the walls themselves were closing in.

Through our conversation that night, I learned that Alex came from a family of privilege. His success—whether in his art or any other area—was always going to be cushioned by his trust fund. It made sense why he could spend his time surrounded by these creepy creations, living a life that seemed detached from the struggles I faced. For someone like him, there was always a safety net. Still, as much as I was fascinated by the masks and molds in his loft, I couldn't wait to leave. The air was too heavy with something I couldn't quite place, but it wasn't good.

Yogi, on the other hand, was determined to build his network. He was focused on his musical journey, constantly looking for ways to connect with artists in the industry. I remember him introducing me to Anthony Michael Hall, of all people. Anthony's breakout roll in acting was playing Rusty Griswold in National Lampoons Vacation. But Anthony wasn't hanging out with Yogi because of an acting gig he was playing harmonica and singing with Yogi. I ended up staying in that house for about four more months, but eventually I had to leave. I could feel the need for a change again—a shift away from that world and the people who occupied it. I wanted to move closer to the members in my band, so that's what I did.

Chapter Forty-Six

A Broken Band

John Calvin

"The surest source of destruction to men is to obey themselves."

I made the decision to move to the valley. Hollywood had its perks, especially in my industry, but the valley was just a few miles away and much cheaper, and the boys in the band were right there. It had a charm of its own, and I found a nice place off Coldwater Canyon that gave me peace and space. And no roommates! It felt like a fresh start in some ways, but my celebration was short-lived.

Somehow, the boys in the band lost their place and asked if they could crash at mine for a while. It wasn't exactly a peaceful existence, but I agreed. The situation didn't last long. Darell, having been on edge for a while, suffered a psychotic break, and he packed up and left for the state of Washington to see his biological father, who lived in a commune. Things were getting stranger. This is when John made the suggestion that we fly up to Washington to find Darell. So off we went. And we found him, at that very commune with all of his half sisters and brothers, cousins and people just living there. It was a very hippie vibe. John had told us Darell's dad was violent and unstable, so we proceeded with caution and went in stealth mode, and got out of there quickly. When we got back, all of us were pretty beat up, but that couldn't stop the music—as they say the show must go on. we played a couple of gigs and a few coffee shops right when we got back from Washington. One time, I remembered, we were on Vetura BLVD playing a small coffee shop when two members of the grunge band Alice and Chains were having coffee and listening to us. When we finished, they approached Darell, explaining who they were. It was a small place, so I overheard the conversation. I was stunned when they asked Darell if he wouldn't mind recording some acoustic guitar tracks on their next project. This is when I new Darell was not all there. He said flat out he couldn't do it. He gave the men no explanation. It was just a stern no. They looked perplexed. And the craziest part was Alice in Chains was probably one of Darell's favorite bands at the time. This gives you some insight to how difficult it was playing with the guy. We were always astounded by his gift, but on the flip side would have to deal with mood and erratic temper changes. This is the time where his mental state was at a point where he just couldn't handle normal every day to day tasks and he parted ways with us. Fortunately, Darell had a close friend that was also an immense talent on guitar. His name was Jerry, and he showed up to join us. We jumped right back into it, playing shows, opening for acts like The Mighty Mighty Bosstones and bands in that vein. That year, the band Sublime's lead singer passed away from a heroin overdose, and their record company, Red Ant, was on the lookout for a band to fill that gap. They came out to see us rehearse one evening. It was our big break, and we were all pretty psyched to have this exposure. Something unfortunate happened during that session with Red Ant. I can't remember exactly what happened but I remember John got really angry, and things got physical, and the record company walked out before we even had a chance to show them what we had.

In hindsight, I genuinely believe it was a blessing in disguise. Had they signed us and we gained traction, I don't think I would have handled it well. My ego was fragile, and the fame and success might have only fed the demonic grip I was already under. My spiral would have been quick, and who knows where I would've ended up. God had bigger plans for me. But at that moment, all I could think about was the missed opportunity.

A few weeks later, Jerry's older brother, Zack, came to stay with us. Jerry had told me Zack would only be there for a week, but that wasn't the case. Zack was a full-blown drug addict and a criminal. I didn't know what I was getting into when I agreed to let him stay. One night, we had a small show at a bar in the valley. It was a two-room establishment—one room for drinks and the other with a stage for performances. We were busy setting up our instruments when things started to go south.

Apparently, the bouncers asked Zack to show ID, and when he handed them a driver's license that had gone through the wash, rendering it unreadable, they refused to let him in. Zack snapped. From what I heard, he completely lost control. The bouncers were practically cowering in the corner as Zack picked up a large barstool chair and threw it over the bar, shattering whiskey and wine bottles everywhere. The crash of glass filled the air, and by the time we came out to see what was going on, Zack was already gone. He stormed out, leaving chaos in his wake. The police were called, but we were all instructed to deny knowing him. We did not want to see him go to jail. At that point, though, it was becoming harder to ignore the type of person Zack was.

The band had been living with me for over three weeks, and I was starting to see the cracks. I learned from one of the bandmates that Zack was no stranger to criminal activity. He'd been involved in armed robberies—robbing liquor stores, 7-Elevens, and smaller places with cash on hand. In fact, I discovered stolen bikes—Mountain bikes, 10-speeds—piled up outside our apartment complex. It was getting out of control.

Eventually, I had no choice but to ask Zack to leave. I tried to be polite about it, but he wasn't having it. He told me he'd think about it, but I could tell his mind was made up. Things were quickly spiraling, and none of us were feeling safe anymore.

Later that same day, something unexpected happened. Darell showed up out of the blue. None of us had heard from him since he left, so we were all curious about where he had been. His return was mysterious, and we wondered what kind of shape he was in. The tension in the apartment grew thicker as we tried to figure out what had led to his sudden reappearance. Darell wouldn't tell us where he'd been or what had happened to him during his absence. He asked if he could stay with us for a while until he found a place. The apartment was crowded already, but I couldn't turn him away. It felt wrong to do that, so I told him he could sleep on the rug in the living room until things settled down.

A week went by, and Zack became more and more unpredictable. He had this new habit of flashing his gun around—one I assumed he either stole or bought illegally from someone. He'd talk about the money he was making from his latest crime spree, bragging like it was some kind of accomplishment. It wasn't long before things started to escalate, and the tension in the apartment became unbearable.

The next day, Darell came into my room, pale and wide-eyed, shaking. He'd woken up from a deep sleep to find the barrel of Zack's .45 just inches from his face. He told me that Zack did just for laughs. My stomach dropped. I had enough. I understood that Zack was Jerry's brother, but that didn't matter anymore. This wasn't some family drama. This was a dangerous man who could kill someone without a second thought. Everyone in the house was on edge, constantly fearing for their lives.

I couldn't take it anymore. I made plans to call the police the next day after work. I had to get Zack either arrested or evicted. But I'll admit, I was scared. If the police couldn't find grounds to arrest him, he'd still be there, and worse—he'd know I had called the Police. The consequences of that could be dangerous for all of us. As I drove home, I played over and over in my mind what I would say to the officers, how I would explain everything. When I pulled up to the apartment, just about all of the parking spaces were taken.

When I finally found a spot my heart skipped a beat. There weren't just three police cruisers parked in front of the building—there was also a firetruck and a large-looking vehicle I hadn't recognized, but it definitely looked like a city or state vehicle. A wave of dread washed over me as I walked up the walkway and saw a commotion by the side of the building. I rushed toward it, my mind racing, thinking Zack had hurt or even killed someone.

As I got closer, two large men were pushing a gurney out of my door. My pulse pounded in my ears as I saw what was on the gurney—someone zipped up in a black body bag. My stomach turned, and fear overwhelmed me. Who was it? Who had died? I didn't stop to talk to the men pushing the gurney; I just had to know. Inside, the bandmates were there, gathered together in the living room. They told me Zack had overdosed—he'd done a speedball, mixing heroin and cocaine. The news hit me like a punch to the gut. They told me what had happened, but I could barely process it. Zack had always been reckless, but this was too final, too real.

I had a strange feeling of guilt. I still wasn't a believer, but somehow, I felt responsible. I had been planning to call the police that night. I had been pushing for Zack to be evicted. The anger I had towards him, the hatred I'd built up, felt like it might've somehow contributed to his death. It was irrational, but it gnawed at me. I know now that this isn't true, but in that moment, it felt real.

I've come to realize, though, that God gives us all chances to redeem ourselves. Zack had his chances, but he chose recklessness. His choices, his free will, led him down a path that ultimately destroyed him. Whether Zack went to hell or went to be with the Lord, I can't say. But I pray for his soul, hoping that somehow, somewhere, he found redemption. After everything had settled, I couldn't stay there any longer. I moved out, leaving the bandmates in the apartment. It was just too much for me to handle. I needed to get away from the mess, from the darkness that seemed to be surrounding me. So, I found a new place just a few hundred yards up the street. It wasn't much, but it was mine. And for the first time in a while, I felt like I could breathe again.

Chapter Forty-Seven

Strings Of Fate

A.W. Tozer

"God never uses anyone greatly until He tests them deeply. Every great opportunity will come with a challenge."

By the time we'd gotten a solid foothold in the local music scene, things were beginning to look up. Our band was playing some pretty decent venues, and somehow, we managed to land ourselves a manager. Her name was Sasha. Our new manager was a very attractive blonde girl from New Orleans. There goes that New Orleans thing again. She had a natural instinct for the music business, something she inherited from her mother, who had managed iconic acts like The Meters and The Neville Brothers. She immediately liked our music and took us under her wing, guiding us with a firm but caring hand.

Soon after connecting Sasha helped us get into a decent music studio, where we recorded a five-song CD. That CD was our ticket to bigger venues—places like the Whisky, Roxy, Troubadour, and even the Viper Room. For a while, it seemed like everything was falling into place. But one night at a street fair, something happened that would lead me further down a dark path.

I remember walking past a booth where a fortune teller—a clairvoyant—was reading tarot cards. I was intrigued. The curiosity inside, pushed me to sit down and see what he had to say. Maybe it was a bad idea, it was definitely a bad idea, but I was drawn to it. He started by reading my palm, he traced his index finger down the lines of the center of my hand, explaining what each line represented. He indicated that I would only have 2 women in my lifetime that I would truly love and that I would become very ill later in life. I'm in my fifties, and I can contest to both predictions as being accurate. He then laid out his tarot cards.

I'm not sure why, but the way he spoke felt off, like there was something more to it than simple fortune telling. He then told me our band would have a big show coming up—one that would be a turning point—but that drugs would tear the band apart.

The part that stuck with me, though, was when he said that later in life, I would face a serious medical issue. He said it wouldn't kill me, but it would slow me down, leaving me weakened for a period. In the back of my mind, I thought to myself, "That sounds like something out of a bad horror movie," but at the same time, I couldn't shake the feeling that something had changed inside me after the reading. I couldn't explain it, but I felt like another unclean spirit had latched onto me in that moment, pulling me into a deeper darkness. I'm not saying this guy new the future but that dark meeting was more than accurate.

After the incident with Zack, things began to unravel for the band. Our drummer Eddie was the first to come to me. He said he wasn't feeling it anymore and wanted to head back to Northern California. "You know," he said, "the straw broke the camel's back, and Zack was the straw." After Eddie left, the bass player John joined a hip-hop group, and soon after, Darell and Jerry headed north as well. It was clear that the band was falling apart.

I was left feeling defeated, with no band and no direction. But Sasha stayed by my side. She told me she could find some new players to form a new group, so we put out ads in the classifieds and started the search. Within a month, we had a new lineup: a drummer, guitarist, and bass player—each of them a pro. These guys were no joke. We had a couple of practices, and they learned our songs in one sitting. It was incredible.

Let me tell you a little about the new guys. There was Shane, the guitarist. He was a session player for film and television and was even listed in the *Monsters of Rock Hall of Fame*. Frank, the drummer, was no slouch either—he'd played in the industry, notably with Dean Parks from Steely Dan. And then there was Steve, our bassist. Steve was a touring and recording musician who had played with everyone. He'd been in the band Squeeze, toured with Jeff Healey, Boz Scaggs, Quit Riot, and recorded albums with Alan Holdsworth and Stewart Copeland. Honestly, I was by far the weakest musician in the band, but I was just happy to be playing with these pros.

We started gigging around town, and soon enough, clubs were calling us back to open for some bigger acts. I'll never forget one particular song that became a fan favorite. We played "I'm a Believer" by The Monkees at every show, and for some reason, people went wild for it. It became our signature tune, and even the band Smash Mouth—who we opened for one night—loved our version of it.

A year later, Smash Mouth released their own version of "I'm a Believer," and it became their number-one hit for a solid year. Now,

I can't say for sure that they copied us, but I'll always assume they did. It felt like a vindication of sorts, like maybe we had something special, even if the world didn't recognize it just yet.

But with all the attention came the usual distractions—drugs, alcohol, and women. The band was getting offers, and one of the big ones came from Madonna's label. They liked our sound, but there was a catch—they wanted us to replace Steve, our bassist, because of his age. He was only around ten years older than the rest of us, and they didn't think he fit the image. I couldn't believe it. I turned them down. To me, it wasn't about age—it was about ability. Steve was an incredible musician, and that was all that mattered. To them, though, it wasn't enough. We returned to the studio to record a new demo as the songs sounded much different with pro players. We recorded at another decent studio. This studio was owned and run by a man named Andy. Andy gained fame when he became Jimi Hendrix's guitar tech in the sixties and seventies. He later modified guitars for just about everyone in the business. But his bread and butter was the carting industry, Andy loaned amps and music equipment to artists that needed gear for live and recording events. Andy had a great little recording studio at his warehouse. The producer who recorded us at Andy's studio was one of Sasha's friends a guy named Micajah Ryan. Micajah was an exceptionally gifted audio engineer. He worked on albums for artists such as Guns N Roses "Appetite For Destruction", Bob Dylan, Commodores, Megadeath, and many more. To pay for the recording time at Andy's studio, Andy's fee was an 8-ball of cocaine. And because I was the only musician dabbling in that realm, I was commissioned to get it for him. I can't remember how I connected with this dealer, but let's call him Tony, as I do not want to use his real name for many reasons. We met outside of the Roxy theater. He had two massive Rottweilers with spiked collars standing at both hips. He was an incredibly intense-looking Colombian with a gigantic, what looked like a knife scar running down his face. He was scary. I was amazed when he said he had heard my band and liked our music. I was slightly comforted, but not much. He basically bragged and said he was the boss in LA for the cocaine seen. I did not know what to say. We made the exchange, and we were both on our way. It was almost impossible to not sample some of this stuff before I gave it to Andy, so I did. Andy was pleased when I handed it to him, and we were given the green light and a block time in the studio. It was off hours, and we knocked out five songs in around eight hours. It was a masterclass watching Macajah record and mix. And let me preface this, Macajah was not involved in any drug transactions he was a Christian, which I did not know at the time. But all of Slash's recorded guitar tones and solos were thanks to Macajah. He took our guitarist Shane's solos and used the same technique. When it was completed, we had Dave Collins, the lead masterer at A&M Records, master our final product. It was a decent-sounding demo, so we started getting it out to all of the clubs to get more gigs. Sasha told me that her mother's group, the Neville brothers, were coming to Hollywood to play at the Greek theater with BB King and Earth Wind and Fire. She said she gave one of our demos to her mom, who then gave it to the Neville Brothers, and they wanted to meet the band. That was a big moment for us, to possibly tour with a well-known group. We all went to the show that weekend and hung out backstage with the acts. Art and Aaron Neville were extremely friendly men. BB King was also a nice guy. It was Sitting off stage and watching BB up close and personal that I won't forget.

Chapter Forty-Eight

A Broken Wing

Charles Spurgeon

"You are never so broken that God cannot heal you, never so lost that He cannot find you, and never so hurt that He cannot comfort you."

Around this time, I started dating a lovely woman named Carmelita. She worked as a bartender at a Little bar just two buildings down from Rocky's. The bar was called Residuals, a name that held a certain charm. It had a unique history, mainly because it was a popular spot for actors, directors, producers, and other locals in the entertainment industry. They would come in, bringing with them residual checks from their acting gigs. But here was the catch: the checks had to be for ridiculously low amounts—sometimes as little as fifty cents. The owner would tack the checks to the wall for everyone to laugh at. It was a quirk of the Hollywood scene that made the place feel like a little underground gem. In fact they had the Seinfeld wrap party at the bar.

Out of all the women I had dated, Carmelita stood out. She was genuinely the kindest person I had ever met. She was a beautiful mix of Mexican and Irish heritage. Her mother, who lived in the valley, came from the Irish side of the family, while her father was Mexican. Carmelita's family history was heavy, especially when it came to her father.

Her dad had been incarcerated with a twenty-year prison sentence for killing a man in the 1970s. He had been living in Oakland at the time of the incident, just walking down the street with a friend when the two had a violent altercation with five white men. It was a terrifying situation, and out of sheer desperation and self-defense, they fought back. In the chaos, Carmelita's father ended up killing one of the attackers.

This happened during a time when racism ran rampant, and though we may feel it doesn't play a huge role today, back then, it was an entirely different world. The courts were not forgiving, especially when it came to minorities, and Carmelita's father was sentenced to prison for defending himself. He was just twenty years old at the time, facing a sentence that would change the entire course of his life.

Carmelita never spoke ill of her father, despite his troubled past. Instead, she painted a picture of him as someone trying to survive in a system that seemed determined to break him. And in her eyes, he wasn't just a man who had made a mistake—he was a symbol of the oppression her family had endured for generations.

It was hard not to feel sympathy for her father's story. But Carmelita's life wasn't just shaped by her father's past. Her mother, too, played a significant role in the person Carmelita became.

Her mother had been a professional dancer in her youth. In fact, she was one of the five dancers who had toured with Elvis Presley throughout his career. Carmelita often spoke of her mother's stories, claiming that Elvis had once been allegedly in love with her, and even had proof in the form of old letters and mementos. It all seemed like something straight out of a Hollywood film, yet there was an undeniable truth in Carmelita's eyes when she told these stories.

But beneath the glittering tales of fame and success, there was something darker in Carmelita's family dynamic. Her mother, as strange as it sounds, had the vibe of someone who was involved in occultic practices. Carmelita's mother's home was filled with dark energy—her mother had cats, herbs, pagan art and pagen jewelry, oh, and an entire wall adorned with photographs of herself. She wore nothing but black, and the air in her house felt heavy, like something was always watching you. It was the kind of house where you'd feel a chill even if the heat was on.

And then to make things even more contorted there was her mother's boyfriend, Bryan—Carmelita's high school classmate and best friend. Yes, her mother's boyfriend was Carmelita's best friend from her high school days. He was about twenty years younger than her mother, and there was something just off about him. I wasn't familiar with Bryan's past but I assumed with his strange behavior it was rocky.

Carmelita had been through a lot in her life, much of which I didn't know at the time. When she was just fourteen, she had been kidnapped at gunpoint by her mother's abusive boyfriend—note, not Bryan. This boyfriend, a big six foot something man, put her in the trunk of his beat up old car and drove her from Los Angeles to Lake Tahoe, where he savagely sexually abused her. Young Carmelita spent nine hours, in her nightgown, in that trunk. He was eventually caught, but not before wreaking Physical and emotional damage on Carmelita.

The man was sentenced to sixty years in prison, but his prison time was not going to heal the scars he had inflicted.

Afterward, life didn't get any easier for Carmelita. Her mother remained entangled with troubled men, and the chaos only escalated. When you think things couldn't get any crazier, the story about how Bryan won Carmelita's mom's affection is beyond anything rational. Carmelita's mom was in another abusive relationship, and Bryan, having feelings for Carmelita's mom decided he would protect her by getting rid of this new boyfriend. Bryan confronted the new boyfriend head-on. In a moment of raw tension, Bryan ambushed him, shooting him in the back of the head in an effort to defend Carmelita's mother from the man being potentially violent towards her. Miraculously, the man survived, the bullet grazing the unsavory boyfriend's head. Bryan's actions led to a strange bond between him and Carmelita's mother.

I couldn't fathom the twisted web Carmelita had grown up in. But I couldn't deny the powerful hold these dark energies had on her. It was as though she had been born into a family where chaos was normal, and violence was just another part of the landscape. I had never experienced anything like it before.

One day, out of the blue, Bryan showed up at my work, uninvited. He started accusing me of not treating Carmelita right. And I probably should not have egged him on by jokingly begging him not to shoot me in the back of the head. Because let's face it this was possible with this guy. The confrontation quickly escalated into a fistfight. I had no idea why he was so upset, but I had the distinct feeling it was about Carmelita. And let me state I did not throw the first blow, this guy just came at me, I was only defending myself. I honestly did not want to hurt the disturbed man so I mainly fended off his punches while trying to DE-escalate the situation. Maybe he held some deep seated affection for Carmelita and thought I was taking her away from him. Maybe he was just jealous. Whatever the reason, it felt like he was trying to force some kind of twisted power dynamic between us. Fortunately, the fight didn't go too far, and no one was seriously hurt. But the encounter left me confused.

I couldn't help but wonder: What kind of person would act like that? What kind of energy would drive someone to such extremes? I began to realize that when you're dealing with these kinds of unclean spirits, anything—absolutely anything—was possible. And nothing seemed too strange, too horrifying, or too unbelievable. Carmelita's life was a constant swirl of chaos, and I had become a part of that.

Things were getting darker by the day. I wasn't sure how long I could keep my head above water in the midst of all the madness. But Carmelita was in it, and I couldn't just walk away. Not yet.

Chapter Forty-Nine

A Black Crow And The Last Show

Charles Spurgeon

"All the pleasures of this world will fade away, and nothing can satisfy the soul except the love of Christ."

So, the partying was in full gear; I was drinking, smoking weed, and more. And the thing was, I thought my behavior was totally normal. I mean, here I am, a musician, a wannabe rock star. This was expected, right? No one was calling me out on my behavior. I mean, my girlfriend was an addict, and she seemed perfectly OK with my behavior. And she joined me on most of my outings. My band mates did not say anything but were disappointed in my behavior. I think Steve, the bass player, actually gave me a tongue-lashing, but the other guys were quiet about it. And right about this time, Sasha informed us that we had a surprise show coming up. She told us we'd be opening up for the Black Crows and Oingo Boingo. And that's not what the big part was; the surprise was that we were going to be playing with these headlining acts in none other than the Roxy Theatre, mind you, on New Year's Eve. The Troubadour, the Whiskey, and the Roxy were the three most prominent clubs in Los Angeles on New Year's Eve. Not just any group got this gig. We were all jazzed. I know the band mates were worried if I'd be fit for the show. The owner of the Roxy, Mario, liked my band. I'm not sure why, but He just did. A couple days before the show, Mario hosted a party for my group in the Rainbow Room. We had a whole section for us. It was pretty wild. the Rainbow Room was having our party. That's when I noticed a strange little man in the other section of the room, an old guy with a glass eye. It was non other than Jack from Telecast. He was just staring at me. I had long hair past my shoulders, but he knew it was me. He held his drink up and smiled at me to cheer me from across the room. I held my beer up and smiled back. He finished his drink, and I watched him leave. It was a strange bitter sweet moment. Another character that was there that night was a Rainbow Room regular—Lemme from Motor Head and a few other actors and musicians were there. The rainbow room was about 50 feet from the Roxy. They were almost connected and on the same property. After a couple of hours, I wanted to check out who was playing at the Roxy, so Carmelita and I headed there. When we entered the front door, a person was taking a cover charge of $20. It was a little steep. But what caught my eye as we were about to leave was the four large photographs that hung side-by-side over the entrance inside the building. The first photo was of Jimi Hendrix, the second was Eddie Van Halen, the third was of me, and the fourth one was Roger Daltrey. I was blown away. Exiting the building was hard, and

I didn't think my head would fit through the door. My ego was now blown out of proportion. Looking back on this, I am so glad God led me out of that city. I would not have survived if my ego got any bigger. Carmelita couldn't believe the photograph of me on the nightclub's wall. A couple days passed, and New Year had arrived. We got to the club an hour early for a sound check. We played a couple songs as the sound man mixed our instruments and vocals. When we finished, he called me over and complimented the band. He told me he had been the House sound engineer for nearly 15 years, aside from Steve Winwood, we were the best sounding band he had ever mixed during his time there.

Again, there went my head expanding. Sasha told us that the line went down the street and around the corner. The Roxy on New Year's Eve was one of the places people wanted to be. We went to the green room to hang out before the show. We were The first to go on, and we had a thirty-minute set. Then it was Oingo Boingo, then the Black Crows to ring in the new year. It was 7, and they were now letting people flow into the iconic club. I was not going to drink till after the show. I promised myself and the boys. They were pleased about that. My acoustic was set up that week by a luthier who worked on guitars for folks like Kenny Loggins, so it sounded amazing. The time came, and the sound guy called us out onto the stage. When we walked out, I had to admit that I was nervous. And being from a small town, I was not a hog caller or crowd rouser. It was a simple "Hello folks, thank you for coming out to the Roxy for New Year's Eve. We're Coldwater, and I hope you connect with our music," We began to play. I was honestly surprised at the positive reaction from the packed house that night. The energy was electric, and the applause felt like a warm embrace. We had just finished our set, and the crowd went wild. It was one of those moments where you could feel that we had done something special. I had played many shows, but this was different—the sound was incredible. It was by far the best-sounding stage I'd ever been on. Every note seemed to resonate perfectly.

As we stepped off stage, the sound guy made an announcement: Oingo Boingo would be performing in half an hour. But before I could process that, I was already being approached by people asking for my autograph. That, in itself, was surreal. Here we were, a complete unknown band, and people were treating us like we were rock stars. I didn't understand it. We were just a group of guys playing our hearts out. But there they were, eagerly handing me napkins and scraps of paper to sign. I guess they assumed we were an established act, and in that moment, it felt kind of nice to let them think that.

I made my way out into the crowd, the adrenaline still pumping through me. But I wasn't going to let the high fade too quickly. No, I had Bacardi 151 waiting for me backstage, and I was going to drink away the buzz—maybe even push the edges of the night into something a little darker. I went straight for the hard stuff.

If you've heard about people blacking out from drinking, you probably have an idea of what happened next. I don't remember much after that. I can vaguely recall a few songs from Oingo Boingo's set, but nothing substantial. Like the day, eleven years earlier, when I woke up in the bushes up in Applegate. My next memory was waking up the next morning, disoriented, lying in bed in nothing but my underwear. Luckily I was in my apartment. My head was pounding, and I couldn't for the life of me figure out how I had gotten there.

Carmelita was there, her presence a comforting contrast to the chaos of the night. She told me that both she and Sasha had gotten me home, making sure I was safe and put to bed. But what really stuck out was what she said about Chris, the lead singer of the Black Crowes. He had also gotten drunk during the show and almost fell off the stage. I laughed at the thought of that, but I couldn't help but feel terrible for not ringing in the new year the way I should have. The whole night had slipped away from me in a haze of poor decisions.

Later that week, I met with Sasha to talk about our future. She told me that we had an incredible opportunity to tour with the Neville Brothers, a chance that could take us to the next level. But, of course, there was a catch. She wanted us to sign a management contract with her. She was asking for 20%.

Now, Steve, our seasoned bassist knew the business better than anyone in the band. He had been in the game long enough to understand how management worked, and he immediately said that 20% was too high. It would make Sasha a member of the band in a sense, and the highest-paid person in the group at that. That wasn't something we could just accept.

I took a couple of days to think it over. The bandmates and I discussed it, and after some back-and-forth, I went back to Sasha with a counteroffer: 10%. She didn't even flinch. She stood firm, her position unchanged. I could feel the pressure building inside me. It wasn't just a business decision at that point. It felt like a test of my resolve. I knew what I had to do.

I told her, calmly but firmly, that we wouldn't be able to go that high. Walking away from her felt like stepping off a ledge. She had every right to ask whatever she felt she was worth. And she did in fact land us our best shows so I understood her wanting to be compensated. At that moment, everything just seemed to crumble around me. The band mates didn't want to continue without her. They didn't think the band could survive without management, and they weren't willing to keep playing with me if the whole thing was falling apart.

The reasons they gave me were harsh, but I understood, even if I didn't want to. They told me that my drinking had become too much of a risk, and they didn't want to invest in something so volatile. The truth stung, but deep down, I knew they were right.

I was angry—angry at them for abandoning me, angry at the situation for spiraling out of control. But looking back now, I can see that I too would have left myself. The way I was living, the choices I was making—they weren't sustainable. Something had to change. And that something was me. It was a crushing blow, but sometimes it takes losing everything to see what you still have left. In the silence that followed, I found myself facing a truth I couldn't ignore. I had to change, or I was going to lose everything, including myself.

Chapter Fifty

Cold Steel Anger

A.W. Tozer

"God is the only safe place in life, and He is with us in every moment of danger. There is no harm that can touch us without His allowance, and nothing can separate us from His love."

The anger was still simmering beneath the surface. I couldn't shake it—the fallout with the band, the manager's betrayal, and the path my life had veered onto after everything fell apart. It gnawed at me like an old wound that refused to heal. The sun had long since dipped below the horizon, and all I wanted to do was drown the sorry shell of a man I'd become in something alcoholic. I knew Carmelita would be game for a night out; she never turned down an opportunity to drink.

We headed to a dive bar just down the street from the barbershop on Vineland Boulevard. I can't recall the name of the place—probably because it wasn't memorable. It was one of those nondescript holes-in-the-wall, frequented by barflies nursing whiskey with trembling hands. When we rolled in around 8:00, the dim lighting and stale air wrapped around us like a worn-out blanket. By 9:00, we were four drinks deep, and there was no sign of slowing down.

Carmelita was getting us VIP treatment, thanks to her connections at Residuals, the bar down the street where she worked. The bartender knew her well and kept the drinks flowing without hesitation. But not everyone was pleased about it. Across the room, a couple of Middle Eastern looking guys with gold chains and flashy watches were eyeing us with disdain. It wasn't long before one of them started making gestures toward Carmelita.

I tried to ignore it at first, but the combination of booze and my already short temper made it impossible. The guy was leaning into the provocation, smirking and muttering under his breath just loud enough for me to catch. When he finally said, "Why don't you leave the loser and come home with me?" something inside me snapped.

I shot up from my seat, my chair scraping loudly against the floor. "You wanna step outside," I barked, motioning toward the door. Carmelita grabbed my arm, pleading with me to let it go. The bartender, his face a mask of concern, gave me a subtle shake of his head. But I was too far gone, fueled by rage and alcohol. I ignored them both.

The man stood up, a slow, deliberate move, and motioned for me to lead the way. Like a fool, I went first, stepping out into the cool night air and heading to a clearing around the corner. My adrenaline was pumping; I was ready for a fight. But then I felt it—the cold, unyielding barrel of a gun pressed against the back of my head.

"Not so tough now, are you?" the man's voice hissed.

I turned slowly, my heart pounding. "It's a good thing you've got that gun," I said, my voice steady despite the chaos in my mind. "You're gonna need it."

That's when I saw it—the look in his eyes. They weren't his. It was like something else was driving him, something dark and sinister. He wasn't just angry; he was possessed. I'd seen enough to recognize it now.

Before anything could escalate further, the bartender and Carmelita came rushing out. They froze at the sight of the gun. The bartender, keeping his voice calm, said, "You don't want to do this. You don't want to spend the rest of your life in prison over something so stupid."

Carmelita chimed in, her voice pleading, "Come on, man, just let it go."

The man hesitated, his grip on the gun tightening, then loosening. Finally, he spat out, "You're lucky they came out here. This was going to be your last night." He paused, narrowing his eyes. "This isn't over. I'm part of Armenian Power, and I'll find you."

Like an idiot, I responded, "If you need to find me, I'm a bartender at Rocky's." I even pointed down the street, giving him my hours. "Does that help?"

The bartender's face was a mix of shock and frustration. The man's friend came out, muttered something Armenian, and dragged him away. They climbed into an older, souped-up Cadillac and sped off into the night.

"Why on earth did you tell him where you work?" the bartender asked, laughing and exasperated. "Do you have any idea who these guys are? They don't mess around. They are in the gang Armenian Power." I thought to myself, what's Armenian Power? I had never heard of this group or gang. The Crips, and the Bloods, yes. But these guys, never.

Two days later, I found out just how serious they were. I was outside the barbershop, taking a cigarette break with a good friend and client the actor Paul Gleason, when the same Cadillac crept down the street. The man who pulled the gun in me was in the passenger seat. He rolled down the window, stuck his hand out, and mimicked firing a gun at me in slow motion before speeding off. Paul Said, "that didn't look good." I said "It's not a big deal." and walked back in the shop.

It should've rattled me. A few years earlier, it would have. But I'd been through so much that it barely registered. The city and its chaos were numbing me. Still, I couldn't help but feel a pang of sadness. I could see it in the guy's eyes after he had the gun to my head—he wasn't a bad person at his core. He was like Carmelita, like me, like so many others in this city: broken, lost, and controlled by forces we barely understood.

It was like a city within a city, a web of spiritual battles being fought in the shadows. And we were all just pawns, blind to the larger war raging around us.

Chapter Fifty-One

The Weight Of Darkness

Mark 5:9

"Then Jesus asked him, 'What is your name?' 'My name is Legion,' he replied, 'for we are many.'"

Looking back on my band days, I've come to realize something that took me years to truly understand. The secular music world, as wild and free as it may seem, is owned, controlled, and manipulated by the Devil. It's a world that celebrates ego, self-absorption, and the pursuit of worldly pleasures. The music itself is saturated with messages about sex, lies, violence, money, drugs, and rock 'n' roll. Men sing about their conquests, their love and battles with their own vices, while women sing about heartbreak and the things that broke them.

It's all about the world and what it can give you. There's nothing but a deluge of the seven deady sins.

What I've come to believe is that demons thrive in environments like this. They are drawn to self-centeredness and arrogance, the very things that define the music industry. Demons know that if you don't know Jesus, if you live your life wrapped up in yourself and the world, they've found their playground. They've hit the satanic jackpot. And here's the thing: I truly believe that demons have actual physical weight. You might think I'm crazy, but hear me out. It's not much, but it's measurable.

When I think back to some of the most broken, possessed people I've encountered, I see a physical heaviness to them, a weight that is beyond just body mass. When people have multiple demons dwelling in them, like the man in the Bible from the Gadarenes, that weight only grows.

Now when I read story's, like the ones in the bible, like the demoniac, it's very telling. When Jesus came across this man who was tortured by demons, the man's response was chilling. Jesus asked, "What is your name?" and the possessed man replied, "Legion, for we are many." In Roman times, a "Legion" referred to a group of three thousand to six thousand soldiers. That's how many unclean spirits this man was carrying. And if we believe demons have weight, then the collective weight of three thousand to six thousand demons is something you can almost quantify.

After much thought and some investigation, I found that people were already thinking about this very subject in our distant past. In 1907, a doctor named Duncan MacDougall conducted an experiment with terminal patients. He placed them on a sensitive scale just before they died, and to his amazement, all of them lost exactly 21 grams right when they died. This experiment led him to propose that the soul, or the life force, had mass—21 grams to be exact. Now, if we extend that idea, what if the demons themselves had a physical body at some point in time, and when they expired, their soul or spirit left their bodies? Could these unclean spirits have a measurable weight? What if the man in the cave had three thousand demons, each one weighing 21 grams? That's an additional 142 grams or about 6 extra pounds. If he had six thousand demons in him, that's an extra 13 pounds.

Think about that. When someone has been carrying demons around for years, decades even, that weight must add up. The heaviness in their spirit manifests physically. And beyond that weight, there's the constant, suffocating pressure demons place on a person. Their goal is simple: to drag you into sin, to make you lose your salvation, to keep you trapped in darkness.

I remember feeling this weight in my own life. It was as though I was being crushed under an invisible burden, a pressure that I couldn't escape. And those demons, they're relentless. Every choice you make that leads you further from God, they celebrate. Their whispers are constant, coaxing you to stay in the darkness. They try to numb you, twist you, make you forget who you really are. But the beauty of it all is that these parasites, these demons, they flee at the name of Jesus.

There's power in His name. And when you decide to go through deliverance you feel lighter afterward. Lighter in a physical sense. It's as though something that had been weighing them down, something dark and oppressive, was finally gone.

The people I've seen in the hard rock scene, the ones who carry the most visible burden, always seem physically heavy. It's why we hear the term Hard Rock, or Heavy Metal, being used. Even when they're thin, there's this weight in their eyes, in their posture. They're often covered in tattoos, which, in a sense, is a form of self-harm—much like the demoniac who cut himself with stones. Pastors and even priests often say that when they see cutting, they see a demonic infestation. It's a symptom, a sign that there's something much deeper at work. But here's the good news: when you call on the name of Jesus when you invite Him into your life, they flee. They cannot stand in His presence.

Chapter Fifty-Two

A Father's Final Chapter

John Calvin

"We must learn to say, 'The Lord gave, and the Lord has taken away. Blessed be the name of the Lord.' We must humble ourselves under His mighty hand, trusting that He does all things for our good."

Amid all the chaos, the endless cycle of dysfunction, I found myself packing up yet again. This time, it was into a single-story quadplex—a two-bedroom place where I shared the space with a roommate, a nice guy named Troy. We both had our issues—baggage that we carried around like invisible chains. Our neighbor, Alexandra, was another story. She was a transsexual who had undergone surgery to add breasts, and I assumed, bottom surgery as well. This is over thirty years ago when it wasn't the societal contagion it is today. Alexandra was kind, but there was no hiding the truth. He, like many others in LA, was living a life that didn't align with reality, or the word of God. He was a male pretending to be female, and despite His outward transformation, the space around us just felt... off. It was heavy, dark, and I couldn't explain it, but I felt it in my bones.

And seeing Alexandra and then looking in the mirror at myself was also a realization. Maybe my music pursuit was no different then his adding female body parts to give him the sense that he was something different and new but really he wasn't. And just maybe my music pursuit was something that was also a facade. Unfortunately we were in a city that chewed you up and spat you out, making you believe you could be something, only to leave you emptier than before. Even when it seemed like you were doing the right thing and riding high, on top of the world, you'd crash. You'd always crash.

That was when I made the decision. I knew I couldn't stay. I couldn't let myself be swallowed whole by this corrupt, godless place. Something deep inside told me that if I stayed, I would lose something precious—something I couldn't yet name. I did not want to be like Jack. Back then, I didn't understand what a soul was, or that I even had one, but I felt it. I felt the pull, the tug to leave before LA stole it from me. I didn't know what would happen, but I knew I had to escape, before the city took more from me than I could afford to give. So I decided that if I did not leave this wretched smog filled Sodom and Gomorrah I would lose something. I didn't know what that something was because I was not saved just yet. I had no idea that I had a soul. I didn't know what a soul was. With the stories that I knew about, guys like Robert Johnson, who went to the crossroads and sold his soul to the Devil to become the face of rock 'n' roll, but I thought it was just Hollywood folklore or a screen writers imagination, I was pretty oblivious. Things got more real as I got closer to my exiting the city.

Preparations were underway. I rented a U-Haul, made plans to move out of the city, and started reaching out to friends to let them know I was leaving. I told my parents up north, and they offered me a place to stay while I figured things out. I was grateful for their support. I called Carmelita to tell her my plans, and though I tried to keep things light, it was clear this was a significant moment for both of us. She was an only child, and though she had her own battles—Carmelita was the caretaker, the one who held everything together.

That week Carmelita received great news followed by a staggering blow. She learned that her father had been released from prison, and just before she could re connect with him to heal some old wounds he was senselessly killed by his roommate in a jealous rage. It was very tragic to say the least. Carmelita took me to the crime scene, where we saw the blood-soaked bed where her father had died. It felt surreal, like we were walking through someone else's nightmare. The blood was still there, dried into the sheets, and the clothes—her father's clothes—also had dried blood clinging to it. It was horrific, and I saw the devastation in Carmelita's eyes as she processed the reality of it all. She was holding onto a thread of her sanity, and I didn't want to push her too hard, especially when I was struggling with my own demons.

I had already told her about my decision to move up north, to leave LA behind. I reassured her that we could still be together, that we could make it work, even if she stayed behind or followed me. I saw the conflict in her eyes. She needed time to think, to process, to decide what was best for her. I understood. She had just lost her father, and everything around her felt like it was slipping away.

I felt the weight of it all—the choices I had to make, the life I was leaving behind, and the uncertainty of the future. But the truth was, I couldn't bear the evil, the darkness of LA anymore. It was sucking the life out of me, and I knew I had to leave before it completely consumed me.

And so, I made the decision to go. The weight of it, the heaviness in the air, felt lighter as I took the first step toward a new chapter. But little did I know that leaving this city would not just be an escape from a place—it would be an escape from something far more dangerous. The darkness I had been living in would soon come forward and reveal its self.

Chapter Fifty-Three

A Voice Of Evil

Derek Prince

"The devil cannot speak to you unless you allow him to. The key is not to listen to his lies, but to speak the truth of God's Word. When you resist, he must flee."

The next event that unfolded in my life served as an undeniable, chilling confirmation that I wasn't just dealing with 't the usual chaos. No, what I was experiencing was something far darker, supernatural, and outright terrifying. It happened one afternoon in March when the sun was shining brightly outside, casting a warm glow through the windows. I was folding a large load of laundry in my room, organizing my clothes—socks, shirts, pants, etc. The room was quiet; no TV, no radio, no noise at all. Just silence.

But that silence was broken. Out of nowhere, a voice spoke directly to me. I turned sharply to my right, where the voice had come from, expecting to see someone standing there. But there was no one. Just my CD rack and my guitar on its stand. No one was there.

"What?" I asked, confused.

"You can't leave," the voice said again, and this time, it repeated the words three times.

At first, I wasn't sure what to make of it. But the words, the tone—they weren't from a person. It wasn't a friend, a neighbor, or anyone I knew. This was a voice, a presence, from somewhere dark and far beyond the realm of the ordinary. The more I thought about it, the more certain I became: I was dealing with a spirit. A demon. I wasn't ready to confront it fully, but deep down, I knew the truth. It wasn't going to let me go easily.

Fear gripped me. I wasn't prepared for this, but I wasn't about to back down. "I'm leaving LA," I said aloud, my voice steady despite the knot of fear in my stomach. "And there's nothing anyone or anything can do to stop me."

The voice responded, its tone growing colder, more insistent. "You can't leave. Big things are going to happen for you. I promise."

I was no stranger to demons. I'd dealt with them in different forms for years, and I knew their tricks—how they lied, how they manipulated. I wasn't buying what it was selling. But even though I knew it was a liar, a demonic force, that didn't make the fear go away. It was powerful, persuasive, and terrifying in its own way.

I backed out of my room, still shaken. My roommate, Troy, was in the kitchen eating a sandwich. He saw the look on my face, knew something was off, but I couldn't bring myself to tell him the truth. He'd think I was crazy. I wasn't ready for that.

I left the apartment and walked around the corner to a payphone, we hadn't put in a pone line, and called Carmelita. I didn't tell her what had just happened; I wasn't ready to freak her out. Instead, I just said, "Something serious is happening at my apartment, and I need to stay with you for a couple of days. I'll tell you more when I get to your place."

I wasn't sure what to make of it all. I was on edge, but I needed to grab a few things before I left. I went back to my apartment, hesitant but determined to get what I needed. When I stepped into my room again, the voice greeted me like an old friend. It spoke once more, its words clear, calm, but chilling. Assuring me of success if I just stuck it out.

I couldn't stand it anymore. I shouted down the hall to Troy. "Troy, can you come here," I called out.

Troy came in, looking confused but willing to help. "What's up?" he asked.

I didn't want him to think I was losing my mind, so I asked him to do something simple. "I need you to go into my room and just tell me if you hear anything. Just listen, and let me know what you think."

Troy agreed, though I could see the skepticism in his eyes. We walked into my room together. I held up my finger, signaling him to wait, and we stood in silence for what felt like an eternity. A minute passed. Nothing. No voice, no sounds.

I didn't want to admit what had happened. I wasn't ready to confront this darkness in front of him. "Thanks, man," I said, forcing a smile. "I must be losing it." He said "yep", with a slight laugh as he wondered out down the hall eating the rest of his sandwich sandwich.

But I wasn't losing it. Something real, something evil, had been speaking to me. I didn't need his validation to know what I'd heard and felt.

I grabbed what I needed—my clothes, a box of books, and my guitar—and left the apartment for good. As I was heading to my car, I saw Alexandra, the transgender neighbor, going into his apartment.

Something about the whole situation felt wrong, and I wanted to ask him if he had ever experienced anything like what I had just gone through. But I didn't. I had a feeling It was probably a demon that knew him well.

In hindsight, As I look back on that incident I now know the LGBTQ community is a magnet for these unclean spirits. I'm sure my lifestyle wasn't much better, but for a demon to actually be able to physically talk to me it must have been high in the chain of command, the kind of entity that could influence the very fabric of my reality.

I made my way to Carmelita's place and told her the whole story. She looked at me like I was a little off, maybe crazy even, but she could tell I was sober and serious. She knew I wasn't making this up.

After a couple days at Carmelita's apartment it was time to head back north. I packed the last of my things, I said goodbye to her and promised I'd call once I arrived in a few hours. The journey was starting, but not without its obstacles. When I got to the U-Haul place the attendant apologized and said this has never happened but the trailer I was going to rent was stolen the night before. I couldn't believe it. Was this the same evil spirit influencing someone else to thwart my ability to leave? It certainly felt like it. But I wasn't going to let that stop me. I would find another way to get my belongings back north.

I returned to the apartment and told Troy he could have the things I just couldn't fit in my small car—my bed, my bookshelf, anything he wanted. He'd been sleeping on a mat on the floor, so I knew he'd be happy with what I was offering. I packed up the last of my stuff, a box of books, my guitar, and my clothes, and headed out.

A couple hours on the road I stopped at a truck stop to grab a burger. It was McDonald's, and the workers, all of whom were Mexican, quietly laughed among themselves as they prepared my order.

I didn't think much of it at the time. I ordered a couple hamburgers, and when the worker handed me the bag, I noticed they were all still laughing. It wasn't until I took my first bite as I was speeding down the highway that I understood why. The burger was all bun—no patty, no meat, just two pieces of bread with condiments. I laughed to myself. "Ooooh, slick," I muttered, realizing the prank. But as I sat there eating two pieces of bread, I couldn't help but feel that it was just another odd moment and actually a pretty funny one. So I laughed a little and headed north.

Chapter Fifty-Four

The Dead Speaks?

Smith Wigglesworth

"When we face anything supernatural, whether it's a ghost or a demon, we must recognize that the power of Jesus Christ is greater. We are not to be afraid but to speak the name of Jesus with boldness, and any spirit that is not of God will leave."

I finally made it to my parents' place. They had moved back to Colfax, CA, nestled up the hill from the hustle of city life. My father, ever the dreamer and adventurer, had found a piece of property so remote it felt like the middle of nowhere. It was a good four miles off the main highway, winding down a dirt road that stretched about a quarter of a mile. Don't ask me why anyone would want to live that far out in the wilderness, but this was my father's idea of paradise.

The property had history, too. It was once a Christian camp in the seventies and you could feel that presence, even in the quiet stillness of the land. The center of it all was a massive pond—about the size of three football fields, or so it seemed. The pond stretched out in front of the property like a peaceful, shimmering mirror, reflecting the sky above. Just up the hill, overlooking the pond, was the mobile home my parents had bought from my uncle. It was small and had a nice homey feel—but the land around it was something special.

I stayed with my parents for a few months while I tried to figure things out, waiting for Carmelita to come up to Northern California and join me. But it wasn't just the beauty of the land that stood out during my time there. No, there was something else, something far less tangible, that made the place feel even more unique.

It happened one night, around 1 am. I had been sound asleep in one of the smaller bedrooms on the opposite side of the mobile home. The room was quiet, the only sound being the occasional rustle of leaves from the trees outside. That was until I was abruptly woken by the smell of cigar smoke. It was thick, pungent, and unmistakable. I opened my eyes, disoriented, trying to figure out where it was coming from. The smell was so strong, it felt like it was invading my lungs.

As I rubbed my eyes to clear the fog of sleep, I looked up, and that's when I saw him. A large man, his figure shrouded in the haze of cigar smoke, was standing over me, staring down at me in my bed. I froze, my heart pounding in my chest. I could see him clearly, though his features were a bit hazy around the edges, like a figure from a dream that didn't quite belong in the waking world.

I didn't know what to do or say, but instinctively, I asked, "Who are you?"

The man didn't respond. He just stood there, puffing on his cigar, his eyes fixed on me with an intensity that was both unsettling and oddly familiar. I rubbed my eyes again, thinking maybe I was still in some half-asleep state, but when I looked back, the man was gone. Vanished into thin air, like smoke drifting away in the night. The air felt heavy for a moment, the smell of the cigar lingering just long enough to remind me of what had just happened.

I wasn't surprised. After everything I had seen, all the strange, supernatural encounters in my life, I wasn't about to be amazed or dumbfounded by this. I had come to terms with the fact that we were living in both a physical and spiritual world simultaneously. The boundaries between them were thinner than most people realized, and things could slip through those cracks—things like ghosts?

The next morning, over breakfast, I brought it up to my parents. I told them about the strong cigar odor and the man who had stood over me while I slept. They looked at each other, then at me, as if they had expected me to encounter something like this eventually.

"Oh, that's Gene," my mom said, almost nonchalantly.

"Gene?" I asked, confused. "Who's Gene?"

My father cleared his throat, his voice a little more serious than usual. "That's your uncle's father," he said, as if that should explain everything. "He used to stay in that room when he visited. He passed away in that room, too, many years ago." He also smoked cigars in that room.

I sat there, a little stunned. They went on to explain how Gene had spent the last years of his life in their trailer. It was his room, the room I was using. And as strange as it seemed, it made sense now. The man I had seen, the one with the cigar, was Gene—my uncle's father. It wasn't a random ghost. It wasn't some demonic presence or a dark force. It was just Gene. There were no great cosmic answers, no huge revelations to be had. It was just Gene.

When I thought about it later, I realized how much I had learned about the nature of life, death, and the afterlife. Scripture says that when a person dies, their disembodied spirit doesn't wander the Earth. Instead, their soul goes straight to heaven or hell, depending on their life and choices. The idea of spirits lingering behind, haunting places, was something that seemed at odds with that teaching. Yet, there I was, having experienced it firsthand.

I couldn't explain it. I didn't know what it meant. But I had learned that life, death, and the supernatural were far more complex than most people gave them credit for. There were mysteries that simply couldn't be unraveled. I didn't fear them anymore. I had come to a place of understanding, even if that understanding was incomplete.

As I settled in at my parents' place, waiting for Carmelita to join me, I found myself becoming more and more at peace with the world around me. The land, the quiet pond, the old trailer, and even Gene's lingering presence—they all seemed to fit together, like pieces of a puzzle that, once assembled, made the world a little less strange.

And maybe that was the point. Life wasn't meant to be fully understood. It was meant to be lived, experienced, and sometimes, just accepted as it came. Whether it was the supernatural, the strange encounters, or the quiet moments of clarity, I was beginning to realize that it was all part of the same journey.

Corinthians 5:8 says,

"Yes, we are of good courage, and we would rather be away from the body and at home with the Lord."

It's a beautiful verse, one that fills the heart with peace, knowing that death isn't the end but a passage to be with the Creator. But in reality, the Bible doesn't really talk about ghosts. And we all know there's only one Holy Ghost—and the man smoking the cigar in my room? That wasn't him.

This whole ghost phenomenon remains a mystery, one we'll have to wait to ask the Creator about. It raises questions, of course. Are spirits of the dead real? What happens when a soul lingers behind? If I were to offer a theory on ghosts, it might go something like this: what we see as ghosts are like recordings frozen in time, activated somehow by a mysterious force or energy. Maybe they're not wandering souls, but echoes of past moments playing out in the right conditions. Like on a VHS, DVD, stream, or download.

I was reminded of this theory when my sister shared a strange story about her dog that passed away a few years ago. The day after her dog died, my sister noticed something strange—an unusual mist filled her kitchen. It wasn't fog, but more like smoke, drifting through the air. It was thick, almost tangible, so she took a photo and sent it to her husband, asking if he had any idea where the smoke was coming from. When my nephew, her son James enlarged the photo, he noticed something odd: two shapes in the mist. No editing, no manipulation. Just a photograph capturing something inexplicable. One shape matched her little dog that had just literally passed away the day before, and the second shape—larger, taller—matched the dog she'd had a year before. That was something that I couldn't explain, nor could she. Was it just a trick of light, or something more? This mystery, like so many others, is one we'll have to ask the Creator about when we meet Him face-to-face.

Chapter Fifty-Five

Window To The Soul

T.L. Osborn

"When we allow Christ to live through us, the world can see Him in our actions, our words, and even our eyes. The eyes of believers become a reflection of His light, and when we see one another, we see Christ shining in us."

After a short stay with my parents, Carmelita left LA and moved into a one-bedroom apartment in Roseville, about 15 miles west of Colfax with me. Roseville wasn't too big—about thirty five thousand people at the time in the late nineties—but it had a charm to it. A conservative town, filled with evangelical Christians who took their faith seriously, and it was there that the Lord directed me. I didn't know it then, but this was where my life was about to take a turn.

I had big dreams of opening my own salon and barbershop, but the reality was that I didn't have enough clients to make that jump. So, I decided to work at a national chain salon to build my client base. I chose Great Clips. The work was grueling—I was cutting fifteen to twenty haircuts a day, which was a lot—but it paid the bills, and I met some incredible people there. There were characters, for sure, and some of them I've stayed friends with to this day.

But there was more to it than just cutting hair. You see, when you're doing a lot of haircuts, you get to know people. They talk to you, share their lives, their stories. And the thing that always stood out to me was how different the Christians were. And I don't mean just in their beliefs, but in their eyes. Christians, especially the born-again ones, always had this light in their eyes, this quiet but undeniable presence about them. You could almost see the Holy Spirit shining through them. And I noticed that no one else—no one from other religions—had that same glow. Some of my clients, the born-again Christians, started inviting me to church. And not just once, but repeatedly. I could feel their sincerity. These weren't just casual invitations; they were from people who wanted to share something with me. And like I said it was only the evangelical Christians that offered this invitation. Not Buddhists, Muslims, Mormons, Catholics, Jehovah Witnesses, only Christians. But at the time, I wasn't ready. Carmelita was in my life, and she had her own struggles. She was drinking every day and smoking weed regularly. She was a wake and bake individual. I had cut back quite a bit but I was still partaking on occasion. It was an unfortunate part of our lives, and we weren't ready to let go of it. I just wasn't ready to go to church, not with the life I was living. At that point in my life stepping into church I think I would've burst into flames.

In hindsight Church would have been a nice bucket of water thrown on me. I couldn't bring myself to accept their invitations. I didn't feel worthy. I knew they were good people, but I felt like I was too far gone. My own habits and struggles seemed to disqualify me from the light they carried. The more invitations I got the more I felt convicted to talk to Carmelita about going to church. She told me she wanted nothing to do with church. This is when I confronted Carmelita about her addiction, asking her if she planned on slowing down at all. She told me she had no plans to stop. I understood the trauma she had been through, especially her kidnapping, which had left deep scars on her. But despite the feelings I had for her, I knew we couldn't keep going down the same path. It was hard, but I made the painful decision to part ways. I've prayed that she would find the Lord and that, one day, she would embrace the life she deserved. I knew she would be an amazing believer, if she ever found her way there. Carmelita was now four hundred miles and out of my life.

Chapter Fifty-Six

The Invitation

John Piper

"The first time you hear the gospel and truly understand it, you see the heart of God. You realize that He is not an abstract concept but a living, loving Father who has reached out to you in your weakness. The gospel reveals His love and care for you, a love that will never let you go."

I was questioning everything—God, my relationships, my career. What was the point of it all? Was this really all there was to life?

And then, as if by divine timing, I started getting more invitations to a church. The invitations were coming from a little church just down the street called Bayside. I didn't know much about it, but I kept getting these invitations. One of the members, a down-to-earth guy named Trey who played bass in the worship band, asked me to come.

He wasn't all starched out and uptight like I thought most church people were, so I agreed to check it out.

Oddly enough, this church met at a local high school called Granite Bay High. I wandered in late, unsure of what to expect, and sat in the back by myself. The pastor, a passionate and charismatic man named Ray Johnson, was speaking, and from the moment he began, it felt like he was talking directly to me. I was struck by how relevant and personal everything seemed. The message struck a chord deep within me, igniting a spark I never expected. That day, I heard the story of a man named Paul in the Bible—a ruthless tyrant who hunted down Christians, even to the point of death. And yet, despite his cruelty, God's love for him never wavered. Instead of condemnation, God gave Paul a revelation of hope and a future. That truth hit me like a wave, filling me with hope I didn't even know I was searching for. In that dark, lonely moment of my life, it was exactly what I needed—a reminder that no one is beyond the reach of God's grace and purpose. And believe me up to that point I thought I was beyond repair or redemption.

That morning, I raised my hand, and I felt a genuine shift within me. I knew, without a doubt, that God was real, that He loved me, and that He wanted a relationship with me. It was a turning point. I stopped drinking heavily and started taking small steps toward cleaning up my life. I still smoked, but I wasn't the same person anymore. I left that service knowing that I was loved by God, even if I didn't have it all figured out.

But discipleship? That was where I fell short. I didn't go to The "I Raised My Hand table" off to the side of the stage. I needed to plug into the church. I didn't get the support I needed, and that was my mistake. Discipleship is key—it's essential for growing in faith. The Bible is the instruction manual for life; without it, we're like someone trying to assemble a piece of furniture without the instructions. I'm sure there are some men out there who toss that manual aside. And what do you end up with, a wonky piece of furniture?

Chapter Fifty-Seven

Haircuts To Honeymoon

John Wimber

"When God brings two people together, it is not by accident. Marriage is not just about love; it's about destiny. The wife God gives you is a reflection of His grace, a partner in His calling for your life."

The next day, Monday, I felt like a fog had lifted from my life. The heavy weight I had carried for so long seemed to dissipate with each passing hour. It was as if the path before me had cleared, and for the first time in a long while, I could see the direction I was heading. And that direction, well, it was about to take an unexpected turn.

It was just another ordinary day at the Salon when she walked in—an incredibly attractive woman who needed a haircut. I remember thinking, "What is someone that looked like her doing at Great Clips?" She was just too classy. We were in a rather upscale neighborhood, and I was used to seeing a certain type of clientele, but not *her*—she stood out. I had a client in my chair, but I couldn't help but notice her sitting in the lobby. She was waiting patiently, but it was one of those moments where you can just *feel* the world shift a little.

I didn't usually rush through haircuts, but something about her presence had me turning up the speed just a little. I could tell my current client noticed the same thing as he kept glancing over at her, commenting on how pretty she was. I quickly wrapped up with him and rang him out without wasting any more time.

At the time, my hair was to my shoulders and bleached a platinum blonde. I thought it looked cool, but looking back at photos, it was more like a dumpster fire on my head. But this wasn't about my hair—this was about *her*.

When I called her over to my chair she came with a pleasant smile. I had her name from the computer so I said "Claudia?" She responded in broken English, "Yes Claudia." For the life of me, I couldn't place her accent. French? Spanish? I had worked in Los Angeles long enough to hear just about every accent you could imagine, but this one was new to me. It wasn't until she told me she was from Brazil that everything clicked. I'd met a couple of Brazilians in my life, but I had never met anyone quite like Claudia. And she was a sliver taller than me.

Despite the language barrier, we managed to communicate reasonably well. She was in the States working as a nanny for a wealthy family who lived just a few miles away in an upscale neighborhood by the lake. We talked about music, and I was floored by how many bands she knew. Her enthusiasm for music was contagious, and we hit it off quickly.

I took my time with her haircut, maybe a little too much time, but I didn't care. I was learning more about her with every snip. The shop started to get busier, and I could see Kim, the manager, motioning for me to pick up the pace. She could tell I was getting lost in conversation, but I didn't care—I was enjoying this connection.

Eventually, I finished up the cut and rang her out. But then it hit me. I had forgotten to ask for her number. What an idiot I was!

The rest of the week was a blur. I thought about Claudia constantly, hoping she'd come back for another cut. But deep down, I knew better. Women don't come back to a chain salon as quickly as men do—guys, maybe every four to six weeks. Women? It could be four to six months before she needed another trim. I even thought about fishing her number out of the computer system, but I didn't want to come off as creepy. I had to let it go, or so I thought.

A few days passed, and I was at the salon doing a cut when, to my surprise, Claudia walked back in, this time with a young boy in tow. She smiled at me and asked if I could cut the boy's hair. I assumed he was one of her employer's children. This was my chance. I wasn't going to let her slip away again. I had to ask her out, and this time, I wasn't going to mess it up.

I finished cutting the boy's hair and, in the most eloquent way I could manage, with her limited understanding of English, I asked if she'd like to grab coffee sometime. She smiled and said yes.

That was the start of it all. We met at a coffee shop around the corner from the salon, and instantly, we seemed to click. We had so much in common—it was almost as if we had known each other for years, not just a few hours. Our relationship blossomed, and we spent the next year growing closer, getting to know each other on a deeper level.

But, as is often the case with life, things weren't perfect for long. Claudia had a visa that was quickly coming to an end, and she had to return to Brazil. I could feel my heart sink. I was beginning to truly care for her, and I didn't want her to leave. I wasn't sure what would happen next, but I knew that this was a pivotal moment in both our lives. I was pretty persuasive, so I said, "What if you stay?" Her eyes widened a little, and I could see the conflict inside her. Claudia wasn't sure if she could do this—if she could stay. Her fear was palpable. She didn't have a car, her contract with the family had just expired, and she didn't have a job. It was all very uncertain.

I didn't want her to go. I told her we could figure things out. We could work on getting her an extension on her visa, and I knew she could find something—anything—to get by. That's when she met Lucy, another Brazilian girl. They instantly clicked. Lucy had recently moved to the area and became a part of a new group of friends from Brazil that also resided in and around the area. She asked Claudia if she wanted to get an apartment together, and to my relief, Claudia agreed.

She decided to stay. I was thrilled. I couldn't believe it. She had chosen to stay with me in the States. But there was one big problem: she didn't have a car.

I didn't think twice. I sold my Pontiac Fiero and used the money to buy two used Geo Metros. They were tiny, slow, and practically looked like toys, but they got an impressive forty miles per gallon. I gave one to Claudia, and we both laugh to this day about those cars—Bonafide clown cars. It was one of those things that became a funny story as time passed, but at the time, it felt like a step forward. At least she had wheels now.

Claudia still didn't have a job, and without a social security number, it was tough. So she decided to clean houses for income until we could figure out her legal status. I printed up some simple fliers outlining her cleaning services, and we hit the most upscale neighborhoods in town, hanging them on every door. It was remarkable—within days, people started calling her. She did so well we just couldn't believe it. But the work was tough—physically demanding, with toxic chemicals doing a number on her body. Claudia wasn't one to shy away from hard work, but if she was planning to stay longer, she was thinking about finding something less taxing. She began thinking about an office job, something that would be kinder to her body.

After about a year of living with Lucy, I asked Claudia if she would move in with me. And she did. It felt right. Things were starting to feel like they were settling into place. But there was still something missing.

My clients continued to ask me how I was doing, how things were going, and whether I was attending church. The youth pastor at Bayside, a guy named Greg, had heard that I had attended in the past but had stopped going. He strongly encouraged me to give it another try. So, both Claudia and I decided to go together.

But here's the thing—I still hadn't opened the Bible to read it independently. I relied on the church to feed me, and that was a mistake. If you go to church hoping your pastor will read the Bible cover to cover for you, you're in for a disappointment. It doesn't work that way. You have to commit to reading it on your own. I had felt the pull of God's teachings, but I was too comfortable to put in the work. I was also still heavily self absorbed in my own world. I was still playing music and writing. The Bible took a back seat.

And then there was the guilt—the guilt of living in sin with Claudia. We weren't married, and I felt that weight on my conscience. I had lived with two women in the past , and I had never felt that sense of guilt in those scenarios. But now it was different. I understood the Lord's commandments. The weight of this sin was quantifiable, undeniable. I had to make it right. And I knew Claudia was the one I wanted to spend my life with. She wasn't just some girlfriend. She was much more. This was the moment I knew it was time to take the leap. I bought a ring and came up with a sweet and simple way to propose, one that would hopefully catch her off guard in the best way. We were at a friend's house when I carefully placed the ring in a particular teacup, knowing it would soon hold more than just tea—it would hold a promise. When the time felt right, I casually asked her if she wouldn't mind making me some tea, specifically using that cup. She obliged, utterly unaware of what was waiting at the bottom.

When she finally found the ring, her eyes widened in surprise, and her smile lit up the room. My heart was pounding, but when she looked up at me and said yes, I felt a wave of joy and relief I'll never forget. It could've gone differently, but thankfully, it turned out to be a beautiful moment that marked the start of the rest of our lives.

So, on June 8th, 2003, just a couple of months after I proposed, I woke up with an idea I couldn't shake. I rolled over in bed, looked at Claudia, and blurted out, "Hey, do you want to elope?" She stared at me, half-asleep, looking as confused as ever. After a long pause, she asked, "What's elope?" I couldn't help but laugh as I explained it, telling her it meant we could skip the wait and just get married that day. I didn't want to lose the moment—or her—and thankfully, once she understood, she was all in. I called my parents that day and asked them to come with us to Lake Tahoe, where we were going to get married at Harvey's Casino. It sounds crazy, I know, but it was one of those decisions where you just go for it. The man who married us looked like a version of Don Ho, the Hawaiian singer who sang that sixties song "Tiny Bubbles." It was a quick ceremony, a drive-by wedding of sorts, but it felt like the most natural thing in the world.

We had a small reception a couple of months later in my brother Scott's backyard. It wasn't fancy, but it was full of love and laughter. Our family pitched in, and we were blessed enough to be able to spend a couple of weeks in Brazil. Meeting Claudia's parents was an incredible blessing, one that I'll never forget.

When we were in Brazil, we were going to rent a car in Claudia's home town Santos, just south of São Paulo, where her parents lived. But because half of all car rentals are stolen in Brazil, we decided to buy a used car instead and use it to travel up and around her state. It was a smart move. We put almost a thousand miles on that old car driving two and from the state of Rio back to her parents in Santos. It was breathtaking—the people, the beaches, the food, the places we stayed. It was an unforgettable trip, one that brought us even closer together.

As we said our goodbyes to her parents and headed back to our apartment in the US, Claudia shared her concerns about renting. She had been eyeing a small house just up the street from our apartment and suggested we buy it. It felt right. We were newlyweds, and now, we were homeowners. We pulled the trigger and purchased the house, knowing that this was a huge step in our future together.

Things were heading in the right direction. The life I had been waiting for, praying for, was finally unfolding. And just when everything seemed perfect, there was one more thing I needed to do—one more thing I needed to make right.

Chapter Fifty-Eight

A Stroke Of Reality

A.W. Tozer

"It is doubtful whether God can bless a man greatly until He has hurt him deeply."

I always knew I wanted to start my own business, to open my own shop. But I also knew I couldn't do that without building a solid clientele first. That's why I chose to work at a Great Clips franchise—a place where I could get in a high volume of daily haircuts and hone my craft while building up a loyal customer base. After a few years of paying my dues, and cutting hair at a breakneck pace, I finally had that sizable clientele I'd dreamed of.

That's when one of my clients approached me with an opportunity. He owned some commercial space in Roseville, and he was offering to rent it out to me. I was intrigued. As it turned out, the space was in the oldest part of Roseville. Also the building I'd be renting from was literally the oldest building in Roseville, but It sounded promising—historic, full of character, and, best of all, affordable. The downside, it was a few miles from the Great Clips where I worked, and the neighborhood wasn't exactly the most desirable.

I now know that business success hinges on location. You know the old adage, location, location, location. But back then, I was green, eager, and easily swayed. The guy was a good salesman, and before I knew it, I was hanging my shingle and opening my shop.

Business was slow at first. My clients weren't thrilled about driving the extra five miles to the new shop, but many of them did it anyway. I was deeply appreciative of their loyalty, and I made sure to show it.

The building owner had made it clear that I wasn't allowed to do any major renovations. The structure was considered historic, and he didn't want its integrity compromised. The only thing I was allowed to change was the tile. When I pulled up the old tile, I noticed the floor beneath it was red. Curious, I asked the owner about it. He shrugged and said he wasn't sure what it was.

That's when I brought my dad in to take a look. He took one glance at it, and his face darkened. "That's lead," he said. "It's fine if you leave it alone, but don't mess with it."

I had already messed with it. I told him I had rented an electric tile stripper and chipped away the old tile. He stared at me, his face grim. "Did you at least wear a mask?"

I hadn't.

He sighed, his concern clear. "Well, let's hope you weren't exposed."

At the time, I shrugged it off. But about a year later, that moment came rushing back to me in the worst possible way.

I was at home in the small studio I had built in my garage. Claudia was in Brazil visiting her family for the month, and I was playing music with a drummer and a bass player. We were working on Johnny Cash's "Folsom Prison Blues," and I was in my element, lost in the music.

Right as I hit a high note, there was a sudden, bright flash—like an old Polaroid camera going off. At first, I thought it was a malfunction with the fluorescent lights in the studio. But then I noticed something was wrong.

My left eye had gone strange. It's hard to explain, but my peripheral vision was gone, and my central vision was blurred and split. I waved my hand in front of my face, trying to clear it, but nothing changed.

I turned to the guys and joked, "I think I'm having a stroke." We laughed nervously, but deep down, I knew something was horribly wrong.

They offered to drive me to the hospital, but I waved them off. "I'll just sleep it off," I said. "It'll be fine in the morning."

It wasn't.

When I woke up, my vision was worse. It had narrowed further, and I was essentially down to tunnel vision. I knew I couldn't ignore it any longer. I quickly dressed, called my parents up in Colfax, and then drove myself to the hospital. In hindsight, I probably shouldn't have been driving, but I was desperate to get there.

The hospital admitted me immediately. The doctors confirmed what I had jokingly feared—I was having a stroke. At 36 years old, I was experiencing something I had always associated with old age.

Because it had been over twelve hours since the onset of symptoms, they couldn't give me the clot-busting shot, TPA Activase, which is most effective within the first hour. Beyond that window, the shot could cause more harm than good. The stroke had run its course through the night and damage was done.

I was left with a small, permanent area of white matter in my brain. It was terrifying to think about, but it was my new reality.

My parents rushed to the hospital to comfort me, their presence a balm for my growing fear. But Claudia wasn't there. She was thousands of miles away in Brazil, and that was the hardest part. When I spoke to her on the phone, I could hear the worry in her voice. I told her I was fine, but I really wasn't. After a week of being scanned, scraped, poked, and woken up every hour on the hour to do blood and cognitive tests by the nurse, I was released. My vision was still compromised. It was a combination of dampened peripheral vision and hazy fog-like mist everywhere. And when I walked out that day, the sun was more intense than normal, it blinded me and my head pounded. The doctors were not conclusive on what caused my stroke. They thought it was a clot but were not 100%. I told them it felt more like a collapse of my vessels, which I later read about vasculitis, so that is what I feel it was and what I'm dealing with today. Claudia did not come home for almost a week after my stroke, so it was a tough go. When she got back, she tried to comfort me, but a stroke is a tricky one; you can't see the damage because it's internal. I couldn't explain to her what I was going through. There wasn't a lot of damage to my brain, but there was some, and when you have a brain injury, all you want to do is sleep. Your brain needs sleep to heal. I actually returned to work a couple days later. I couldn't just stay alone in the house. I cut my hours to about four hours a day for a couple months. But I was definitely a different person after the stroke. There is a shift that happens in a person when they come face to face with their Own mortality. After this life-threatening event, my whole perception of life, death, and the afterlife was at the forefront and center of my thoughts. What would have happened to me if I had died. I had been going to church, but was I saved. I had strong doubts about my salvation because I was not living according to God's commandments. I was what we call a carnal Christian. I was still, on occasion, smoking weed, watching highly questionable content online, and using unclean language. I couldn't help but think, was this sudden illness the work of an unclean spirit. As I look back, did the Lord allow a Demonic spirit to bring me to the edge of death to open my eyes to the cliff overlooking the pit. I believe the Lord allowed me to go through that to draw my focus on him. Sometimes, he will enable roadblocks to keep us from going off in the weeds and the weeds being sin. The more we sin, the further away from God we'll be. Galatians 5:19-21"Now the works of the flesh are evident: sexual immorality, impurity, sensuality, idolatry, sorcery, enmity, strife, jealousy, fits of anger, rivalries, dissensions, divisions, envy, drunkenness, orgies, and things like these. As long as I warned you before, I warn you that those who do such things will not inherit the kingdom of God."Like a father with his child, there must be punishment for when we willfully engage in an act of sin. And this is why our creator allows us to go through these trials. Hence Job. I'm not saying every person who goes through trials is dealing with God redirecting them; I'm saying I feel my situation was a redirection. The next couple of years were challenging.

Chapter Fifty-Nine

The Silent Battle Within

Charles Spurgeon

"If your afflictions have brought you to Christ, it was worth it."

Something shifted within me after the first stroke. My health began a steep and terrifying decline, and no conventional doctor or hospital could explain why. I carried a heavy weight, both physical and emotional, that seemed to grow heavier by the day. The man who used to move at one hundred miles an hour now trudged through life at thirty five miles per hour. A shadow of fear loomed over me constantly, an unwelcome companion I couldn't shake. That day in the studio, I lost more than just my vision—I lost a part of myself, a piece of the dream I had worked so hard to build. The barber shop I had poured my heart into was gone, and with it, the sense of ownership and purpose that had once fueled me. Now, I found myself renting a small booth in a crowded salon, surrounded by a constant buzz of noise and motion. The traffic of clients and stylists was relentless, and for someone recovering from a stroke, the flood of visual and auditory stimuli was almost unbearable.

But I couldn't stop. I didn't have the luxury of time or money to rest and recover. I had to keep going, even when every fiber of my being cried out for stillness. As I stood behind the chair, cutting hair in this chaotic environment, my mind was gripped by a deeper, spiritual question: Was I merely facing the consequences of my past choices, the physical toll of a life once lived without restraint? Or was there something darker at work—an unclean spirit clinging to me, exploiting my weakness? Now that I had become a Christian, the weight of these questions pressed heavily on my soul, pulling me into an inward battle between the natural and the supernatural, between my past and the redemption I longed for.

In 2008, just two years after the first stroke, the unthinkable happened again: a second stroke. This time, it happened at the shop where I had been renting a booth, trying to rebuild my life after losing my business in Old Roseville. I was cutting hair, chatting with a client, when it hit—shortness of breath, blurred vision, and a sinking realization that it was happening again.

Panic set in, but there was no time for it to take hold. I swallowed my pride and asked my client if he could drive me to the hospital. They didn't hesitate, and I was deeply appreciative, though the embarrassment lingered. On the way to the hospital, I took an aspirin, hoping it might stave off the worst.

It seemed to help. This second stroke wasn't as devastating as the first, but it was no less terrifying. I found myself back in the hospital, subjected once again to every test the medical community had to offer. Yet, as before, no one could tell me why this was happening or what was wrong with me.

Two years of endless visits to specialists, undergoing scans, pokes, and prods. Two years of doctors shrugging their shoulders, prescribing pills that offered no relief, and giving me answers that weren't answers at all. I realized I was trapped in a cycle of conventional medicine that wasn't working.

So I broke free.

I decided to abandon the mainstream path and venture into the world of alternative therapies and decentralized medicine. I tried acupuncture, rife machines, hyperbaric chambers, and anything else that promised even the faintest glimmer of hope. None of it came cheap, but I was desperate. Desperation has a way of making you open to anything.

Finally, after countless dead ends, I found Dr. Michael Powel in Sacramento. He was different. Instead of dismissing my symptoms or giving me vague platitudes, he listened. He ran tests—different tests, ones I hadn't heard of before—and came back with a diagnosis: CPN.

Chlamydia pneumonia.

Before you jump to conclusions, it's not what you're thinking. It's not a venereal disease. It's a condition caused by pneumonia, one I had likely contracted years ago when I was a child. According to Dr. Powel, the disease had gone dormant in my body, hiding deep in the core of my body. But as I aged and my immune system weakened, it began to wake up, spreading throughout my body and wreaking havoc. He explained that the bacteria had built colonies in my organs, triggering a condition called mast cell activation. My body was essentially attacking itself, inflaming at the slightest provocation—certain smells, foods, temperatures, even seemingly harmless environmental triggers.

It was like my body's natural defense mechanisms, designed to fight off a cold or flu, had turned against me. The inflammation wasn't just uncomfortable—it was dangerous. Dr. Powell told me it could compress my veins, leading to a condition called vasculitis. Blood clots could be forming, or worse, my veins could be narrowing to the point of cutting off circulation. Every day was a balancing act, teetering on the edge of disaster.

And then there was the diet.

To manage my symptoms, I had to strip my meals down to the bare essentials. My body rejected almost everything I put into it, leaving me with only a few safe foods: cooked carrots, broccoli, yams, chicken, and occasionally eggs. That's it. Every meal, every day, was some variation of these four ingredients.

It wasn't a diet—it was survival. Like I tell my friends and family I eat to live not for pleasure.

As grueling as it was, I trusted Dr. Powell. He was the first doctor to give me answers, to offer me a path forward that didn't feel like a shot in the dark. His diagnosis and treatment actually gave me relief. It also gave me something I hadn't had in years: hope.

The road ahead wasn't easy, and the shadow of fear still lingered. But for the first time in a long time, I felt like I was walking toward something instead of away from it.

Chapter Sixty

From Fear To Family

T.L. Osborn

"Before your child hears the world, let them hear the Word."

Two years had passed since I began treatment with Dr. Powell. Life wasn't perfect, and my health hadn't completely rebounded, but I was functional. I could work, provide for my family, and—most importantly—hope. That's when Claudia brought up something that had been lingering in the back of my mind but was too heavy for me to say aloud: having a child.

Her words caught me off guard, not because I didn't want a child, but because I had been too afraid to voice it. What if I had another stroke? What if my health failed entirely? I was self-employed, working as a barber, and Claudia, being from another country, didn't have the safety net I could provide if something went wrong. The weight of those what-ifs was almost too much to bear.

But something inside me had shifted since becoming a Christian. I began to feel the Lord nudging me, calling me to step out in faith. The fear was real, but so was His voice, reminding me that my life wasn't my own anymore—it was His. So, despite my hesitation and doubts, we made the decision.

One year later, on November 10, 2011, we welcomed Nicole into the world. It's impossible to capture the depth of that moment in words. The room was filled with love, with my parents present and Claudia's parents visiting all the way from Brazil. I stood there, overwhelmed by the magnitude of it all, holding this tiny life in my hands. It was more than special; it was holy.

As the years passed, Nicole grew into a vibrant, curious child, and my barbershop clientele grew right alongside her along with a slight improvement with my health. When Nicole was four, approaching her fifth birthday, Claudia and I faced an important decision: public school or private.

We chose the latter.

After much prayer and deliberation, we decided to enroll Nicole in a Christian school. The reasons were clear to us. It was evident that the state and federal government, a secular entity, had taken over the public school system, steering it in directions we couldn't accept within our household. There was a push to introduce ideologies we found contrary to the teachings of Christ. Concepts rooted in Marxist and communist ideologies had crept into classrooms, and we could see the rise of agendas that we believed were harmful to the innocence of children.

The demonic influence we saw through the LGBTQ agenda, among others, was targeting young minds, weaving itself into cartoons, music, and even children's literature. Having lived and worked in Los Angeles, I had seen firsthand the machinations of Hollywood, a place I knew all too well. The content they produced—whether for adults or children—was saturated with ideologies that were, in our eyes, a blatant rebellion against God.

We decided to shelter Nicole as much as we could. Some might call it overprotective, but I saw it as a necessary shield in an increasingly hostile world. After years of talking with clients in my barbershop, learning about their families, and hearing their stories, I had noticed a pattern. The most Christ-centered families, the ones who had poured God's truth into their children, were the ones who sheltered them from the storm. Their kids grew up strong in faith, and those kids went on to raise Christ-centered families of their own.

Psalm 91:1 became our guiding verse: *"Those who live in the shelter of the Most High will find rest in the shadow of the Almighty."*

Nicole thrived. Her laughter filled our home, her curiosity kept us on our toes, and her joy reminded us daily of God's goodness. But even as we worked to set her on a path centered on Christ, there was an uncomfortable truth we couldn't ignore: we weren't living by the same standard we were teaching her.

We were what you might call carnal Christians. Outwardly, we made the right moves—church attendance, Bible verses on the walls, Christian schooling for Nicole—but our hearts weren't fully surrendered to the Lord. I struggled with unclean language, watched things I knew I shouldn't, and battled with lust regularly. Claudia and I weren't leading by example; we were compartmentalizing our faith, living a double life of sorts.

For the next five years, we focused on protecting Nicole from the world's influence. We kept her in Christian school, monitored every cartoon, movie, and song she encountered, and worked hard to ensure she had a foundation of faith. But the truth is, we didn't build that same foundation for ourselves.

Looking back, I see God's mercy in those years. Despite our shortcomings, He protected Nicole, gave us the wisdom to shield her from harmful influences, and planted seeds of conviction in our hearts. We were on a journey, and though we hadn't yet surrendered everything to Him, He was gently leading us toward that place of total trust.

It's funny how God works—He doesn't always hit you with a thunderbolt or a grand revelation. Sometimes, He speaks softly, through the giggle of a child, the nudge of a verse, or the quiet conviction in the still of the night. And while we weren't there yet, the seeds were being sown for the next chapter in our lives, one that would require surrender, faith, and a deeper trust in the God who had never stopped pursuing us.

Chapter Sixty-One

A Wake-Up Call From The Inferno

Leonard Ravenhill

"Five minutes in hell and every lost soul would wish they had spent five years on their knees."

It was 2018, and life seemed relatively stable. My daughter, Nicole, was nine years old, and I had been stroke-free for nearly 11 years. But while I was doing well physically, my mother's health was spiraling. Diabetes had wreaked havoc on her body, and she had developed cirrhosis of the liver. By the end of the year, she was on hospice care at my parents' place up in Colfax. living with pain that ranged between a nine and a ten on the pain scale, she was in a bad way. Watching her suffer was unbearable. Her liver was so damaged that any pain pills would further destroy the small fraction of good liver tissue she had

BEYOND THE HOLLYWOOD SIGN

left. I couldn't just sit idly by, so I racked my brain for anything that might ease her pain. Having been around marijuana for most of my life and using it recreationally in the past, I knew cannabis and CBD oils could help regulate her pain levels, or at the bear minimum just get her mind off the pain. After more thought then prayer, I decided to take matters into my own hands.

I began making cannabis oil for my mom. It worked. Her pain eased enough for her to rest, but the process was costly. this is when a client of mine who owned several marijuana grow warehouses suggested using kief instead of traditional cannabis. He explained that kief, the concentrated resin crystals of the plant, was exponentially stronger—containing between 50% and 80% THC, compared to the usual 12% to 25% in marijuana flower. What I did not know is there is very little CBD in Keif. It's important to understand that marijuana contains two key components: CBD and THC. CBD is responsible for its calming effects, while THC is what induces a detached, psychedelic experience. What I was preparing was a purely psychedelic high, without any of the calming effects.

So I had no idea what I was getting myself into.

The process itself was simple enough. I used coconut oil since my mom didn't like the taste of olive oil. I set up a crock pot, added the kief and oil, and let it cook on low for about 15 hours overnight. The next morning, I strained the mixture through cheesecloth to separate the plant material, leaving only the potent oil. But in my rush, I didn't think to wear gloves.

The oil soaked into my hands as I squeezed it through the cheesecloth. It even ended up in my hair as I absentmindedly ran my fingers through it. I didn't realize the THC could penetrate my skin, seep through my dermis, and enter my bloodstream.

To make matters worse, in my arrogance, I decided to sample the oil. I wanted to ensure it was strong enough to help my mom, and I believed my tolerance was high from all of the past years of use. Without a second thought, I gulped down an entire dropper—roughly twenty drops—of a product containing 80% THC.

What I didn't account for was that between the oil on my hands, my scalp, and the dropper full I ingested, I had absorbed what felt like one hundred times the typical dosage needed to get high.

Five minutes later, I knew I had made a catastrophic mistake.

The effects hit me like a freight train. My muscles began to cramp, and I felt an overwhelming heaviness in my body. Panic set in. I wiped my hands frantically and dried my hair with a towel, but it was too late. The THC was already in my system.

I called for Claudia to come downstairs. She knew I was making oils for my mom, but she hadn't expected me to ingest any myself. I told her what I had done, admitting that I had taken far more than a safe amount. Even as I spoke, I felt my body slipping away from me—my muscles were locking up, and I could barely move.

We lumbard upstairs to the master bedroom. I collapsed onto the bed, shivering uncontrollably despite the warm, 80-degree weather outside. My spine felt like it was made of concrete, and the cramping was relentless. Claudia did her best to massage my back, trying to ease the tension in my muscles, but nothing seemed to help.

Then came the chills. I begged her to throw a blanket over me, but it didn't matter. My body was frozen in a strange, unshakable cold.

And that's when I heard it.

A loud, rhythmic booming noise—*boom, boom, boom*. It was deafening, reverberating through my skull like a drumbeat from the depths of some otherworldly dimension. My heart pounded in sync with the sound, and I couldn't tell if it was real or a hallucination.

The booming grew louder, and with it came a creeping sense of dread. I could feel something—something dark—pressing in around me.

But deep down, I wasn't so sure.

I closed my eyes, trying to pray, but the words wouldn't come. All I could hear was the relentless booming and the whispers of my own fears. It felt like I was standing at the edge of a precipice, staring into the abyss. I asked Claudia if she could hear the sound—*boom, boom, boom*. The rhythmic pounding was so loud I thought it might be coming from outside, or maybe even from deep within the house. She looked at me, her brow furrowed with concern. "What noise?" she asked.

Her words stopped me cold. She couldn't hear it. I stared at her, my chest tightening as realization dawned on me. It wasn't a noise from the world around me. It was my heart.

The booming slowed, the rhythm breaking apart as though something was pulling it to a stop. My breathing became shallow, and I felt an icy fear creep through my veins. "Claudia," I whispered hoarsely, "my heart... it's slowing down."

Her hands gripped mine as she fought back panic. Darkness began to seep into the edges of my vision, swallowing the room whole. My last conscious thought was that I might never wake up again.

And then everything went black.

But just as suddenly as I blacked out, I was awake again—only I wasn't in my bedroom. I wasn't in my house.

I was falling.

The sensation was immediate and overwhelming. I was plummeting at an incredible speed, faster than anything I'd ever experienced. The air whipped around me, but it wasn't cold—it was hot. Intensely hot. The heat grew with every passing second as if I were descending into the heart of a furnace.

The darkness around me was impenetrable, but every so often, fire would erupt on either side of me. The flames were sporadic, licking up from the abyss below in bursts that illuminated the walls of what felt like a tunnel or a vast, endless hole. The fire wasn't like anything I'd seen before. It wasn't just heat or light—it felt alive, malicious, as if it had a purpose beyond burning.

Panic gripped me as I tried to orient myself, but there was nothing to hold onto. No ground, no walls, no sense of control. I was just... falling.

Then, out of nowhere, I heard it.

A voice.

It was loud, echoing through the blackness with authority that shook me to my core. Yet, despite its power, there was a strange tenderness to it—a mix of love and stern warning. The voice spoke directly to me,

If you continue down this path, there will be no room for salvation.

The words hit me like a thunderclap, reverberating in my very soul. I cannot say with certainty that this was the voice of God, but it felt divine. It wasn't condemning—it was calling me back, urging me to turn away from the direction I was heading.

And then, as quickly as it had begun, it was over.

I sat up in my bed, disoriented and drenched in sweat. My body ached, my muscles still tight from the THC overdose, and my head was spinning. Claudia was sitting next to me, her face pale and her eyes wide with worry.

"You were out for three hours," she said, her voice trembling. "I couldn't wake you up. I didn't know what to do. You were breathing so I did not call the ambulance"

I tried to speak, but my throat was dry, and my mind was still reeling from what I had just experienced. I glanced around the room, half-expecting to see remnants of fire or hear the echo of that voice. But there was nothing. Just me, Claudia, and the aftermath of a mistake I would never make again.

That was the last time I ever used marijuana.

I didn't give the oil I had made to my mother. I couldn't bring myself to hand her something I now saw as poison. Instead, I poured it down the drain, watching as it disappeared, just as I had in my fall.

I came away from that experience with a newfound understanding. While CBD may have its uses for those battling cancer or chronic pain, the active ingredient in marijuana—THC—was something I would warn others to avoid.

What I experienced that night felt more than physical, it was spiritual. I believe substances like marijuana can dull our senses, altering our perception of reality and potentially opening doors we were never meant to open. Doors that can compromise our spiritual protection and lead us further from the path of Christ.

This was yet another supernatural encounter that brought me closer to God. I felt Christ calling me to remain present, to face life with a clear mind and a steadfast heart. And from that day forward, I vowed to never let anything cloud my connection to Him again.

It's a lesson I carry with me still: intentions, no matter how noble, can lead us to places we never intended to go. But even in the darkest of falls, there is always his hand reaching out to pull us back—if we choose to take it.

Chapter Sixty-Two

Thundersnow And The Homecoming

John Wesley

"Let your parents' passing not be an occasion for despair, but for gratitude, that God gave them to you for so long."

My father was my mother's rock in her final days, her caretaker and devoted companion, tending to her every need with unwavering love. Though we hadn't grown up steeped in the gospel, I could see clearly that my mom believed in Christ. I hadn't noticed it in my youth, but as her life neared its end, it became undeniable. She was drawing closer to Him.

During the last month of my mom's life, my sister moved in with my parents to help my dad care for her. My mom had become bedridden, her voice reduced to barely a whisper. We had to lean down close to her, placing our ears near her lips to catch her faint words. Her suffering was unimaginable. Months earlier, there was an accident during a hospital stay, a nurse had accidentally dropped her onto a gurney, fracturing her spine in seven places. The pain was relentless, unyielding.

Her decline was rapid and heartbreaking to witness, but in those last days, something happened that filled us all with an unshakable hope—a hope that could only come from Christ.

Two days before her passing, my mom experienced something extraordinary. My sister and father were sitting with her when it happened. My mom stopped breathing. Her skin turned pale, and they couldn't find a pulse. My mom was gone.

My dad and sister were overcome with grief, holding her hands as they said their goodbyes through tears. Minutes passed as they mourned the loss of the woman who had been everything to them. And then, out of nowhere, she gasped—her chest heaving as life returned to her body.

She opened her eyes, and in a whisper, she began to explain what had happened. She said she had met Jesus. Her words were weak but filled with conviction as she described Him. Jesus told her she needed to return and repair some relationships before her time truly came.

It reminded me of the passage in Ephesians: *"Do not let the sun go down on your anger"*—a divine call to resolve conflict and mend what's broken before it festers and grows into something that separates us from God. My mom mentioned one name in particular: Camie, her dearest and oldest friend. They had lived far apart from each other, but now she knew she needed to speak with her.

My dad made sure she got a hold of Camie, and they talked. My mom's voice was faint, but her heart was full as she made peace with her beloved friend. It was a gift, one last act of love and reconciliation in her final days.

The two days passed and it was Saturday. It was 10:00 pm, the same time of night when she had stopped breathing just two days earlier. My dad and sister were sitting with her, the room quiet and calm. Outside, the night was still.

And then—lightning.

A massive flash illuminated the sky directly above my dad's property. My sister said it was unlike anything she'd ever seen. It wasn't just a flicker; it was blinding, electricity. They both turned toward the window, stunned, and almost immediately, they heard the thunder—so loud it shook the house.

When they turned back to look at my mom, they saw something they couldn't explain. A blue mist, faint but undeniable, was rising from her body. It drifted upward, disappearing through the ceiling.

And as if on cue, snow began to fall outside on the tiny mobile home.

It was calm, peaceful, and surreal. Snow in itself wasn't unusual for the area, but this was different. My sister described it as feeling like a blessing, a divine punctuation to the moment. It wasn't just snow; it was *thundersnow*—a rare phenomenon where lightning and snow coexist. It felt like heaven itself had opened to welcome her home.

My mom's earthly journey had come to an end.

She passed with a single tear sliding slowly down her cheek. My dad, her husband of over fifty years, sat there in quiet grief, knowing the love of his life was gone. But there was also an unshakable peace. He knew she was home.

For me, that moment—the lightning, the thunder, the snow—was a sign from our Creator, a beautiful welcoming for a woman whose life was filled with love and faith. It was as though God Himself had marked her passing with something extraordinary, something unmistakable.

And if you had known my mom, you'd understand. She was special. Truly special.

This was the day my mom went home to be with Jesus, and though we mourned her deeply, we also celebrated the incredible life she lived and the unshakable faith that carried her to the end. For those who believe, this story offers hope—hope that even in our darkest moments, Christ is there, waiting to bring us home.

Chapter Sixty-Three

Embrace Christ's Freedom

Proverbs 3:5-6

"Trust in the Lord with all your heart and lean not on your own understanding; in all your ways acknowledge him, and he will make your paths straight"

In 2019, a year after my mother's passing, reports of a global virus began to flood the airwaves, signaling the start of a worldwide pandemic. It was a strange and unsettling time, but before I dive into that, let me take you back a bit.

Two years earlier, in 2017, a client of mine had begun sharing his testimony about Jesus. He brought me videos, books, and conversations about spiritual oppression and possession. I'd been attending church on and off for nearly fifteen years, and I considered myself a solid Christian. But as I began to dig into this material, my eyes were opened to a reality I hadn't expected.

I had always assumed that accepting Christ meant an automatic shield against the forces of darkness. I thought these principalities would fade from my life. Yet, the more I studied, the more I realized that wasn't the case. Influential spiritual leaders like Derek Prince, Isaiah Saldivar, Alexander Pagani, Vlad Savchuk, and Mike Signorelli revealed a sobering truth: when we invite Christ into our lives, malevolent forces often try harder to lead us astray.

I thought I was doing everything right. I believed in Christ with all my heart. But as I examined my life more closely, I realized I hadn't rid myself of the things He deemed unclean. I still held onto remnants of my past—new-age books, secular music, and even items that could be considered occultic.

So, on June 16, 2022, I took a decisive step. During a Bible study I attended, two brothers in Christ, David Pucilowski and Rory Bateman, agreed to perform a deliverance over me.

I'd heard testimonials about what to expect during deliverance, but I wasn't sure what I'd experience. I didn't believe I was possessed, as I understood a believer in Christ couldn't be. However, I was open to the idea that I could be severely oppressed.

The deliverance lasted around ten minutes. As David invoked the name of Jesus and commanded any unclean spirits to leave, I began to feel an intense pressure in my chest. My throat tightened, and I started coughing and choking slightly. Then, suddenly, there was a release.

It's hard to put into words, but I felt lighter—like a weight I hadn't even realized I was carrying had been lifted. Peace washed over me. I hugged both David and Rory, thanking them for standing with me in this powerful moment.

That experience was transformative, but it also came with lessons. I learned that to walk fully in Christ's freedom, we must cleanse our lives of anything that might create contracts or ties to darkness. Books, jewelry, records, digital files, artwork—even emotional connections from past relationships—can serve as gateways for possession and oppression. It's not enough to store them away; they must be destroyed. I believe it's better to discard these items entirely than to pass them on, allowing someone else to inherit what could be a spiritual burden.

Looking back, my journey has been nothing short of extraordinary. There were times I wished I'd known then what I know now. But as I reflect, I realize we don't live in a perfect world. If we did, we'd be in heaven with our Creator. This fallen world, with all its darkness, exists to highlight the brilliance of God's light. It's the contrast that compels us to seek Him.

God, in His infinite wisdom, has given us free will. It's up to us to recognize Him in the beauty of His creation and to turn away from anything that leads us astray. Every twist, turn, peak, and valley of my life has brought me to a place of clarity.

What are we facing? A battle not just of flesh and blood but of spirit. And the solution to every struggle is the same: Jesus Christ, the Son of the living God.

My words may feel heavy, but they come from a place of hope. I want them to inspire growth, understanding, and faith. Every experience—every joy, every heartbreak—is meant to reveal God's presence in our lives.

Think about it: every event, no matter how mundane or catastrophic, carries a message from Him. It might come through a strained relationship, a job you just started, a near-tragic accident, or even a moment of overwhelming despair. God speaks through these moments.

The challenge lies in tuning our ears, eyes, and hearts to hear Him. He's always there, calling out, stretching His arms toward us. He loves us fiercely, even when He disciplines us.

Remember this: the most difficult moments in your life can pave the way for the greatest gifts. Knowledge, truth, and restoration are yours if you're willing to accept them. They come from embracing the life, death, and resurrection of Jesus Christ.

This journey of faith has taught me that every hardship, every blessing, and every revelation is part of a divine plan—to draw us closer to Him. And as my story comes to a close, I pray that yours is just beginning. May you find hope, strength, and joy in the unshakable truth of God's love.

www.ingramcontent.com/pod-product-compliance
Lightning Source LLC
Chambersburg PA
CBHW070136100426
42743CB00013B/2722